STRUCTURED

GW01018938

RUTH ASHLEY

Co-President of DuoTech
San Diego, California

John Wiley & Sons, Inc.
New York • Chichester • Brisbane • Toronto

Publisher: Judy Wilson
Editor: Irene Brownstone
Production Supervisor: Ken Burke
    Artists: Carl Brown, Winn Kalmon
    Makeup: Karla Savage

Copyright © 1980, by John Wiley & Sons, Inc.

All rights reserved. Published simultaneously in Canada.

Reproduction or translation of any part of this work beyond
that permitted by Sections 107 or 108 of the 1976 United States
Copyright Act without the permission of the copyright owner
is unlawful. Requests for permission or further information
should be addressed to the Permissions Department,
John Wiley & Sons, Inc.

Library of Congress Cataloging in Publication Data:

Ashley, Ruth.
    Structured COBOL.

    (Wiley Self-Teaching Guides)
    Includes index.
    1. COBOL (Computer program language) — Programmed
    instruction. 2. Structured programming — Programmed
    instruction. I. Title.
QA76.73.C25A84   1980   001.64'24   79-27340
ISBN: 0-471-05362-7

Printed in the United States of America

80 81 10 9 8 7 6 5 4 3

To my friend and colleague

Judi Fernandez

How To Use This Book

This book has no special prerequisites. If you have taken a course or read a book on data processing, you should have no problem working through this Self-Teaching Guide. If this is your first venture into the world of computers, you may benefit from an introductory overview of the data processing environment. Another Self-Teaching Guide, Introduction to Data Processing (2nd edition) by Martin Harris, provides excellent background for this book.

This Self-Teaching Guide consists of thirteen chapters, each of which will bring you deeper into Structured COBOL, building on the previous information. Each chapter begins with a short introduction, followed by objectives that outline what you can expect to learn from your study of that chapter. Many chapters end with a Summary Exercise, a program for you to write, which lets you pull together and apply the new material you have learned. The Self-Test at the end of each chapter lets you assess how well you have met the objectives.

The body of each chapter is divided into frames—short numbered sections in which information is presented or reviewed, followed by questions that ask you to apply the information. The correct answers to these questions follow the dashed line in each frame. As you work through the Guide, use a card or folded paper to cover the correct answer until you have written yours. And be sure you actually write each response, especially when the activity is statement coding. Only by actually coding COBOL statements and checking them carefully (letter by letter, space by space) can you get the most from this Self-Teaching Guide.

As you code statements and programs throughout this book, you may use the forms provided or you may wish to use actual COBOL coding forms, available in most college bookstores or supply stores.

In the back of the book are three Appendixes. Appendix A lists COBOL reserved words, Appendix B shows the standard collating sequence, and Appendix C summarizes the formats of the Procedure Division statements discussed in this book. An index is also provided, so you can use this book for later reference.

Contents

How to Use This Book

Introduction   1

Chapter 1   The Structure of Programming   3

Chapter 2   The Structure of COBOL   19

Chapter 3   Beginning COBOL   37

Chapter 4   Using Unit Record Files   61

Chapter 5   COBOL Arithmetic   78

Chapter 6   The First Three Divisions   94

Chapter 7   COBOL Conditions   128

Chapter 8   Sequential Files I   142

Chapter 9   Sequential Files II   163

Chapter 10   More COBOL Programming Techniques   193

Chapter 11   Tables   218

Chapter 12   Random Access Files   242

Chapter 13   Running COBOL Programs   267

Appendix A   COBOL Reserved Words   284

Appendix B   Collating Sequence   288

Appendix C   Summary of Formats   289

Index   293

Introduction

COBOL is a computer programming language that was designed to solve the data processing problems of business. A number of years ago, a national committee, under the auspices of the U.S. government but with representatives of most computer manufacturers, studied the many versions of COBOL. (Almost every large installation had its own version at that time.) The standardized COBOL that was adopted by that committee became American National Standard, or ANS COBOL. Many compilers today have variations, but they are extensions or modifications to the basic ANS COBOL. Reference manuals clearly indicate where the variations differ from the standard.

Structured COBOL deals with the COBOL language—the same COBOL that programmers and computers have been using for years. "Structured" here refers to programming, and, as such, is independent of the COBOL language. Structure is an approach to programming in which we are concerned with clarity as well as effectiveness. A structured approach to learning COBOL makes a complex subject easier to learn and will help you develop good coding habits automatically. Most computer installations ask all their COBOL programmers to use structure. Since Structured COBOL programs are clear and easy to read, they are much easier to modify than "traditional" COBOL programs. This is an important distinction since as much as fifty percent of programmers' time may be spent in modifying old programs.

Programs written in Structured COBOL make sense to all COBOL programmers and COBOL compilers. In fact, one of the major advantages of structured programming is that it is readable by human beings. A person who isn't a programmer at all can read a Structured COBOL program and figure out what is happening.

When you complete this Self-Teaching Guide, you will be able to write COBOL programs that will require no alterations to run on most systems, and only a few changes for others. The Environment Division in the COBOL program, because it describes the machines and equipment used, contains most of the material that varies among systems. When you begin actually running programs, therefore, you will have to find out what Environment Division entries are standard for the system you will be using. The majority of the COBOL program, however, is machine independent and will run equally well on almost any computer system.

The COBOL program you write is called a source program. This source program is then fed into a source computer, where it is compiled or translated into a machine-language program, the object program. One COBOL statement may be translated into as many as fifty consecutive object statements, since extremely detailed instructions must be given to the computer in terms it understands. At the compilation stage, many of the errors (or bugs) in a program become apparent. Errors in spelling of the special COBOL words, omission of required spacing or punctuation, and use of incorrect formats are just some of the factors that can hinder the compilation of your source program into the machine-language object program. Learning to program in machine language does not circumvent these problems; machine-language format, syntax, and sequencing require even more attention to the details of both the language and the system. When you program in a higher level language, such as COBOL, the compiler provides error messages from the source computer, which will help you correct your program. The object computer is used then to execute your mechanically correct program.

In this guide, we shall stick as closely as possible to ANS COBOL, using a structured approach. Structured COBOL is self-contained, including all the materials necessary for you to study ANS COBOL; you do not need access to a computer to learn how to write a program in COBOL. Of course, you will need access to a computer to develop what you learn here into actual programming.

This book includes an introduction to the problems you'll encounter when you first begin to compile, test, and run your Structured COBOL programs. Until you begin that process, you may not really appreciate the benefits of Structured COBOL, even though you know the statements and can code the control structures. Structured coding makes the testing and debugging part of programming much more manageable.

Since we don't know what system is used in your installation, we can't tell you exactly how to go about it. You will probably need guidance from an instructor, a fellow student, or a congenial programmer. And before you run any programs, you may find it useful to review the COBOL reference manual for your installation. Beyond the basics presented in this book, you will find that COBOL has many more options, some more statement types, and various aids for testing your programs, which will be useful as you actually begin to apply what you have learned in Structured COBOL.

CHAPTER ONE
The Structure of Programming

The first chapter of Structured COBOL deals not with COBOL, but with structured programming in general. Before we can begin to apply coding rules, we
need to get an overview of the structure of programming in a business environment. Virtually all programming problems can be seen as combinations of
three structures. We will see how these three simple structures can be com-
bined to solve most business programming problems. In this chapter we'll
look at a few ways to describe the general structure of a problem.

All of this will help you to begin thinking about programming as a method
of creating procedures, called programs, to solve business problems.

When you have completed this chapter, you will be able to:

- state two advantages of structured programming over traditional
  programming;

- identify the type of programming problem represented by an example;

- identify examples of sequence, selection, and repetition in a program
  structure;

- interpret a simple hierarchy chart; and

- interpret a simple pseudocode design.

1. The basics of programming can be diagrammed like this:

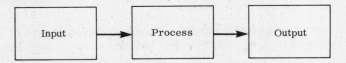

When you write a program, you specify an exact procedure the computer
will follow to solve a problem. In essence, you tell the computer what it
will get as input data, what to do with it, and what you want as output
data. Everything between the input data and the output data is processing.
In a business environment, a great deal of data is handled. Problems
such as inventory control, personnel file maintenance, and payroll processing all involve input of data, processing, and output of the results.

Consider a payroll problem—any payroll problem.

(a) Give one example of input information that is needed.

_____

(b) Give one item of processing.

_____

(c) Name one piece of possible output data.

_____

- -

(a) hours worked, rate per hour, person's name, etc.
(b) multiply hours times rate, figure tax, etc.
(c) a paycheck, records, etc.

2. Consider a situation in which a department store has a large file (or col-
    lection) of customer account records. Every day the accounting depart-
    ment receives several hundred payments in the mail. Clerks keypunch
    a set of data cards, each with customer number and amount paid. These
    cards become the input data for a program that looks up each customer
    from whom a payment was received, and subtracts the payment from the
    current balance. Finally, it prints out names of any customers who paid
    too much, and it also prepares a daily "income statement" of the total
    amount received that day by mail.

    (a) Name two items of input to this problem.

    _____   _____

    (b) Name two elements of processing.

    _____   _____

    (c) Name two items of output.

    _____   _____

- -

(a) customer file, payment cards; (b) look up accounts, subtract payments, add up all payments, check if balance is less than zero; (c) new
balances, total of payments, list of overpaid customers

3. Most business problems fall into four general categories. Update prob-
    lems involve modifying master sets of data. Summary problems use
    input data to find specific information or totals. Report problems use
    input data to produce printed reports in a specific format. Editing prob-
    lems require a detailed "edit" or verification of input data, often as a
    preparation for its use as input to still another program.

Indicate whether each problem below is a summary, update, report, or editing problem.

(a) Go through a set of patient records and print each patient's name, length of hospital stay, and total bill. _____

(b) Process a set of patient records to find out the average cost per day per patient. _____

(c) Process a set of patient records to change attending physician "Sweeney" to "McDowell". _____

(d) Process a set of payment records to make sure each is in correct format and includes an eight digit patient number. _____

- - - - - - - - - - - - - - - - - - -

(a) report; (b) summary; (c) update; (d) edit

4. Many business problems contain elements of all four general problem types. In the situation described in frame 2, which aspect of the problem, if any, is of each type?

(a) Summary _____

(b) Update _____

(c) Report _____

(d) Editing _____

- - - - - - - - - - - - - - - - - - -

(a) income statement (total amount in); (b) changing customers' balances; (c) list of overpaid customers; (d) none indicated in the problem statement

5. Each problem, no matter what type, involves input, processing, and output. Every program—which is the procedure for solving the problem—must include at least one input function, one processing function, and one output function. A given program may include many of each type of function, depending on the complexity of the problem. In addition, every program has an overall control function which calls in any of the other functions, as needed. Structured programming is based on these control functions. They control the sequence in which all other functions are executed.

(a) What type of program would require a control function? _____

(b) What type of function is involved in the tax computation in a payroll problem solution? _____

(c) What type of function would call on a tax computation function?

_____

- - - - - - - - - - - - - - - - - - -

(a) all types; (b) processing; (c) control

6.   In a program, flow of control dictates which instruction the computer
     considers next. Most high-level languages, including COBOL, offer
     various ways to specify flow of control. Traditional programming is
     based on flow of control, and takes full advantage of all the ways of modi-
     fying flow that are available. Some of these ways require very little in-
     ternal storage and/or very little time. Some are "elegant" and allow the
     programmer to code fewer lines. The result may be an efficient program,
     but it often communicates very poorly with human readers. In structured
     programming, we restrict ourselves to a very few ways to control se-
     quence of execution in programs. The enhanced clarity of coding that
     results means programs can be written more quickly, debugged and
     tested more quickly, and revised much more easily in the future.

     (a) Which generally uses more ways to control sequence of execution—

         traditional or structured COBOL? _____

     (b) Which are generally easier for you to read—traditional or structured

         COBOL programs? _____

- - - - - - - - - - - - - - - - - - -

(a) traditional; (b) structured

7.   Data processing problems have been programmed using traditional tech-
     niques for many years. You may be familiar with flowcharts, for example.
     Let's look more closely at the special features of structured programming.
        Structured programming looks at a problem as a hierarchy of func-
     tions to be performed. Higher level functions are control functions; they
     control the execution of lower level functions, which may be more control
     functions, input functions, processing functions, or output functions.
     Each function, sometimes called a module, is invoked only by higher
     level control functions.

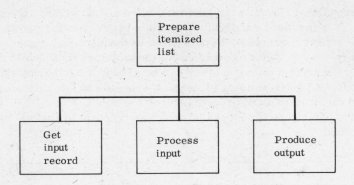

This example shows a high-level module with three lower level modules. What modules shown could be invoked by each of these?

(a) Get input record _____

(b) Prepare itemized list _____

- - - - - - - - - - - - - - - - - - -

(a) none (no function is shown at a lower level than Get input record);
(b) Get input record, Process input, and Produce output (all of the lower level functions)

8. Structured programming enables you to follow a structured design and produce a program more quickly than would traditional programming. And the structured program will be easier to test and, most important, considerably easier to read than a traditional program. In a typical business computer installation, more programmer time is spent maintaining (which includes modifying) old programs than is spent writing new ones. And programmer costs are the largest expense category in many computer installations. Computer time costs are coming down, while salaries go up. Therefore many installations have decided against micro-efficiencies of "elegant" programming in favor of the more efficient use of human resources available through structured programming.

   Which of the following factors contribute to the demand for structured programming?

   _____ (a) Computer time is more expensive these days.

   _____ (b) Computer personnel are more expensive these days.

   _____ (c) Efficient use of machine resources is critical.

   _____ (d) Readable programs are easier to maintain.

- - - - - - - - - - - - - - - - - - -

   b, d

9. Each module of a structured program has one entry point and one exit point. This makes it relatively easy for a programmer to read, write, or understand a program. Names given to modules and pieces of data are easier to read if they are meaningful. Instructions that have some meaningful relationship to one another can be grouped together by spacing or indentation. You'll be using all these techniques in later chapters as you code structured COBOL programs.

   Name two characteristics that make a structured program easy to understand.

   _____

   _____

- - - - - - - - - - - - - - - - - - - -

   (any two of these) meaningful names for data and modules; indentation and spacing to group instructions; separate modules for different functions

10. Traditional programming relies on the flowchart to show the "flow of control" in a program. Although flowcharts can be (and often are) adapted for structured programming, flowcharts focus on control rather than on functions so we will not use them in this book. We will use narrative descriptions along with structured hierarchy charts and a pseudocode (which you'll see shortly) to express program designs in this book.

   Examine the following hierarchy chart.

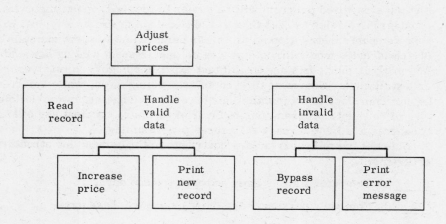

   Which narrative below fits the structure shown in the chart?

   _____ (a) Records that contain valid data will be bypassed.

   _____ (b) Records will be processed under the control of either Handle valid data or Handle invalid data.

_____ (c) Prices in valid records only will be adjusted.

- - - - - - - - - - - - - - - - - -

b, c (both fit the chart)

11. Hierarchy charts show the general structure of a problem. Recall our earlier discussion of types of programming problems.

(a) Which type of problem does the hierarchy in the last frame represent— summary, update, report, or editing? _____

(b) Name the control functions in that chart. _____

_____

- - - - - - - - - - - - - - - - - - -

(a) update (we're changing something in the record)
(b) Adjust prices, Handle valid data, Handle invalid data

CONTROL STRUCTURES

Sequence Structure

12. In the normal way of operating, the computer executes one statement after another, in sequence, unless it receives an instruction to the contrary. The sequence in which the instructions are given to the computer determines the sequence in which they are executed—we can call this a sequence structure. For example, suppose you want the computer to print a line with your name. Your instructions (in everyday English) might be

1. Here is my name
2. Print it

No other sequence for these two instructions would make sense. Below are some English instructions to find and print the total price. Number them (from 1) in the correct sequence.

_____ (a) Multiply quantity by unit price to get total price

_____ (b) Unit price is 7.00, quantity is 5

_____ (c) Print total price

- - - - - - - - - - - - - - - - - -

(a) 2; (b) 1; (c) 3

Selection Structures

13. Sometimes we don't want every instruction executed in sequence, but want to select some instructions to be executed only under certain conditions.

For example, if an item is not food, we may have to add tax to its price. In this case, we use a selection structure. The standard selection structure is the IF-THEN-ELSE, often simply called the IF structure. Here is how we can show a selection control structure:

```
IF item is not food
THEN
        add tax
    ELSE
        don't add tax
    ENDIF
```

We use IF to specify a selection criterion—a condition. When the condition is true, we want the computer to do whatever we have written under THEN. When the condition is false, we want the computer to do whatever we have written under ELSE. The ENDIF marks the end of the IF control structure.

The condition, whether it is true or false, determines whether the THEN or ELSE action will be done. In no case will they both be done. As you'll see later, either can be omitted, however. The selection structure above will have the same functional effect if it is written like this:

```
IF item is food
THEN
        don't add tax
    ELSE
        add tax
    ENDIF
```

See if you can write a selection structure (condition and general actions) based on the chart in frame 10. We've included the special words for you.

IF _____
THEN

_____

ELSE

_____

ENDIF

- - - - - - - - - - - - - - - - - - - -

There are two ways you might have answered this. Both are equally correct.

IF data is valid	IF data is not valid
THEN	THEN
handle valid data	handle invalid data
ELSE	ELSE
handle invalid data	handle valid data
ENDIF	ENDIF

14. The way we write the instructions here is not really computer code, so we generally call it pseudocode. It simulates the sequence of statements as you will code them in a computer program. A pseudocode segment can be translated into COBOL, or almost any computer language.

   Another item worth noting in the pseudocode selection structure is that the THEN and ELSE sections can each contain many actions. For example, the THEN action "handle valid data" from the last frame could be replaced with:

```
THEN
      increase price
      print new record
ELSE
   .
   .
   .
```

Referring to frame 10, indicate here what sequence of actions would replace "handle invalid data" in the selection structure.

_____

- - - - - - - - - - - - - - - - - - -

   bypass record; print error message

15. The next action in sequence after an ENDIF will be executed whether the condition was true or false. The pseudocode below combines the sequence and selection structures. Examine it, then answer the questions that follow.

```
Get a card
IF employee is full-time
THEN
      add 1 to full-time count
ELSE
      add 1 to part-time count
ENDIF
Print name from card
```

(a) Suppose the result of "Get a card" indicates a part-time employee.

   Which instruction will be selected—THEN or ELSE? _____

(b) What instruction will be executed after "add 1 to full-time count"?

   _____

(c) What is the purpose of ENDIF? _____

   _____

- - - - - - - - - - - - - - - - - - -

   (a) ELSE (the condition—employee is full-time—is not true); (b) print name from card; (c) it marks the end of the selection control structure

Repetition Structure

16. Besides sequence and selection, we often want to specify repetition, or iteration, to have instructions executed repeatedly. We can specify that a statement or group of statements will be executed repeatedly until a condition becomes true. The control structure is called PERFORM UNTIL. We specify that some actions will be performed until a condition becomes true. Here is a simple COBOL repetition structure.

```
PERFORM UNTIL no more cards
    add 1 to card-counter
    print line
    get card
ENDPERFORM
```

The structure specifies that the action statements will be executed repeatedly until no more cards are in the file. Here "no more cards" represents a condition. The ENDPERFORM marks the end of the PERFORM control.

(a) How many times will the statements be executed if the input deck has no cards at all? _____

(b) How many times will the statements be executed if there are 12 cards in the deck? _____

(c) What two control structures are represented in this example?

_____

- -

(a) none; (b) 12; (c) sequence and repetition

17. The following pseudocode uses all three control structures—sequence, selection, and repetition.

```
Get a card
PERFORM UNTIL no more cards
    IF  employee is full-time
    THEN
        add 1 to full-time count
    ELSE
        add 1 to part-time count
    ENDIF
    Print name from card
    Get a card
ENDPERFORM
Print count totals
```

The PERFORM UNTIL sets up a repetition of all the instructions up to the ENDPERFORM. Notice that "Get a card" is last in the PERFORM UNTIL structure. That is because, in COBOL processing, the system knows when it tries to read beyond the last record in the file. (You'll learn why later in this book.) Suppose you have 8 cards, 5 for full-time employees and 3 for part-time.

(a) How many times will the first "Get a card" be executed? _____

(b) "Print name from card"? _____

(c) The last instruction "Print count totals"? _____

(d) If the beginning values of full-time count and part-time count were zero, what will be their ending values?

_____

- - - - - - - - - - - - - - - - - -

(a) one; (b) eight; (c) one; (d) full-time 5, part-time 3

18. The instructions you have been interpreting are called pseudocode. They are not actually code for the computer but a structure for preparing to code in any computer language. We tailor it to COBOL, of course, but the structure could be applied to other languages as well. The crucial elements of pseudocode are the structure words (IF, THEN, ELSE, ENDIF, PERFORM UNTIL, and ENDPERFORM) and indentation. As you can see in the last frame, we use indentation to show control. The selection structure is under the control of the repetition structure here, so the IF is indented under PERFORM. The action statements in THEN and ELSE are also indented. We won't be asking you to write pseudocode in this book, but you may want to do it on scratch paper to help you see the logic of programs. Where problems are quite complex, we will give you pseudocode to work from.

Another pseudocode segment is shown below. Study it before answering the questions that follow.

```
Get an input record
PERFORM UNTIL no more records
    IF  state is California
    THEN
        print name of customer
    ELSE
        add 1 to other-states
        add quantity to total quantity
    ENDIF
ENDPERFORM
Print count and total
```

(a) Which structured words make up the selection control structure?

_____

(b) Which structured words make up the repetition control structure?

_____

(c) What type of control structure is included within the selection control structure? _____

- - - - - - - - - - - - - - - - - -

(a) IF, THEN, ELSE, ENDIF; (b) PERFORM UNTIL, ENDPERFORM;
(c) sequence (under ELSE)

19. Decide which control structures are required by each description below.

(a) Read a card, then print its contents. _____

(b) Read a card, print its contents when the salary is under 7000.

_____

(c) Read all the cards and list them. _____

(d) Read all the cards and list all that have salary under 7000.

_____

- - - - - - - - - - - - - - - - - -

(a) sequence; (b) sequence, selection; (c) sequence, repetition;
(d) sequence, selection, repetition

20. A general overview of a structured program can be presented in a hierarchy chart. The hierarchy is often sequenced left to right, but that may vary. The hierarchy shows the functions to be performed by a program, not necessarily the logic to perform them. The pseudocode, which is logic oriented, acts as a guide to coding a program.

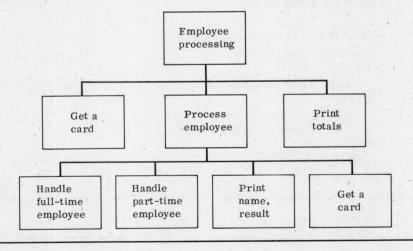

(a) What module(s) in this hierarchy chart represent a selection control structure? _____

_____

(b) What module(s) represent a repetition control structure?

_____

- - - - - - - - - - - - - - - - - - - -

(a) Handle full-time employee and Handle part-time employee;
(b) Process employee (This is a control module—all four modules it controls are repeated.)

In this chapter you have been introduced to programming as a structured approach to problem solving. The concepts you have learned here will be applied throughout this Self-Teaching Guide. In the next chapter, we will turn our attention to COBOL as a language, and we will look at its structure. You will see how the sequence, selection, and repetition control structures are expressed in the COBOL language.

SELF-TEST

Each chapter in this Self-Teaching Guide includes a self-test that will let you pull together what you have learned, so you can see how well you have met the objectives of the chapter.

After you have written your answers to the Self-Test, check your answers in the Answer Key that follows. Be sure you understand any differences between your answers and ours before you begin the next chapter. Following each suggested answer is a frame reference in parentheses, in case you need to review.

1. Cite two advantages of structured programming over traditional programming. _____

_____

2. Name the type (or types) of problem represented by each brief problem description below.

   (a) You need to change the addresses of all students who have submitted change-of-address cards. _____

   (b) You need to find out the total value of your company's inventory.

   _____

   (c) You need to check that each payment card is in the correct format.

   _____

(d) You need to print a list of all customers who haven't used their charge cards for six months. _____

3. Consider a "module" of a structured program.

    (a) Does it represent control or function? _____

    (b) How many entry and exit points does it have? _____

4. Suppose you need a program to read input records and find the total of payments to all suppliers who are located within the city limits. You also need a list of those suppliers.

    (a) What type of problem is this? _____

    (b) What part of the problem will require a selection control structure?

    _____

    (c) What part of the problem will require a repetition control structure?

    _____

5. Which of the following hierarchy charts represents the problem described in question 4? _____

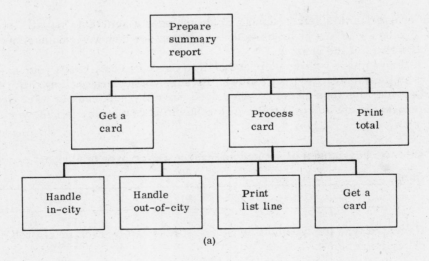

(a)

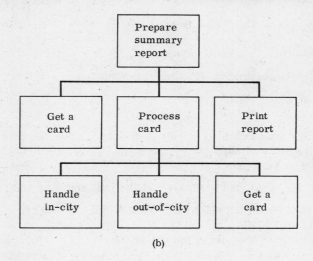

(b)

6. Examine the following pseudocode:

```
Get input record
PERFORM UNTIL no more input records
     Add up hours
     IF total hours more than 40
     THEN
          Calculate overtime hours
          Calculate overtime pay
     ELSE
          Set overtime pay to zero
     ENDIF
     Calculate regular pay
     Write output
     Get input record
ENDPERFORM
```

(a) What part represents an iteration structure?

_____

(b) What part represents a selection structure?

_____

(c) Which part of the selection structure will be executed if the total hours
    is 39? _____

(d) Under what circumstances will "Calculate regular pay" be done?

_____

Answer Key

1. quicker to write, easier to change   (8)

2. (a) update; (b) summary; (c) edit; (d) report   (3)

3. (a) function   (7)
   (b) one of each   (9)

4. (a) summary and report   (3)
   (b) check location of supplier   (13)
   (c) add totals; read all cards   (16)

5. chart (a); the other one will only list the last supplier and the total   (11)

6. (a) from PERFORM UNTIL to ENDPERFORM   (16)
   (b) from IF to ENDIF   (13)
   (c) the ELSE part "Set overtime pay to zero"   (14)
   (d) all circumstances (It is outside the selection structure.)   (15)

CHAPTER TWO
The Structure of COBOL

COBOL is a high-level programming language specially designed for writing procedures to solve business problems. COBOL is an acronym for COmmon Business-Oriented Language. As a language, COBOL has always had an internal hierarchical structure that makes it easily adaptable to coding structured solutions to problems in a business environment. COBOL is flexible enough that we can use a structured format with indentation to follow our pseudocode standard.

In this chapter, we will cover the hierarchy of COBOL, general coding rules, and format requirements, and we will explore how to relate the control structures you learned in Chapter 1 to the COBOL programming language. When you have completed this chapter, you will be able to:

- identify the divisions of a COBOL program;

- arrange the major components of a COBOL program in a hierarchy;

- specify the type of entry coded in the coding form areas A and B;

- determine whether user-supplied names are valid;

- recognize COBOL coding for sequence, selection, and repetition control structures;

- trace control through a COBOL IF or PERFORM;

- differentiate between COBOL rules and structure conventions regarding coding format; and

- interpret format statements to identify correct statement coding.

THE COBOL HIERARCHY

1. Every COBOL program contains divisions, sections, paragraphs, and statements. These represent a hierarchy as shown in Figure 2-1. At the highest level of the hierarchy are divisions; each COBOL program includes the same four divisions. Within each division may be sections and/or paragraphs. Within paragraphs may be entries or statements.

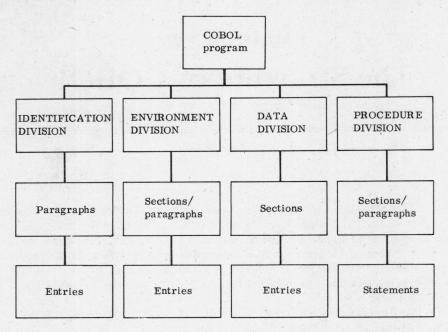

Figure 2-1

Match the following:

_____ (a) Divisions

_____ (b) Sections

_____ (c) Paragraphs

_____ (d) Statements

1. Highest level of a COBOL hierarchy.
2. Lowest level of a COBOL hierarchy.
3. May be included in a division.
4. May include sections.

- - - - - - - - - - - - - - - - - - - -

(a) 1, 4; (b) 3; (c) 3; (d) 2, 3

2. Every COBOL program includes four divisions, in this order: Identification Division, Environment Division, Data Division, and Procedure
Division.

   The Identification Division is used to identify the program. It may
include paragraphs for such information as program name, author, date,
security, etc. The Environment Division is used to give information
about the system and requirements, such as equipment, needed to run
the program. The Data Division is used to describe all the data and files
used by the program. The Procedure Division includes the actual procedure that will solve the business problem.

   Name the division that would:

(a) tell which hardware (printers, card readers, disks, etc.) the program needs. _____

(b) include sequence, selection, and iteration control structures.

_____

(c) describe the input and output data. _____

(d) tell who wrote the program and when. _____

- - - - - - - - - - - - - - - - - - -

(a) Environment; (b) Procedure; (c) Data; (d) Identification

3.   The four COBOL divisions make up each COBOL program, and they always appear in the same order. Each is introduced by a division header, like this:

```
IDENTIFICATION DIVISION.
ENVIRONMENT DIVISION.
DATA DIVISION.
PROCEDURE DIVISION.
```

The Identification Division, which occurs first, includes one or more paragraphs that help identify the program. The Environment Division usually has one or more sections that include paragraphs for hardware information. The Data Division can include two sections, one to describe data from the files and one to describe any other data the program uses. The Procedure Division, which occurs last, uses paragraphs and, in advanced programs, may use sections as well.

(a) Which Divisions may include sections?

_____

(b) Which Divisions may include paragraphs?

_____

(c) List the COBOL Divisions in order.

_____

_____

_____

_____

- - - - - - - - - - - - - - - - - - -

(a) Environment, Data, Procedure; (b) Identification, Environment, Procedure; (c) Identification, Environment, Data, Procedure

THE CODING FORM

4. Figure 2-2 shows a COBOL coding form. Examine it to find the answers to these questions:

    (a) How many columns are accounted for on the form? _____

    (b) What columns are used for IDENTIFICATION? _____

    (c) What columns are used for SEQUENCE [(PAGE) and (SERIAL)] ?

    _____

- -

    (a) 80; (b) 73-80; (c) 1-6

5. Here is a "framework" for a COBOL program, written on part of a COBOL coding form.

SEQUENCE		CONT. COL	A	B							COBOL STATEMENT		
(PAGE)	(SERIAL)												

```
010010  IDENTIFICATION DIVISION.
010020  PROGRAM-ID.    name entry.
010030 *
010040  ENVIRONMENT DIVISION.
010050  INPUT-OUTPUT SECTION.
010060        SELECT entry.
010070        :
010080 *
010090  DATA DIVISION.
010100  FILE SECTION.
010110        :
010120 *
010130  WORKING-STORAGE SECTION.
010140        :
010150 *
010160  PROCEDURE DIVISION.
010170  paragraph-name
010180        statements
010190        :
```

Notice that the form has two general areas A and B. Column 8 is called the A margin, and column 12 is called the B margin. (Area B extends to column 72, as you can see in Figure 2-2.) COBOL restricts various program components to begin, or be contained, in specific areas. Examine the framework. In which area does each of the following start?

_____ (a) Division headers

_____ (b) Section headers

_____ (c) Paragraph names

_____ (d) Statements

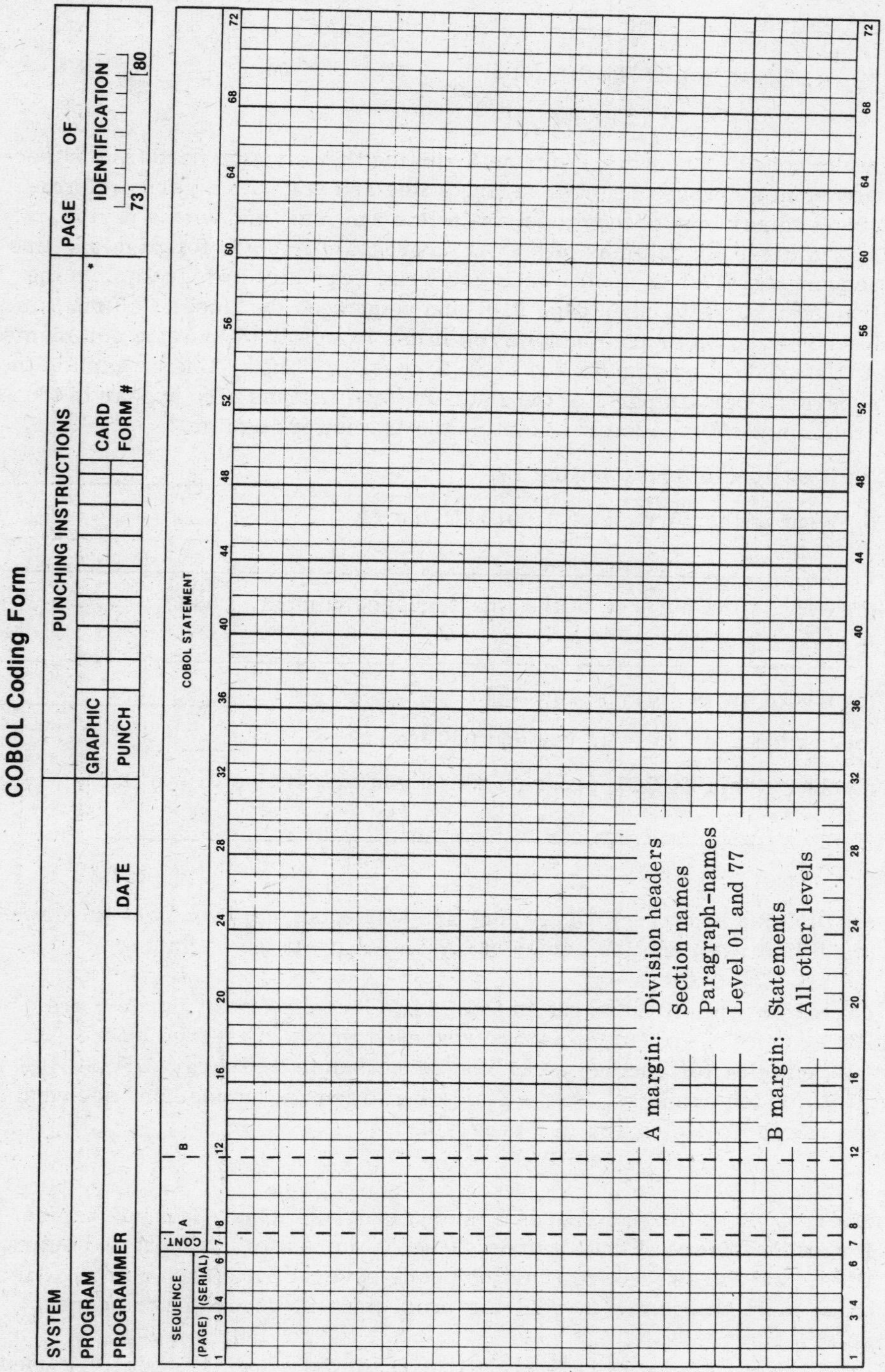

Figure 2-2. COBOL Coding Form

_____ (e) Entries

- - - - - - - - - - - - - - - - - - -

(a) A; (b) A; (c) A; (d) B; (e) B

6. In the coded framework in frame 5, notice that division headers and section names always occupy a separate line and end with a period. Paragraph names may occupy a separate line and must end with a period.

   The first six columns of a COBOL program line are for page and line sequencing. This is useful when you write very large programs. In the framework, we've used page 010, and sequenced the lines. Column 7 is for continuation or comments. You'll use it mostly to indicate comments. An asterisk in column 7 allows you to insert a "blank" line or explain the program. Certain parts of the Data Division Entries also appear in the A area, as you'll see later. Examine the framework again.

(a) What type of entry is line 1? _____

(b) What is the purpose of 010010 in line 1?

   _____

(c) What is the purpose of the line sequence numbered 030?

   _____

(d) What type of entry is line 130? _____

(e) In what area do lines 010 and 020 begin? _____

(f) Where in a COBOL program would you expect line 010 to fit?

   _____

- - - - - - - - - - - - - - - - - - -

(a) Division header; (b) Page and line sequence; (c) Comment (insert a blank line); (d) Section name; (e) Area A; (f) At the beginning

All of the capitalized words in the COBOL framework of frame 5 are specific to COBOL—in fact, they are reserved words—reserved by the COBOL compiler for special uses. You cannot name a program DIVISION— even if it divides numbers. Now we're going to look at names, and see what you can use to create names in a program.

7. Every COBOL program needs a unique program name. It needs names for all the pieces of data it uses. It needs names for its input and output files. And the Procedure Division needs several paragraph names. All of these must be created by you, the programmer, according to specific rules.

   First and foremost is the rule that reserved words are not to be used as programmer-supplied names. They can be part of such a name, however. FILE is a reserved word, yet, MASTER-FILE and FILECHECK are both valid names. In general, names:

- can be from 1 to 30 characters in length
- must use at least one letter
- must start with a letter or digit
- may use any digits, letters, and hyphens
- must be unique.

Mnemonic names, which have meaning, are best, because they help to make the coded program self-explanatory. None of the names below are reserved words. Check to see if each is a valid programmer-supplied word.

_____ (a) ABC

_____ (b) 17-20-AGE-RANGE

_____ (c) -40-YEARS

_____ (d) $COST

_____ (e) GROSS-PAY

- - - - - - - - - - - - - - - - -

(a) valid; (b) valid; (c) not valid (- at beginning); (d) not valid ($);
(e) valid

8. Appendix A includes a reasonably complete list of reserved words. As you will see, few reserved words include hyphens, so if you use hyphens liberally in your names, you won't have to refer to the list very often. But when in doubt, refer to the list to make sure you haven't used a reserved word as a name. For practice, check which of the words in the list below are reserved:

_____ (a) VALID   _____ (e) COUNT

_____ (b) INVALID   _____ (f) COUNTER

_____ (c) PRINT   _____ (g) TIME

_____ (d) PRINTER   _____ (h) TIMER

- - - - - - - - - - - - - - - - -

b, c, d, f, h

In this book, we are going to concentrate first on the Procedure Division. You will learn to code the most common statements and routines in Chapters 3 and 4, for which you will have to create paragraph names. You'll be given the first three Divisions, so you won't have to create file and data names in these early chapters. In the rest of this chapter, we'll look at how those three control structures we discussed in Chapter 1 are implemented in

COBOL. You'll learn much more about using these control structures in later chapters.

Sequence Structure

9. Statements in COBOL are executed in sequence until something occurs to direct control elsewhere. These are valid COBOL statements.

```
MOVE 7.00 TO UNIT-PRICE.
MOVE 5 TO UNIT-QUANTITY.
MULTIPLY UNIT-PRICE BY UNIT-QUANTITY GIVING TOTAL-PRICE.
```

In what order would these statements be executed?

_ _

in the sequence in which they appear

Selection Structure

10. A pseudocode selection structure is shown on the left below. On the right, you can see how the structure can be coded in COBOL.

```
IF employee is full-time            IF EMP-TYPE = 'FULL'
THEN                                    ADD 1 TO FULL-COUNT
        add 1 to full-time count    ELSE
ELSE                                    ADD 1 TO PART-COUNT.
        add 1 to part-time count
ENDIF
```

Notice that COBOL does not include the words THEN and ENDIF. The THEN action immediately follows the IF condition. And the period (after the ELSE action here) acts as the ENDIF—it ends the selection and control passes to the next statement in sequence, after the period.

The COBOL IF includes other statements within it. The entire structure must be completely contained in area B. The indentation you see above helps to show the structure of the program. Which of the coding examples on the next page is functionally equivalent to the selection

structure above? _____

```
 7|8    12    16    20    24    28    32    36    40    44    48
(a) |IF EMP-TYPE = 'FULL'
    |    ADD 1 TO FULL-COUNT
    |ELSE
    |    ADD 1 TO PART-COUNT.
    |
(b) |    IF EMP-TYPE = 'FULL'
    |    ADD 1 TO FULL-COUNT
    |    ELSE ADD 1 TO PART-COUNT.
    |
(c) |        IF EMP-TYPE = 'FULL'
    |            ADD 1 TO FULL-COUNT
    |        ELSE
    |            ADD 1 TO PART-COUNT.
    |
(d) |            IF EMP-TYPE = 'FULL'
    |                ADD 1 TO FULL-COUNT.
    |            ELSE
    |                ADD 1 TO PART-COUNT.
```

- - - - - - - - - - - - - - - - - - - -

b, c (a begins in area A; d is not equivalent, because an extra period
follows the THEN action.)

Notice that b is not indented, but is entirely within area B; c is
indented farther, but is still within area B.

11. Here is another example of a COBOL selection structure.

```
IF ITEM-TYPE NOT = 'FOOD'
    MULTIPLY ITEM-PRICE BY TAX-PERCENT
        GIVING TAX-PRICE
    ADD TAX-PRICE TO ITEM-PRICE
ELSE
    NEXT SENTENCE.
MOVE ITEM-PRICE TO OUT-PRICE.
```

In this IF statement, a sequence of statements are executed only if the
condition (ITEM-TYPE NOT = 'FOOD') is true. The ELSE NEXT SEN-
TENCE is optional in COBOL, but we often include it to make visually
clear that this is an IF-THEN-ELSE construction. Here, if the condition
is false (if the item IS food) control passes to the next sentence—after the
period.

Examine the coding, then answer these questions.

(a) In what area should the IF and ELSE be coded? _____

(b) How would control change if the period were placed after ITEM-
PRICE, and ELSE NEXT SENTENCE were omitted?

_____

(c) What statement above is not a part of the selection structure?

_____

(d) What statements, of those shown, are executed if ITEM-TYPE = 'FOOD'? _____

(e) What statements are executed if ITEM-TYPE = 'DRUG'?

_____

- - - - - - - - - - - - - - - - - - -

(a) B; (b) no change—ELSE NEXT SENTENCE is optional; (c) the MOVE statement; (d) MOVE; (e) MULTIPLY, ADD, and MOVE

12. A statement (or sentence, which is one or more statements and ends with a period) may be continued on another line anywhere a space occurs. Although we commonly use one space to separate words, any number of spaces could be used.

   Here is the earlier IF again, and another statement. See if you can figure out the control.

```
IF EMP-TYPE = 'FULL'
      ADD 1 TO FULL-COUNT
ELSE
      ADD 1 TO PART-COUNT.
DISPLAY EMPLOYEE-NAME.
```

(a) If EMP-TYPE on a card is PART, where would 1 be added?

_____

(b) If EMP-TYPE were RETD, where would 1 be added? _____

(c) What type of employee names will be displayed? _____

(d) What would happen if the period were omitted after PART-COUNT?

_____

- - - - - - - - - - - - - - - - - - -

(a) PART-COUNT; (b) PART-COUNT; (c) all; (d) no full-time employee names would be displayed.

Repetition Structure (COBOL PERFORM)

13. In COBOL, we sometimes want to execute a sequence of statements that is not in sequence! The program segment in Figure 2-3 shows several paragraphs with statements. Notice the PERFORM statement in PARA-GRAPH-2. The effect of this statement will be to immediately execute all the statements in PARAGRAPH-7, then return control to the statement following the PERFORM. Thus, the paragraphs will be executed in this sequence: 1, 2, 7, 3, etc.

```
PROCEDURE DIVISION.
PARAGRAPH-1.
        statements.
PARAGRAPH-2.
        statements.
        PERFORM PARAGRAPH-7.
PARAGRAPH-3.
  .
  .
  .
PARAGRAPH-7.
        statements
PARAGRAPH-8.
  .
  .
  .
```

Figure 2-3.   PERFORM Statement

Suppose you want PARAGRAPH-5 to be executed immediately after PARAGRAPH-7 is performed from PARAGRAPH-2.

(a) What statement would you use? _____

(b) Where would you insert the statement? _____

_____

- - - - - - - - - - - - - - - - - - - -

(a) PERFORM PARAGRAPH-5.
(b) You have several choices here. You could insert it immediately after the original PERFORM in PARAGRAPH-2, as the last statement in PARAGRAPH-7, or as the first statement in PARAGRAPH-3.

14. The basic PERFORM statement executes a sequence of statements else-where in the program, then returns control to the statement following PERFORM. It can be used as a THEN or ELSE action in an IF statement. Let's see the effects on control.

```
IF ITEM-TYPE NOT = 'FOOD'
    PERFORM FIGURE-TAX
ELSE
    NEXT SENTENCE.
MOVE ITEM-PRICE TO OUT-PRICE.
```

When the computer encounters PERFORM FIGURE-TAX, control goes immediately to a paragraph in the program named FIGURE-TAX, and all the statements in that paragraph are executed. Then, after the last statement of FIGURE-TAX is executed, control returns to the statement immediately following PERFORM. In this example, control will pass to the statement following the IF structure. A paragraph that is PERFORMed can PERFORM any paragraph except the one that PERFORMed it. It can include IFs, and often does. An IF may include PERFORMs, as you saw above. An IF may even include more IFs. We'll be looking into all of these later in this book.

```
IF ACCOUNT-NUMBER VALID
     ADD 2 TO TOTAL-COUNT
     PERFORM CHECK-TOTAL
     MOVE CHECK-FLAG TO TOTAL-FLAG
ELSE
     PERFORM BAD-ROUTINE.
```

(a) Name a paragraph referenced in the coding above? _____

_____

(b) If CHECK-TOTAL includes 7 statements, how many statements are represented by the THEN action above? _____

(c) After the statements in CHECK-TOTAL are executed, what statement is executed next? _____

- - - - - - - - - - - - - - - - - - -

(a) CHECK-TOTAL and BAD-ROUTINE; (b) 9; (c) MOVE

15. Now let's look at a chart of the general COBOL repetition structure and see how a PERFORM can repeat a section of code.

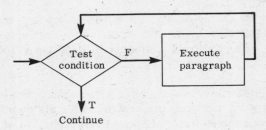

```
format:  PERFORM paragraph-name
         UNTIL condition.
```

When the computer sees the UNTIL clause, the first thing it does is test the condition. If the condition is true at the beginning, the paragraph isn't executed at all. If the condition is false, the paragraph is executed once. Then the condition is tested again. Before every execution of the named paragraph, the condition is tested. As soon as the condition is true, control will fall through to the statement following the PERFORM.

(a) How many times will a paragraph be executed if the condition is true when PERFORM UNTIL is first encountered? _____

(b) What will happen (theoretically) if the condition never becomes true?

(c) Is the condition tested before or after the first execution of a paragraph? _____

- - - - - - - - - - - - - - - - - - - -

(a) none; (b) theoretically, the paragraph will be repeated endlessly
(Actually, the computer won't let you run forever but will cut you off
after a certain amount of time.); (c) before

16. The PERFORM UNTIL is a very powerful COBOL statement. Here is an
    example.

```
PERFORM COUNT-RECORDS
    UNTIL END-OF-CARDS = 'Y'.
```

END-OF-CARDS is set equal to 'Y' when an input file has reached the
end.

(a) What paragraph is executed as a result of the statement above?

_____

(b) Where will control return after that paragraph is sufficiently executed?

_____

(c) When will control return? _____

- - - - - - - - - - - - - - - - - - - -

(a) COUNT-RECORDS; (b) the statement following PERFORM; (c) when
the condition is true (when END-OF-CARDS = 'Y', or end of file is reached)

17. The COBOL language allows a great deal of flexibility in spacing. The
    minimal requirements are simple.

    - No spaces may be used within words or components.
    - At least one space must separate words or components.
    - At least one space must follow each period.
    - Statements must be entirely contained in the B area.

In structured COBOL, we add a few conventions to these rules.

    - Write only one statement or major segment per line.
    - Use indentation to show control.
    - Use spacing to align related parts.

The coding you have seen in this chapter adheres to COBOL rules and
structure conventions. Examine each segment below, and indicate if it
adheres to COBOL rules. If so, indicate whether it adheres to structure
conventions.

(a)

```
7 | 8    12      16      20      24      28      32      36      40      44      48      52
  |       ADD 7 TO LINE-COUNT  DISPLAY LINE-COUNT.
```

COBOL _____   Structure _____

(b)

```
  |       IF LINE-COUNT = 50 PERFORM NEW-PAGE
  |       ELSE NEXT SENTENCE.
```

COBOL _____   Structure _____

(c)

```
  |       IF ITEM-TYPE = 'F' PERFORM TAX-FOOD ELSE
  |       PERFORM NO-TAX.DISPLAY ITEM-NAME.
```

COBOL _____   Structure _____

(d)

```
  |       IF A = 500
  |           PERFORM MAXIMUM-A
  |       ELSE
  |           PERFORM MINIMUM-A.
```

COBOL _____   Structure _____

- - - - - - - - - - - - - - - - -

(a) yes, no (two statements on the line); (b) yes, no (more than one segment per line); (c) no (no space following period); (d) yes, yes

As you continue in this book, you will look more closely at each statement or entry you have seen in this chapter. By now, you should have a fairly good grasp of the structure of COBOL as a language. You should know how the three control structures are handled in a COBOL program. And you have seen a variety of relatively self-explanatory COBOL statements. Before we get into the details of COBOL in the next chapter, let's look at the format notation we will be using to introduce statements.

FORMATS FOR COBOL STATEMENTS

18. Below is a sample format statement for a simple PERFORM.

PERFORM paragraph-name

The capitalized word is always required, as written. The lower case word is supplied by you.

Here is another sample. Notice that it is laid out one segment per line.

IF condition
$$\begin{Bmatrix} \text{statement} \\ \text{NEXT SENTENCE} \end{Bmatrix}$$
[ELSE
$$\begin{Bmatrix} \text{statement} \\ \text{NEXT SENTENCE.} \end{Bmatrix}]$$

The brackets [ ] indicate a part that is optional—you use it if needed or desired. The entire ELSE segment can be omitted if you have no ELSE action. The braces { } indicate a choice—use one and only one of the items in braces. We will be using this notation throughout the book to indicate format choices.

Which of the IF statements below would be valid according to the above format?

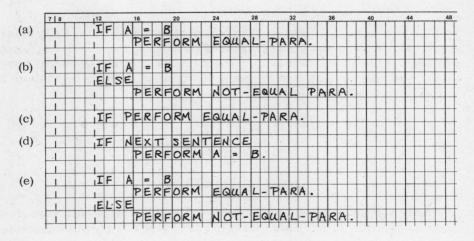

a (b omits the option after condition; c omits the condition; d omits the condition and uses both choices; e has an extra period before the ELSE.)

19. Here are some more format statements that show additional features of format notation.

MOVE $\begin{Bmatrix} \text{data-name} \\ \text{literal} \end{Bmatrix}$ TO data-name

SUBTRACT $\begin{Bmatrix} \text{data-name} \\ \text{literal} \end{Bmatrix}$ FROM data-name

[GIVING data-name]

Literals (or constants) are numbers (with or without decimal point and sign) or characters—characters are enclosed in quotes, as you may have noticed in COBOL statements earlier. We'll talk more about literals later. For now, decide which of the following adhere to the format statements above, to make sure you can interpret the format notation.

_____ (a) MOVE ITEM-TYPE TO 'FOOD'.

_____ (b) MOVE 'FOOD' TO ITEM-TYPE.

_____ (c) MOVE 12.98 to ITEM-PRICE.

_____ (d) SUBTRACT 7.98 FROM ITEM-PRICE.

_____ (e) SUBTRACT 7.98 FROM ITEM-PRICE GIVING DISCOUNT-PRICE.

- - - - - - - - - - - - - - - - - - - -

b, c, d, e (a has a literal after TO)

You now have an overview of the structure and rules of the COBOL language and basic conventions of structured COBOL. In the next chapter, you will learn to use enough basic COBOL statements to complete a short program. Now take the Self-Test to ensure that you are ready to begin learning to code structured COBOL.

SELF-TEST

After you have written your answers to the Self-Test, check your answers in the Answer Key that follows. Be sure you understand any differences between your answer and ours before you begin the next chapter. Following each suggested answer is a frame reference in parentheses, in case you need to review.

1. Code the first and last division headers on the form below.

2. Which is at a lower level in a COBOL program—a statement or a paragraph? _____

3. In what area of the COBOL coding form does a statement begin? _____
A paragraph name? _____

4. Which of the paragraph names on the next page are valid for programmer-supplied names?

_____ (a) INPUT-OUTPUT

_____ (b) PRINT-REPORT

_____ (c) $VALUE-CALCULATION

5. Which type of control structure is represented by the COBOL statement below?

```
7│8    │12    16    20    24    28    32    36    40    44    48    52
│          PERFORM ADD-BALANCES
│                  UNTIL EOF-CARD = 'END'.
│
```

_____

6. Examine the coding segment below.

```
7│8    │12    16    20    24    28    32    36    40    44    48    52
│         IF A = B
│              DISPLAY A
│         ELSE
│              DISPLAY B
│              PERFORM CHECK-RECORDS.
│         MOVE SPACES TO LINE-OF-PRINT.
```

If A has the value 7 and B has the value 6, which of the statements after the condition will be executed?

_____

_____

7. Examine the coding segment below. Indicate whether each line adheres to COBOL rules and structure conventions. The IF begins in column 12.

```
      7│8    │12    16    20    24    28    32    36    40    44    48
(a)   │         IF A=B DISPLAY A.
(b)   │         ELSE
(c)   │         DISPLAY B
(d)   │         PERFORM CHECK-RECORDS.
(e)   │         MOVE SPACESTO LINE-OF-PRINT.
```

(a) _____ , (b) _____ , (c) _____ , (d) _____ , (e) _____

8. Here is the format for a COBOL WRITE statement.

WRITE record-name   [FROM identifier]

$$[AFTER\ ADVANCING \left\{ \begin{matrix} n\ LINES \\ mnemonic\text{-}name \end{matrix} \right\}]$$

Which of the following are valid WRITE statements? (Assume all programmer-names are valid.)

_____ (a) WRITE PRINT-A-LINE.

_____ (b) WRITE 2 LINES FROM PRINT-A-LINE.

_____ (c) WRITE PRINT-A-LINE FROM LINE-OF-PRINT.

_____ (d) WRITE PRINT-A-LINE
        AFTER ADVANCING TO-TOP-OF-PAGE.

Answer Key

1.   IDENTIFICATION DIVISION.
     PROCEDURE DIVISION.   (3)

2.   statement   (1)

3.   B, A   (7)

4.   b (a is a reserved word; c starts with $)   (9)

5.   repetition (or iteration or looping)   (17)

6.   DISPLAY B
     PERFORM CHECK-RECORDS
     MOVE SPACES TO LINE-OF-PRINT   (12)

7.   (a) doesn't adhere to rules (period after A) or conventions (two major
         parts of statement on one line)
     (b) okay
     (c) doesn't adhere to indentation convention
     (d) doesn't adhere to indentation convention
     (e) doesn't adhere to COBOL rules (no space after SPACES)   (19)

8.   a, c, d   (20)

CHAPTER THREE
Beginning COBOL

Now you are ready to start writing structured COBOL programs. In this chapter and the next we will focus on the basic Procedure Division coding needed for programs involving card input and printer output. You will be learning about the first three divisions as well, but you won't actually code these divisions until Chapter 5. Instead, when you write the Procedure Division, you'll be given the necessary parts of the Identification, Environment, and Data Divisions. You'll learn to interpret them and to code a structured COBOL Procedure Division to solve problems that involve counting and selecting input records and printing messages on a system device.

When you complete this chapter, you will be able to:

- interpret one- or two-level record descriptions in the Working-Storage Section of the Data Division;

- specify the meaning of PIC X, FILLER, VALUE, and SPACES entries in the Data Division;

- write statements to input cards (ACCEPT) or print a line (DISPLAY) on standard devices;

- write statements to move data and/or literals (MOVE) to data items;

- write an IF statement to execute a selection control structure;

- write a simple PERFORM statement to cause one execution of a paragraph;

- write a PERFORM statement using the UNTIL option to execute a repetition control structure;

- write a statement to terminate execution (STOP RUN); and

- write a statement to cause an arithmetic operation to take place (ADD).

DATA IN THE COBOL PROGRAM

1. Every COBOL program involves data—as input, as output, often as temporary or working data. In this chapter, we're going to focus on working

data. Much of the data originates as punched cards. Let's look at a typical 80-column computer card to see how COBOL is used to describe data.

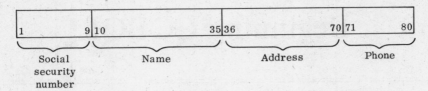

This card represents an input record; we'll call it IN-RECORD. In COBOL, a record-name is a level 01 data-name. That means it is coded with level 01 in the Data Division. The four major components, or fields, shown above are the next level down—they may be called level 02 when they are coded in the Data Division. The name and address fields can be broken down further, to level 03. Here is how the data structure might look as coded in a COBOL program.

```
01  IN-RECORD
    02  IN-SSNO
    02  IN-NAME
        03  IN-LAST
        03  IN-FIRST
    02  IN-ADDRESS
        03  IN-STREET
        03  IN-CITY
        03  IN-STATE
        03  IN-ZIP
    02  IN-PHONE
```

(a) The field labeled IN-NAME includes IN-LAST and IN-FIRST. What fields are included in IN-ADDRESS?

_____

(b) What fields are included in IN-PHONE? _____

(c) In which area is level number "01" coded? _____

(d) In which area are other level numbers coded? _____

(e) In which area are all data-names coded? _____

- -

(a) IN-STREET, IN-CITY, IN-STATE, IN-ZIP; (b) none; (c) area A;
(d) area B; (e) area B

2. The coding structure in frame 1 gave names to all the data fields. When we are writing a program, we must not only name the fields but also tell the system how long each field is and what kind of characters it has.

COBOL does this with a PICTURE clause—abbreviated PIC. In a PIC-TURE clause, we indicate the type of character in each position of a field. The character X indicates that the field position may contain any character at all, a 9 indicates that a position will contain a numeric digit, and an A indicates only letters or spaces. A field that is four character positions long could be described as PIC XXXX or PIC X(4). A nine-digit field can be described as PIC 9(9) or PIC 999999999. A part number field might be described as XX999—the first two characters can be anything, but the last three are digits. (In practice, A is little used. You'll learn many more useful PICTURE characters later.)

Only fields at the lowest level defined are described with pictures. A data-name that is subdivided, such as IN-RECORD or IN-NAME, doesn't get a separate picture.

To describe the first item in the structure of frame 1, we could use either IN-SSNO PIC X(9) or IN-SSNO PIC 9(9). We generally use X rather than 9 when no arithmetic will be done using that data.

```
7|8   12    16    20    24    28    32    36    40    44    48    52
 01   IN-RECORD.
      02   IN-SSNO              PIC  X(9).
      02   IN-NAME.
           03   IN-LAST    PIC  X(13).
           03   IN-FIRST   PIC  X(13).
      02   IN-ADDRESS.
           03   IN-STREET  PIC  X(18).
           03   IN-CITY    PIC  X(10).
           03   IN-STATE   PIC  X(2).
           03   IN-ZIP     PIC  X(5).
      02   IN-PHONE        PIC  X(10).
```

Examine the structure above. How many positions are represented by:

(a) IN-RECORD _____   (c) IN-STATE _____

(b) IN-ADDRESS _____   (d) IN-PHONE _____

- - - - - - - - - - - - - - - - - - -

(a) 80; (b) 35; (c) 2; (d) 10

3. Sometimes we want to use only part of the data on an input record in our program. Then we don't have to describe all the specific fields. If we only want the name from our record, for example, we could code the record description like this:

```
7|8   12    16    20    24    28    32    36    40    44    48    52
 01   IN-RECORD.
      02   FILLER                PIC  X(9).
      02   IN-NAME.
           03   IN-LAST     PIC  X(13).
           03   IN-FIRST    PIC  X(13).
      02   FILLER           PIC  X(45).
```

FILLER is a reserved word that is used to set aside storage positions without naming them. These FILLER areas cannot be referred to in the program.

(a) As written on the preceding page, how many fields can be accessed by name? _____

(b) How many positions are included in IN-NAME? _____

(c) How many positions are included in IN-RECORD? _____

- - - - - - - - - - - - - - - - - -

(a) 3 (IN-NAME, IN-LAST, IN-FIRST); (b) 26; (c) 80 (the typical input card length)

4. We must also provide record descriptions for output data. Each line of printed output is considered a record—the lines range up to 150 positions. We often insert spaces between fields to make the page easier to read. A line of output can be any length, limited only by the size of the printer. Let's say we want to print the first name and the last name, separated, in a 100-position line called OUT-RECORD.

```
01    OUT-RECORD.
      02    FILLER          PIC X(10).
      02    OUT-FIRST       PIC X(13).
      02    FILLER          PIC XXXX.
      02    OUT-LAST        PIC X(13).
      02    FILLER          PIC X(60).
```

(a) How many positions are occupied by the data in the record description above? _____

(b) How many fields can be referred to by name? _____

(c) How many columns will appear between the first and last name? _____

- - - - - - - - - - - - - - - - - -

(a) 26; (b) 2; (c) 4

5. We can set fields of working data to specific values by using a VALUE clause following PIC. COBOL provides figurative constants that you can use to give values to data items. Some of the more useful figurative constants can be used to set a data item to blanks or zero. Either SPACE or SPACES will set all the positions in a data item to blanks—we generally use this with fields described with character X. ZERO, ZEROS, or ZEROES will set the value to zero—this is especially useful for fields described with all nines in the PICTURE.

In an output line, we can use the VALUE clause with SPACES to make sure blanks appear where we want them. For example, the first FILLER in the preceding frame could read:

    02 FILLER   PIC X(10) VALUE IS SPACES.

Notice that the period appears after the last entry for the field. In this case, VALUE IS SPACES puts spaces as the first ten positions of the record.

(a) Rewrite the second FILLER from frame 4 so that blanks will separate the first and last name.

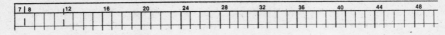

(b) How many blanks does this clause insert? _____

- - - - - - - - - - - - - - - - - -

(a) 02 FILLER   PIC XXXX   VALUE IS SPACES.
(b) four

6. The VALUE clause has the format shown below:

    VALUE [IS] value

The word IS is optional, so you could write VALUE SPACES, if you like. We'll use the VALUE clause for other purposes besides inserting spaces and other figurative constants later in this book.

The VALUE clause takes effect the moment the program begins. If you change a data item, the VALUE won't be reset. That's why we don't use VALUE for input records—reading data would overlay it and eliminate the value. Suppose your program includes:

    02 OUT-NAME   PIC X(30)   VALUE SPACES.

In the program, you might put a name in that field, say,

    'ANDERSON, JOSEPH'.

What will be the value of OUT-NAME then? _____

_____

- - - - - - - - - - - - - - - - - -

the name you put in (SPACES were overlaid)

THE COBOL PROGRAM

7. Figure 3-1 shows a complete, though short, structured COBOL program. The program takes a small deck of cards as input. Each card includes information about one person—last name, first name, and year of birth.

The last card in the deck has 9999 as year of birth—this is our end-of-deck marker. Each line of print will include the first and last name.

```
IDENTIFICATION DIVISION.
PROGRAM-ID.  LIST-NAMES.
ENVIRONMENT DIVISION.
DATA DIVISION.
WORKING-STORAGE SECTION.
01  IN-DATA.
    05  I-LAST-NAME      PIC X(12).
    05  I-FIRST-NAME     PIC X(12).
    05  I-YEAR-OF-BIRTH  PIC 9(4).
    05  FILLER           PIC X(52).
01  OUT-DATA.
    05  FILLER           PIC X        VALUE SPACES.
    05  FIRST-NAME       PIC X(12).
    05  FILLER           PIC X        VALUE SPACES.
    05  LAST-NAME        PIC X(12).
    05  FILLER           PIC X(54) VALUE SPACES.
*
PROCEDURE DIVISION.
SET-UP-PROGRAM.
    ACCEPT IN-DATA.
    PERFORM PROCESS-CARDS
        UNTIL I-YEAR-OF-BIRTH = 9999.
    STOP RUN.
PROCESS-CARDS.
    MOVE I-LAST-NAME TO LAST-NAME.
    MOVE I-FIRST-NAME TO FIRST-NAME.
    DISPLAY OUT-DATA.
    ACCEPT IN-DATA.
```

Figure 3-1. Structured COBOL Program

(a) The Procedure Division here includes two paragraphs. What are their

names? _____

(b) What control structures are represented?

_____

- - - - - - - - - - - - - - - - - -

(a) SET-UP-PROGRAM and PROCESS-CARDS; (b) sequence and repetition

8. Let's look at the input and output statements in the program—ACCEPT and DISPLAY. These statements are generally used for small amounts of input and output data or for small systems. In the next chapter you'll learn to use files for larger amounts of data. Then we'll need more coding in the Environment and Data Divisions as well.

On the next page are the usual formats of ACCEPT and DISPLAY.

```
ACCEPT    data-name   [FROM CONSOLE]
DISPLAY   data-name   [UPON CONSOLE]
```

The CONSOLE options refer to the computer room terminal—these options aren't much used in large installations today because the computer operator is much too involved and busy to read messages or enter data. The simple "ACCEPT data-name" statement generally reads one card, or accepts one record from the system input device. When the record is read in, the appropriate positions on the card are assigned to the various data-names. The "DISPLAY data-name" statement generally prints one line on the system printer.

Refer back to Figure 3-1.

(a) Which statement(s) input data? _____

(b) Which statement(s) output data? _____

(c) After the ACCEPT statement is executed, what data-names can you

refer to? _____

(d) What is printed by the DISPLAY statement? _____

_____

- - - - - - - - - - - - - - - - - - -

(a) ACCEPT (2); (b) DISPLAY; (c) I-LAST-NAME, I-FIRST-NAME, and I-YEAR-OF-BIRTH; (d) first and last names with spaces

9. The ACCEPT and DISPLAY statements, like all statements, must be entirely contained in the B area. Refer back to the formats if necessary, and try writing some COBOL statements.

(a) Write a statement to cause the computer to input one card, described as INVENTORY-UPDATE, from the system input device.

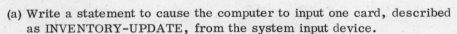

(b) Write a statement to cause the computer to print one line, described as UPDATE-REPORT, on the system output device.

- - - - - - - - - - - - - - - - - - -

(a)
(b)

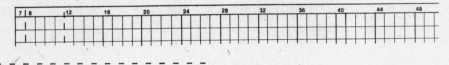
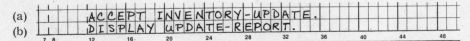

10. When a second ACCEPT is executed, new input data overlays the old. The second card, in effect, destroys the data read in by the first card. After a DISPLAY statement is executed, the output data remains in the record, so you can still refer to it if you need to.

(a) Suppose your program ACCEPTs three cards using the same record name, in succession. How many, and which one(s) are still present after the third ACCEPT? _____

(b) Suppose your program issues two ACCEPTs, followed by two DISPLAYs. What would you expect to be printed?

_____

- - - - - - - - - - - - - - - - - - -

(a) one, the last; (b) the second data, twice

Move Statement

11. Let's look back at paragraph PROCESS-CARDS in Figure 3-1. Here we have, in addition to ACCEPT and DISPLAY, two MOVE statements. Here is the basic format of MOVE.

$$\text{MOVE} \quad \left\{ \begin{array}{l} \text{data-name} \\ \text{literal} \end{array} \right\} \quad \text{TO data-name}$$

The MOVE statement causes the data represented by the first data-name or literal to be copied (or duplicated) into the second data-name. (We'll look at literals shortly.) The second data-name determines the number of characters moved—if the first is longer, some characters are dropped, if the first is shorter, the second is filled with blanks or zeros. (We'll see which in a moment.) Here, though, our data items are the same length.

(a) How many characters are moved by each MOVE statement in Figure 3-1? _____

(b) How does the value of I-FIRST-NAME change when it is MOVEd?

_____

(c) What are the relative positions of first and last names in the record after they are MOVEd? _____

- - - - - - - - - - - - - - - - - - -

(a) 12; (b) same as before; (c) reversed

12. Data items, or fields, can be of various types. We've been considering those described with 9, X, or a combination. A data item described

with all 9's is a numeric data item—it is treated differently in a MOVE than is an alphanumeric data item, which may be all X's or a combination.

When an alphanumeric (or non-numeric) field is moved, it is aligned on the left, and padded with blanks if necessary. When a numeric field is moved, it is aligned on the right (or at the decimal point if it has one) and padded with zeros, if necessary.

(a) When numeric values are moved, where is the data aligned?

_____

(b) What character is used to pad numeric values? _____

(c) When non-numeric values are moved, where is the data aligned?

_____

(d) What character is used to pad non-numeric values? _____

(e) Which of these pictures describe numeric fields?

    XXXX   X(4)   X(9)   XX99   9999   9(7)

- -

(a) on the right, or at decimal point; (b) zero; (c) on the left; (d) blank;
(e) 9999 and 9(7) (if any X occurs, it's not numeric)

Literals

13. The format of MOVE (frame 11) shows that you can move a data-name to a different data-name. You can also move a "literal" to a data-name. In COBOL, we can use three distinct types of literals.

Figurative constants can be moved to data-names. Thus, you could code MOVE SPACES TO OUT-DATA to set the entire record to blanks. You could code MOVE ZERO TO YEARS to set the value of YEARS to zero. You'll learn to use other figurative constants later.

Numeric literals are numbers; they can include a decimal point and can be preceded by a plus or minus sign. These are all valid numeric literals: 99, 100.00, -72.63. They can't contain commas or any other characters. And they can only be moved to numeric fields. (You'll learn to code pictures for decimal point and sign in the next chapter.) Thus, you could code MOVE 14.98 TO PRICE, or MOVE 1981 TO YEAR.

Non-numeric literals can contain any characters you wish, as long as they are enclosed in quotes—either single or double, depending on the computer system. We're using single enclosing quotes in this book, since that is most common. These are valid non-numeric literals: 'ERROR', 'SWEENY', '1981'. If you happen to need to include quotes within your non-numeric literal, use double ones.

Match the following literals with the literal types:

_____ (a) 000
_____ (b) 997
_____ (c) COUNT
_____ (d) 'COUNT'
_____ (e) ZEROS

1. Figurative constant
2. Numeric literal
3. Non-numeric literal
4. None of these

- - - - - - - - - - - - - - - - - -

(a) 2; (b) 2; (c) 4; (d) 3; (c) 1

14. MOVE statements can send data from the various formats, but it always goes TO a data-name. Here are some examples (FIRST-NAME has 13 positions).

    (1) MOVE IN-FIRST TO FIRST-NAME.
    (2) MOVE SPACES   TO FIRST-NAME.
    (3) MOVE 'RUTH'   TO FIRST-NAME.

    After example (1), FIRST-NAME contains whatever IN-FIRST contains. After example (2), FIRST-NAME contains 13 spaces. After example (3), FIRST-NAME contains RUTHøøøøøøøøø—RUTH padded with nine blanks to fill out the 13 positions. We use ø for blank.

    Now you write MOVE statements to accomplish the following: (Be sure to start in the B area.)

(a) Assign your last name to LAST-NAME.

(b) Put the value of IN-YEAR in OUT-YEAR.

(c) Set a numeric field called MARKER to zero without using a figurative constant.

- - - - - - - - - - - - - - - - - -

(a) MOVE 'ASHLEY' TO LAST-NAME. (write your name)
(b) MOVE IN-YEAR TO OUT-YEAR.
(c) MOVE 0 TO MARKER.

15. The DISPLAY statement can be used to print literals and the value of specific data items, as well as complete records of data.

```
DISPLAY 'MY NAME IS ' FIRST-NAME.
```

This statement will cause both the message (the literal) and the current value of FIRST-NAME to be printed on the device. Non-numeric literals are often used to print messages during program execution.

(a) Write a statement to print the current value of a data item named LINE-COUNTER.

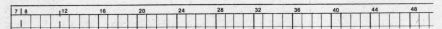

(b) Write a statement to print your name as a literal.

- - - - - - - - - - - - - - - - - - -

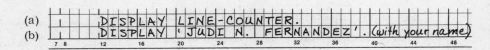

```
(a)    DISPLAY LINE-COUNTER.
(b)    DISPLAY 'JUDI N. FERNANDEZ'. (with your name)
```

16. You can also use ACCEPT to input just a few fields from a card or console. For example, ACCEPT NAME-IN will input one record. A specific number (N) of characters were set aside for NAME-IN in the Data Division. The first N characters on the input record are assigned to NAME-IN when the ACCEPT statement is executed. A program might include the following sequence:

```
DISPLAY 'ENTER YOUR NAME' UPON CONSOLE.
ACCEPT NAME-IN FROM CONSOLE.
```

Of course, the console must be available for someone to input the name.

Write a statement to print the literal "GOOD MORNING", and the value of NAME-IN on the console.

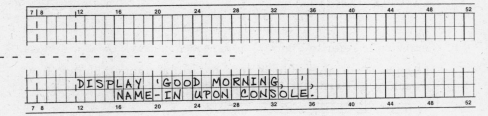

```
DISPLAY 'GOOD MORNING, '
        NAME-IN UPON CONSOLE.
```

17. Let's consider the main paragraph in Figure 3-1, repeated here:

```
SET-UP-PROGRAM.
    ACCEPT IN-DATA.
    PERFORM PROCESS-CARDS
        UNTIL I-YEAR-BIRTH = '9999'.
    STOP RUN.
```

The paragraph controls the logic of the program, including the first input, the controlling PERFORM, and a terminating statement, STOP RUN. As you can see, most of the processing will be done in the PERFORMed paragraph.

(a) How many times will PROCESS-CARDS be executed if the first

ACCEPTed card has year of birth of 9999? _____

(b) If "UNTIL condition" had been omitted, how many times would

PROCESS-CARDS be executed? _____

(c) Suppose the deck has 8 real data records plus an end card with '9999'.

How many times will PROCESS-CARDS be executed? _____

(d) What statement causes the program to end? _____

- - - - - - - - - - - - - - - - - -

(a) none; (b) one; (c) eight; (d) STOP RUN

18. Refer back to Figure 3-1 as needed, and answer these questions.

(a) What is the last statement executed in the program? _____

(b) What is the purpose of the * in column 7? _____

_____

(c) In what area do paragraph names begin? _____

(d) What paragraph contains the control logic? _____

- - - - - - - - - - - - - - - - - -

(a) STOP RUN; (b) to indicate a comment (blank) line; (c) A; (d) first (SET-UP-PROGRAM)

19. Continuing to refer to Figure 3-1 as needed, answer these questions.

(a) Suppose the last card to be accepted will contain all blanks. How would you rewrite the PERFORM statement?

7	8	12	16	20	24	28	32	36	40	44	48

(b) Suppose, in addition, the paragraph to be PERFORMed had been named OUTPUT-ROUTINE. Rewrite the PERFORM again.

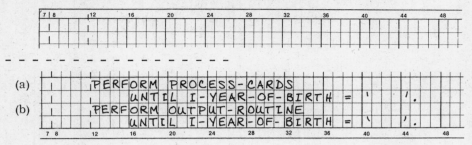

20. Suppose you have a set of cards, each containing information about one part in your inventory. The last card is marked by a "dummy" part number of 99999. You want to list the part number, part name, and quantity-on-hand for each card. The relevant Data Division entries are shown below.

```
01  PARTS—RECORD.
    02   PART—NUM              PIC X(5).
    02   PART—NAME             PIC X(10).
    02   PART—DESCRIPTION      PIC X(25).
    02   PART—ON—HAND          PIC 9(3).
    02   PART—PRICE            PIC 9(5).
    02   FILLER                PIC X(32).
01  PARTS—LIST.
    02   FILLER                PIC XX       VALUE SPACES.
    02   OUT—NUM               PIC X(5).
    02   FILLER                PIC XX       VALUE SPACES.
    02   OUT—NAME              PIC X(10).
    02   FILLER                PIC XX       VALUE SPACES.
    02   OUT—ON—HAND           PIC XXX.
    02   FILLER                PIC X(56)    VALUE SPACES.
```

Here is a pseudocode for your program.

Main-logic: Get a record
              PERFORM UNTIL no more records
                  move input fields to output fields
                  put out one line
                  get a record
              ENDPERFORM
              End program

Write the Procedure Division in structured COBOL. Be sure to include the division header, and create paragraph-names.

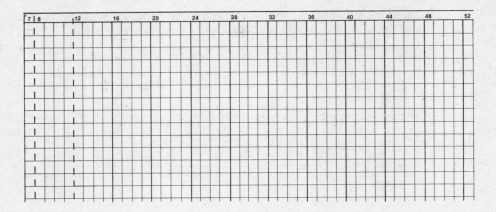

```
PROCEDURE DIVISION.
MAIN-LOGIC.
    ACCEPT PARTS-RECORD.
    PERFORM PROCESS-PARTS
        UNTIL PART-NUM = '99999'.
    STOP RUN.
*
PROCESS-PARTS.
    MOVE PART-NUM TO OUT-NUM.
    MOVE PART-NAME TO OUT-NAME.
    MOVE PART-ON-HAND TO OUT-ON-HAND.
    DISPLAY PARTS-LIST.
    ACCEPT PARTS-RECORD.
```

In checking your answer, pay attention to punctuation, spelling, and spacing. Did you use the same paragraph-name in your PERFORM that you used to name your processing paragraph? Did you use the right data-names from the Data Division?

COBOL Selection

21. The program you have just written used sequence and iteration control structures. Here is a modified form of the processing paragraph that uses a selection structure to select the appropriate action.

```
PROCESS-PARTS.
    MOVE PART-NUM TO OUT-NUM.
    MOVE PART-NAME TO OUT-NAME.
    IF PART-ON-HAND GREATER THAN 10
        MOVE PART-ON-HAND TO OUT-ON-HAND
    ELSE
        MOVE SPACES TO OUT-ON-HAND.
    DISPLAY PARTS-LIST.
    ACCEPT PARTS-RECORD.
```

This paragraph will result in the quantity-on-hand being printed only if it is greater than 10. If the quantity-on-hand is 10 or less, the output field will be filled with blanks. Here, as a review, is the IF format:

IF   condition
$\left\{ \begin{array}{l} \text{NEXT SENTENCE} \\ \text{statement} \end{array} \right\}$
[ELSE
$\left\{ \begin{array}{l} \text{NEXT SENTENCE.} \\ \text{statement} \end{array} \right\}$]

Write an IF statement that will use PART-NUM=1000 as the condition. When the condition is true, the field OUT-NAME should be filled with blanks. When the condition is false, OUT-NAME should hold the PART-NAME.

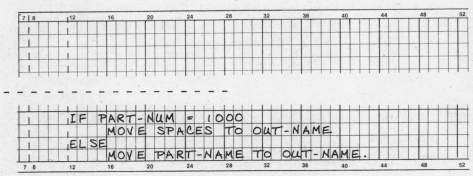

```
IF PART-NUM = 1000
    MOVE SPACES TO OUT-NAME
ELSE
    MOVE PART-NAME TO OUT-NAME.
```

22. Here is another modification of the processing paragraph from frame 20.

```
PROCESS-PARTS.
    IF PART-ON-HAND LESS THAN 25
        MOVE PART-NUM TO OUT-NUM
        MOVE PART-NAME TO OUT-NAME
        MOVE PART-ON-HAND TO OUT-ON-HAND
        DISPLAY PARTS-LIST
    ELSE
        NEXT SENTENCE.
    ACCEPT PARTS-RECORD.
```

This could also be coded like this:

```
PROCESS-PARTS.
    IF PART-ON-HAND LESS THAN 25
        PERFORM SET-UP-LINE
    ELSE
        NEXT SENTENCE.
    ACCEPT PARTS-RECORD.
SET-UP-LINE.
    MOVE PART-NUM TO OUT-NUM.
    MOVE PART-NAME TO OUT-NAME.
    MOVE PART-ON-HAND TO OUT-ON-HAND.
    DISPLAY PARTS LIST.
```

What does this version do that the original (frame 20) doesn't do?

_____

_____

- - - - - - - - - - - - - - - - - - -

It prepares and prints the line only if the quantity-on-hand is less than 25. It doesn't print anything otherwise.

23. Several COBOL statements require a condition—you've seen conditions in PERFORM UNTIL and in IF. Table 3-1 shows the symbols we use to write one type of condition. These are called relational condition operators, and we use them to compare two fields. The operator words and symbols are equivalent; use whichever is more comfortable for you.

Table 3-1.   Relational Condition Operators

operator	symbol	example
EQUAL TO	=	A = B
NOT EQUAL TO	NOT =	A NOT = B
GREATER THAN	>	A > B
NOT GREATER THAN	NOT >	A NOT > B
LESS THAN	<	A < B
NOT LESS THAN	NOT <	A NOT < B

- A space is needed before and after each operator or symbol.
- Either field may be replaced by a literal, but not both.

Write COBOL conditions for the situations described below.

(a) A field named EMP-NUM is 7500 or lower.

_____

(b) A field named TOTAL-HOURS is larger than 40.

_____

(c) A field named PART-NUM is the same as a field named PART-SALE.

_____

(d) A field named PART-NUM is larger or smaller than PART-SALE.

_____

- - - - - - - - - - - - - - - - - - -

(a) EMP-NUM NOT GREATER THAN 7500   (or NOT >)
(b) TOTAL-HOURS GREATER THAN 40   (or >)
(c) PART-NUM EQUAL TO PART-SALE   (or =)
(d) PART-NUM NOT EQUAL TO PART-SALE   (or NOT =)

24. Look back at Figure 3-1 on page 42. Suppose we want to print only the records in which the person was born before 1940. Modify PROCESS-CARDS to accomplish this.

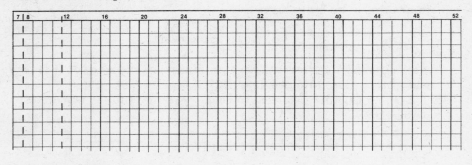

or

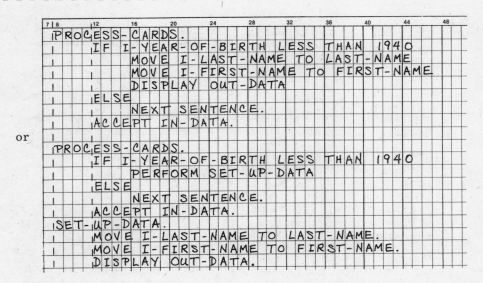

```
PROCESS-CARDS.
    IF I-YEAR-OF-BIRTH LESS THAN 1940
        MOVE I-LAST-NAME TO LAST-NAME
        MOVE I-FIRST-NAME TO FIRST-NAME
        DISPLAY OUT-DATA
    ELSE
        NEXT SENTENCE.
    ACCEPT IN-DATA.

PROCESS-CARDS.
    IF I-YEAR-OF-BIRTH LESS THAN 1940
        PERFORM SET-UP-DATA
    ELSE
        NEXT SENTENCE.
    ACCEPT IN-DATA.
SET-UP-DATA.
    MOVE I-LAST-NAME TO LAST-NAME.
    MOVE I-FIRST-NAME TO FIRST-NAME.
    DISPLAY OUT-DATA.
```

COUNTING RECORDS

25. It is often useful to be able to count things in a program—perhaps all the input records, perhaps only a certain type. In this next section you'll learn to use a numeric field and one form of an arithmetic statement to count records. Then you'll print out a message giving the total.

Numeric fields can be used for arithmetic. Let's say we have this item:

01   MARK-COUNTER   PIC 999   VALUE ZERO.

Here the value clause initializes COUNTER to zero. Since COUNTER is defined with 9's, it is numeric and can be used for arithmetic, which we'll do often later in this book. One way to count is to set a variable, called a counter, to zero, then add 1 to it each time we encounter one of the items we're counting. The ADD statement is the easiest way to do this. Here is its basic format:

$$ \text{ADD} \quad \left\{ \begin{array}{l} \text{data-name} \\ \text{numeric-literal} \end{array} \right\} \quad \text{TO} \quad \text{data-name} $$

We'll be using the literal here, then in the next chapter you'll learn to use ADD in more involved arithmetic.

Write a COBOL statement to count by adding 1 to the numeric field defined above.

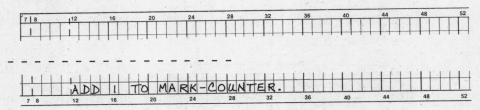

26. The program shown in Figure 3-2 counts the number of input records. Examine the program, then answer the questions which follow.

```
IDENTIFICATION DIVISION.
PROGRAM-ID.  COUNT-RECORDS.
ENVIRONMENT DIVISION.
DATA DIVISION.
WORKING-STORAGE SECTION.
01  CARD-COUNTER                    PIC 999    VALUE ZERO.
01  CARD-RECORD.
    05  CARD-MARK                   PIC 9(4).
    05  FILLER                      PIC X(76).
PROCEDURE DIVISION.
CONTROL-PARAGRAPH.
    ACCEPT CARD-RECORD.
    PERFORM COUNT-CARDS
        UNTIL CARD-MARK = 9999.
    DISPLAY 'NUMBER OF CARDS IS ' CARD-COUNTER.
    STOP RUN.
COUNT-CARDS.
    ADD 1 TO CARD-COUNTER.
    ACCEPT CARD-RECORD.
```

Figure 3-2. Counting Program

(a) What field is used as a counter? _____

(b) What statement does the counting? _____

(c) What statement tells you how many input records there were?

_____

- -

(a) CARD-COUNTER
(b) ADD 1 TO CARD-COUNTER.
(c) DISPLAY 'NUMBER OF CARDS IS ' CARD-COUNTER.

27. The program in Figure 3-2 can be modified to count only certain cards.
Suppose you want to count only cards with 1111 in CARD-MARK. Review
the program.

(a) Which paragraph would need to be changed? _____

(b) What control structure will accomplish the change?

_____

(c) Rewrite the paragraph to count only the cards with 1111 in CARD-
MARK, and print the CARD-MARK from the other cards.

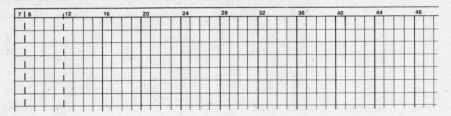

- -

(a) COUNT-CARDS
(b) selection (IF)
(c)

```
COUNT-CARDS.
    IF CARD-MARK = 1111
        ADD 1 TO CARD-COUNTER
    ELSE
        DISPLAY CARD-MARK.
    ACCEPT CARD-RECORD.
```

SUMMARY

In this chapter you have learned to use many of the common statements of
COBOL. The MOVE, IF, and PERFORM are the key statements in most

COBOL applications. While we are still using fairly simple forms of these statements, the principles you have learned hold true in more complex forms as well. The input and output statements you have been using are not the major ones in COBOL. ACCEPT is seldom used in large card-oriented computer installations but is common in terminal setups and small computer systems. DISPLAY continues to be used for messages and testing. But files are used for most input and output. You'll learn to use files for your card input and print output in the next chapter.

As a summary exercise for this chapter you will write a Procedure Division that uses all the statements you learned to code in this chapter. Use the coding form segment provided or a separate coding form. After you check your solution, you'll be ready to take the Self-Test for this chapter.

Summary Exercise

28. In this Exercise you will write a Procedure Division to complete a structured COBOL program. You will use all the statements you learned in this chapter. The program will use a set of cards as input. Each card will have a class code, a student name, a student number, and a grade. Processing will involve counting the total number of cards and listing the names of students with grades of A. At the end, print the message "THE NUMBER OF STUDENTS IS " and the total count. The last card has a dummy class number of all 9's. The first three divisions and a pseudo-code for the Procedure Division are given below and on the next page.

```
IDENTIFICATION DIVISION.
PROGRAM-ID.
    LISTACE.
ENVIRONMENT DIVISION.
DATA DIVISION.
WORKING-STORAGE SECTION.
01   STU-COUNT              PIC 999      VALUE ZERO.
01   STU-REC.
     02   STU-CLASS         PIC X(6).
     02   FILLER            PIC X.
     02   STU-NAME          PIC X(25).
     02   FILLER            PIC X.
     02   STU-NUM           PIC X(9).
     02   FILLER            PIC X.
     02   STU-GRADE         PIC X.
     02   FILLER            PIC X(36).
01   NAME-LIST.
     02   FILLER            PIC X(10)    VALUE SPACES.
     02   NAME-OUT          PIC X(25).
     02   FILLER            PIC X(45)    VALUE SPACES.
```

Pseudocode:

```
    Get a record
    PERFORM UNTIL no more cards
         count card
         IF  grade is A
             write name
         ELSE
             don't write name
         ENDIF
         Get a record
    ENDPERFORM
    Write message total
    End program
```

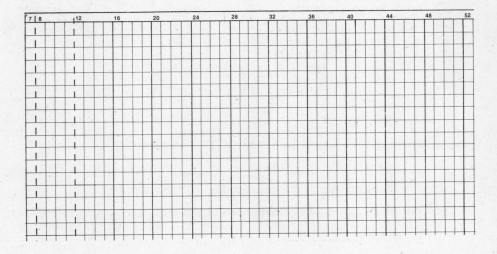

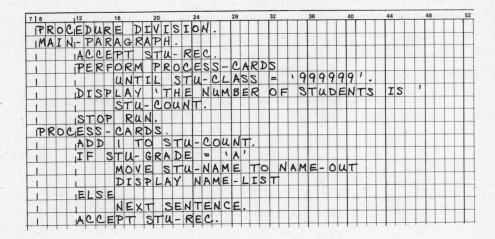

```
PROCEDURE DIVISION.
MAIN-PARAGRAPH.
    ACCEPT STU-REC.
    PERFORM PROCESS-CARDS
         UNTIL STU-CLASS = '999999'.
    DISPLAY 'THE NUMBER OF STUDENTS IS '
         STU-COUNT.
    STOP RUN.
PROCESS-CARDS.
    ADD 1 TO STU-COUNT.
    IF STU-GRADE = 'A'
         MOVE STU-NAME TO NAME-OUT
         DISPLAY NAME-LIST
    ELSE
         NEXT SENTENCE.
    ACCEPT STU-REC.
```

Check your coding. Did you use spacing and punctuation correctly? Did you use the data-names exactly as they were defined in the Data Division? Did you create valid paragraph names? Check your coding of the selection structure (IF) and repetition control (PERFORM UNTIL) carefully.

SELF-TEST

After you have written your answers to the Self-Test, check your answers in the Answer Key that follows. Be sure you understand any differences between your answers and ours before you begin the next chapter. Following each suggested answer is a frame reference in parentheses, in case you need to review.

1. Examine the coding below.

```
01  DETAIL-RECORD.
    02  PART-NUMBER    PIC  9(6).
    02  DEPARTMENT     PIC  9(4).
    02  FILLER         PIC  X(12).
    02  INVENTORY.
        03  ON-HAND    PIC  999.
        03  ON-ORDER   PIC  999.
    02  FILLER         PIC  X(24).
```

(a) Which of these could be a value of DEPARTMENT?

_____8888   _____LING   _____77MB

(b) How many positions are represented by INVENTORY? _____

(c) How many elementary fields here can be referenced in the Procedure Division? _____

2. Write a COBOL statement to receive a data record named IN-DATA from the system input device.

```
 7 | 8    12      16      20      24      28      32      36      40      44      48      52
  |        |
```

3. Write a COBOL statement to print a message (THE VALUE IS) and the value of a field named QUANTITY-ON-HAND on the system printer.

```
 7  8    12      16      20      24      28      32      36      40      44      48      52
```

4. Write statements to assign the values on the next page to a field described as NAME-DEPT PIC X(10).

(a) the value of IN-NAME

(b) the word EMPEROR

(c) all blanks

5. Write a COBOL selection structure to print the message "ERROR ON INPUT" and the IN-RECORD if the value of IN-DEPT (999) is more than 780. If the value is less than or equal to 780, print "record ok" and continue processing.

6. Modify your answer to question 5 to cause the system to execute NORMAL-INPUT when the value of IN-DEPT is not greater than 780.

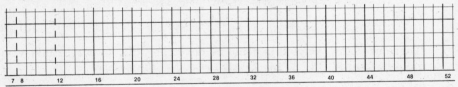

7. Write a COBOL statement to cause PROCESS-DATA to be executed repeatedly until the value of DATA-END is "YES".

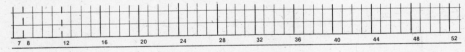

8. Write a COBOL statement to cause a program to terminate execution.

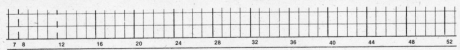

9. Write a COBOL statement to count by two's, using COUNT-BY-TWO as a counter.

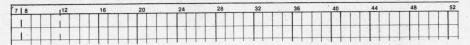

10. In question 9, how would COUNT-BY-TWO be described in the Data Division? _____

Answer Key

1. (a) 8888 (only digits)   (2)
   (b) 6 (ON-HAND plus ON-ORDER)   (2)
   (c) 4 (no FILLER items)   (3)

2. ```
   ACCEPT IN-DATA.
   ```
   (8, 9)

3. ```
   DISPLAY 'THE VALUE IS ', QUANTITY-ON-HAND.
   ```
   (9, 15)

4. (a) ```
       MOVE IN-NAME TO NAME-DEPT.
       ```
       (12, 13)
   (b) ```
       MOVE 'EMPEROR' TO NAME-DEPT.
       ```
       (12, 13)
   (c) ```
       MOVE SPACES TO NAME-DEPT.
       ```
       (12, 13)

   or
   ```
       MOVE ' ' TO NAME-DEPT.
   ```
   (It will be padded with more blanks.)

5. ```
   IF IN-DEPT > 780
        DISPLAY 'ERROR ON INPUT ', IN-RECORD
   ELSE
        DISPLAY 'RECORD OKAY'.
   ```
   (21, 23)

   (There are other ways this could be coded as well. In particular, you could have used GREATER THAN instead of the symbol >.)

6. Change ELSE segment to:
   ```
   ELSE
        PERFORM NORMAL-INPUT.
   ```
   (22)

7. ```
   PERFORM PROCESS-DATA
        UNTIL DATA-END = 'YES'.
   ```
   (17, 19)

8. ```
   STOP RUN.
   ```
   (17)

9. ```
   ADD 2 TO COUNT-BY-TWO.
   ```
   (26)

10. All 9's   (25)
   ```

CHAPTER FOUR
Using Unit Record Files

In the last chapter, you learned to use ACCEPT and DISPLAY statements for small amounts of input and output data. These statements are not generally used as the primary means of input and output in large computer systems. To handle the masses of data generated today, most business and industrial applications use files. Input files are generally entered on cards or from terminals, and the printer serves as the output terminal. Of course, data files may be stored on tape or disk as well. Later in the book, you'll learn to handle data on other media, but in this chapter we're going to deal with card and printer files. Since the records are all separate, these are called unit record files.

As you learn about card and printer files, you will become familiar with end-of-file processing. At the end of the chapter, you'll write program segments that use what you learn here.

When you complete this chapter, you will be able to:

- interpret card and printer file description entries in the Environment and Data Divisions;

- code COBOL statements to OPEN and CLOSE files;

- code COBOL input statements, including action to be taken when the end-of-file has been reached;

- code COBOL output statements;

- use the INTO option of READ and FROM option of WRITE; and

- code a complete Procedure Division that does a card-to-print operation.

FILES IN COBOL

1. When input data is punched on cards, we generally use it as an input file. Each card is one record, 80 characters long. The record has fields, as you saw earlier. Processing a deck of cards as a file is much more efficient for the system than ACCEPTing them as single cards.

    Indicate whether each item on the next page refers to cards to be ACCEPTed or to a card file.

_____ (a) used for large amounts of input
data

_____ (b) has 80 character records

_____ (c) more efficient for the computer

- - - - - - - - - - - - - - - - - -

(a) file; (b) file or ACCEPT; (c) file

2. Just as input cards are more efficient to process as files than as single
cards, so are printer files more efficient to handle than DISPLAYs. In a
printer file, each line generally represents one record. Both card and
printer files are often called unit-record files, since the unit or device
used determines what constitutes a record. The usual print record has
133 positions, but they can range in length from a few columns to 150 or
more positions in some printers.
    Which of the areas below is different for printer files than for lines
printed by DISPLAY statements?

_____ (a) line length

_____ (b) record size

_____ (c) efficiency of execution

- - - - - - - - - - - - - - - - - -

c

3. In order to tell the system about a file, you have to include some extra
entries in your COBOL program. An INPUT-OUTPUT SECTION is needed
in the Environment Division and a FILE SECTION in the Data Division.
In the Procedure Division, each record is accessed by a READ or WRITE
statement, after the file is prepared with an OPEN statement. Then before the program ends, the file must be finished with a CLOSE statement.

(a) In what three divisions is file-related coding needed when a COBOL
program uses files?

_____

(b) In what division do you tell the system what devices are used?

_____

(c) In what division do you describe the records associated with input and
output files? _____

- - - - - - - - - - - - - - - - - -

(a) Environment, Data, Procedure; (b) Environment; (c) Data

4. Figure 4-1 shows the framework of a COBOL program that uses card and printer files. Let's consider the Environment Division entries first.

```
ENVIRONMENT DIVISION.
INPUT-OUTPUT SECTION.
FILE-CONTROL.
    SELECT file-name1
        ASSIGN TO system-name1.
    SELECT file-name2
        ASSIGN TO system-name2.
DATA DIVISION.
FILE SECTION.
FD  file-name1
    LABEL RECORDS ARE OMITTED.
01  record-name1.
    02  record description.
FD  file-name2
    LABEL RECORDS ARE OMITTED.
01  record-name2.
    02  record description.
WORKING-STORAGE SECTION.
```

Figure 4-1. File-Related Entries

Notice that we use an INPUT-OUTPUT SECTION. Within that, we have a FILE-CONTROL paragraph. Each of these is coded on a separate line, beginning in area A, and ending with a period.

In the FILE-CONTROL paragraph is a SELECT entry for each file. Each SELECT entry gives a name to a file to be used in the program and uses an ASSIGN clause to assign it to a device in the system. The system-name is different for most systems—it can range from simply CARD or PRINT to a series of codes. One very common form uses a series of codes and a control file-name that ties it to a control statement elsewhere. UR-S-CARDS means that a unit-record (UR) file, sequential (S), named CARDS in the control language, will be used. We'll use this type of system-name here, but you'll have to check it out for your system.

Here is a sample Environment Division entry:

```
ENVIRONMENT DIVISION.
INPUT-OUTPUT SECTION.
FILE-CONTROL.
    SELECT INVENTORY
        ASSIGN TO UR-S-CARDS.
    SELECT REPORT-INVENTORY
        ASSIGN TO UR-S-PRINT.
```

(a) What names will be used to refer to files in the program?

(b) What is the system-name for the printer file? _____

(c) What indentation above is a convention rather than a COBOL rule?

_____

- - - - - - - - - - - - - - - - - -

(a) INVENTORY and REPORT-INVENTORY; (b) UR-S-PRINT;
(c) the indenting of the ASSIGN clause.

5. The Data Division in Figure 4-1 shows two sections. The File Section is always needed to describe the file organization and the data record associated with each file. Up to now, you've used the Working-Storage Section for data—that is still used, but the File Section must be coded first. You can't generally use a VALUE clause in the File Section, but otherwise data records are described much as in Working-Storage. Working-Storage is used for various things, including end-of-file indicators, output lines that need spacing, and fields to be used for arithmetic.

(a) Name two sections in the Data Division.

_____

(b) Which section is coded first? _____

(c) In which section is data initialized with VALUE clauses?

_____

(d) In which section are records associated with files defined?

_____

- - - - - - - - - - - - - - - - - -

(a) File Section and Working-Storage Section; (b) File Section;
(c) Working-Storage Section; (d) File Section

6. The File Section entry for each file consists of two parts. The first part describes the file, the second part the record.

The FD (File Description) names the file, using the name as in the SELECT entry. And it gives the status or type of file labels. Computer systems assume that every file has labels that contain information about the file-name, organization, size, etc. But in reality, card and printer files don't have labels, so we need to tell the system that label records have been omitted. This satisfies the system, and it will proceed to process the files without label records. Later, you'll learn that files on other devices always have labels. Notice that the FD is in area A while the rest of the entry is in area B. A period follows the last clause.

Refer to Figure 4-1, and write an FD entry for the card file that was SELECTed in frame 4.

```
 7 | 8     |12     16     20     24     28     32     36     40     44     48     52
   |         |
   |         |
   |         |
- - - - - - - - - - - - - - - - - - - - - - -
   | FD   INVENTORY
   |      LABEL RECORDS ARE OMITTED.
 7  8       12     16     20     24     28     32     36     40     44     48     52
```

Note: We'll be using typed rather than handwritten answers except when the areas or columns are the focus of the exercise from now on. You'll still get forms for your coding, however.

7. The description of records for a file always immediately follows the FD entry for that file. For a card file, exactly 80 positions must be accounted for in the record description. For a printer file, the number of print positions must be accounted for.
    Refer to Figure 4-1 as necessary to answer these questions.

    (a) What entry in the Environment Division gives the file-name?

    _____

    (b) What entry in the Data Division includes the file-name? _____

    (c) Where, physically, is the record description for a file placed in a

    program? _____

- - - - - - - - - - - - - - - - - - - -

    (a) SELECT (in the FILE-CONTROL paragraph); (b) FD (in the FILE SECTION); (c) immediately after the FD entry for that file

8. In the Procedure Division, all files must be OPENed before use, and CLOSEd before the program ends. The OPEN statement prepares the named files for use in the programs. You won't be able to use any file for input or output until it has been OPENed. The CLOSE statement tells the system you're finished, and the devices can then be used by another program. OPEN is generally one of the first statements in the Procedure Division, while CLOSE is one of the last.
    Let's consider the OPEN statement. Here is its format:

$$\text{OPEN} \begin{Bmatrix} \text{INPUT} \\ \text{OUTPUT} \end{Bmatrix} \text{file-name} \quad [\begin{Bmatrix} \text{INPUT} \\ \text{OUTPUT} \end{Bmatrix} \text{file-name}[\dots]]$$

You may open as many files as you wish with one OPEN statement, or use a separate OPEN for each file. We'll use one OPEN for all files when we can. On the next page is an example.

```
OPEN   INPUT    CARDFILE
       OUTPUT   PRINTFILE.
```

The statement could also be written on one line.

```
OPEN   INPUT   CARDFILE   OUTPUT   PRINTFILE.
```

Suppose you have files named INCARD and REPORT-OUT.

(a) Write a statement to prepare the files for use in the program.

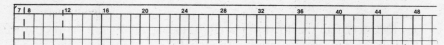

(b) Where in the Procedure Division would you locate an OPEN statement?

_____

- - - - - - - - - - - - - - - - - - - -

(a) `OPEN INPUT   INCARD`
        `OUTPUT REPORT-OUT.`   (Be sure you started in area B.)
(b) near the beginning

9. The format for the CLOSE statement is:

CLOSE file-name [file-name]...

Notice that the use of the file (INPUT or OUTPUT) is not repeated in the CLOSE. As with OPEN, more than one file may be specified in CLOSE.

(a) Write a statement to CLOSE the files you OPENed in the last frame.

(b) Where in the Procedure Division would you probably locate a CLOSE

statement? _____

- - - - - - - - - - - - - - - - - - - -

(a) CLOSE INCARD
        REPORT-OUT.   (You could have put the statement on one line.)
(b) near the end

10. You have seen how to OPEN and CLOSE a file. Now let's look at the state-ments we use to do input and output. We'll look at the output statement—WRITE—first. The simple WRITE format is:

WRITE record-name

Figure 4-2 shows part of a program in which WRITE is used. Notice that the paragraph READ-INPUT isn't shown—we'll add it a bit later. This example shows an output record size of 80, but the size can vary from just a few positions to the line length of the printer.

```
         :
         :
DATA DIVISION.
FILE SECTION.
FD  IN-FILE
     LABEL RECORDS ARE OMITTED.
01  IN-REC                PIC X(80).
FD  OUT-FILE
     LABEL RECORDS ARE OMITTED.
01  OUT-REC          /    PIC X(80).
WORKING-STORAGE SECTION.
01  EOF-READ              PIC XXX   VALUE 'NO '.
PROCEDURE DIVISION.
FIRST-PARAGRAPH.
    OPEN INPUT IN-FILE
         OUTPUT OUT-FILE.
    PERFORM READ-INPUT.
    PERFORM LIST-RECORDS
         UNTIL EOF-READ = 'YES'.
    CLOSE IN-FILE OUT-FILE.
    STOP RUN.
LIST-RECORDS.
    MOVE IN-REC TO OUT-REC.
    WRITE OUT-REC.
    PERFORM READ-INPUT.
```

Figure 4-2. Program Segment

(a) What is the name of the output file? _____

(b) What statement prepares the file for use?

_____

_____

(c) What statement puts a record in the output record area?

_____

(d) What statement actually puts the output record in the output file?

_____

(e) What statement tells the system you are finished using the file?

_____

- - - - - - - - - - - - - - - - - -

(a) OUT-FILE
(b) OPEN INPUT   IN-FILE
         OUTPUT OUT-FILE.

(c) MOVE IN-REC TO OUT-REC.
(d) WRITE OUT-REC.
(e) CLOSE IN-FILE OUT-FILE.

11. In the OPEN and CLOSE statements, you specify the file-names. In the WRITE statement, however, you specify the record-name. Notice in Figure 4-2 that we have OPEN...OUT-FILE, but we WRITE OUT-REC. Suppose the file had been described as:

```
FD  REPORT-OUT
    LABEL RECORDS ARE OMITTED.
01  LINE-OF-PRINT.
    02
       :
       :
```

Write statements to accomplish the following:

(a) Prepare the file for output.

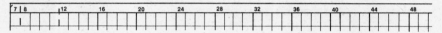

(b) Output the record.

(c) Tell the system you are finished with the file.

- - - - - - - - - - - - - - - - - - -

(a) OPEN OUTPUT REPORT-OUT.
(b) WRITE LINE-OF-PRINT.
(c) CLOSE REPORT-OUT.

12. Notice in Figure 4-2 that a Working-Storage item named EOF-READ is defined and given a value of 'NO '. We'll use this field to indicate when the program has reached the end-of-file (EOF) on the input. In a program, we often have extra processing to do when the input is finished. At the very least, we need to CLOSE our files. For this reason, the READ statement includes an AT END clause. The READ-INPUT paragraph for Figure 4-2 is as follows:

```
READ-INPUT.
    READ IN-FILE
        AT END  MOVE 'YES' TO EOF-READ.
```

The system knows when it attempts to read beyond the last data card, and the AT END clause is only activated when that occurs. The process is equivalent to:

IF the file is all gone
THEN
      do these things after AT END
ELSE
      continue as normal
ENDIF

Notice that AT END is not activated by the last card but by the READ than follows it. That is why the READ is often the last statement in a paragraph—in Figure 4-2, the PERFORM UNTIL causes the system to test for the end-of-file indicator before it starts each repetition of LIST-RECORDS.

Refer back to Figure 4-2.

(a) What will be the result if no records at all are in the input file?

_____

(b) What will be the result if the input deck contains three data cards

before the end of the file? _____

_____

- - - - - - - - - - - - - - - - - - -

(a) LIST-RECORD won't be executed, and nothing will be printed.
(b) Three lines will be printed, then the files will be closed and the program will end.

13. The basic format for the READ statement is

    READ file-name
          AT END statement.

Notice that READ uses a file-name, as OPEN and CLOSE do.

The "statement" can be any number of statements; but you can't use IF in an AT END clause. PERFORM, MOVE, DISPLAY are all valid, though, as are arithmetic statements, such as ADD. For example, you could use

```
READ TRANSACTIONS
     AT END  MOVE 'Y' TO EOF-TRANS
             DISPLAY '#TRANSACTIONS IS ' TRAN-COUNT.
```

The next period after AT END marks its end. If we had an extra period after EOF-TRANS above, the DISPLAY would be executed after every read! Write a statement for the BILLING file that will print the message

"NO DATA FILE--BILLING" and set EOF-BILLING to "Y" if the end-of-file is found on the first READ.

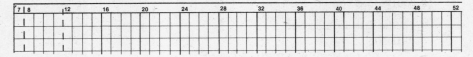

```
READ BILLING
     AT END DISPLAY 'NO DATA FILE--BILLING'
          MOVE 'Y' TO EOF-BILLING.
```

14. If much processing will be done on data, it is safer to move it out of the input area before processing. Data is vulnerable while it resides in the record described for the file. If an equivalent record is described in Working-Storage, you can MOVE the entire record, then process as usual.

    For example, suppose you have an input file (IN-FILE), described with IN-RECORD. You have an equivalent record in Working-Storage (WS-RECORD). Write COBOL statements to access a record and store it in Working-Storage. Use EOF-IN as an end-of-file indicator.

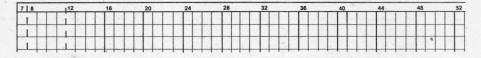

```
READ IN-FILE
     AT END MOVE 'Y' TO EOF-IN.
MOVE IN-RECORD TO WS-RECORD.
```

15. In COBOL programs, we often build lines for output in Working-Storage, since we can then use VALUE clauses to help format the data. When a line is built, we MOVE it to the output record and WRITE it.

    Suppose you have an output file named WRITE-FILE, described with WRITE-RECORD. You've built a line in Working-Storage called ONE-LINE. Write the COBOL statements to print the line.

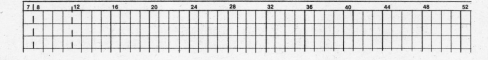

```
MOVE ONE-LINE TO WRITE-RECORD.
WRITE WRITE-RECORD.
```

16. The READ and WRITE statements can both be used to effect a MOVE of the entire record as well as the appropriate input or output.

> formats: READ file-name [INTO data-name]
> AT END statement
>
> WRITE record-name [FROM data-name]

The data-name here is a record-name or data-name usually of the same length as the input or output record. The implied MOVE works like a non-numeric MOVE—aligning on the left and padding with blanks or truncation if needed.

The program in Figure 4-2, for example, could have included the following READ-INPUT paragraph:

```
READ-INPUT.
    READ IN-FILE INTO OUT-REC
        AT END MOVE 'YES' TO EOF-READ.
```

In this case, the LIST-RECORDS paragraph would not have needed MOVE IN-REC TO OUT-REC, because the input record was placed in the OUT-REC spot at the time of the READ.

Suppose you want, instead, to omit the MOVE statement and use the FROM option on the WRITE. How would you code the output statement?

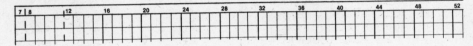

- - - - - - - - - - - - - - - - - - -

```
WRITE OUT-REC FROM IN-REC.
```

17. Refer back to frames 14 and 15.

(a) Recode your answer to frame 14 using a single statement.

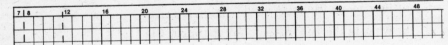

(b) Recode your answer to frame 15 using a single statement.

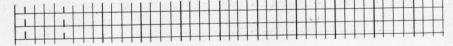

- - - - - - - - - - - - - - - - - -

```
(a) READ IN-FILE INTO WS-RECORD
        AT END MOVE 'Y' TO EOF-IN.
(b) WRITE WRITE-RECORD FROM ONE-LINE.
```

18. Figure 4-3 shows the first three Divisions of another program.

```
IDENTIFICATION DIVISION.
PROGRAM-ID.
    FILEDEMO.
ENVIRONMENT DIVISION.
INPUT-OUTPUT SECTION.
FILE-CONTROL.
    SELECT STUDENTS
        ASSIGN TO UR-S-CARDS.
    SELECT LISTOUT
        ASSIGN TO UR-S-PRINTER.
DATA DIVISION.
FILE SECTION.
FD  STUDENTS
    LABEL RECORDS ARE OMITTED.
01  STU-RECORD.
    02  STU-NUM              PIC X(9).
    02  STU-NAME             PIC X(30).
    02  FILLER               PIC X(41).
FD  LISTOUT
    LABEL RECORDS ARE OMITTED.
01  LIST-REC                 PIC X(90).
WORKING-STORAGE SECTION.
01  END-OF-STUDENTS          PIC X        VALUE 'N'.
01  LIST-WORK-AREA.
    02  FILLER               PIC X        VALUE SPACE.
    02  LIST-COUNT           PIC 999      VALUE ZERO.
    02  FILLER               PIC X        VALUE SPACE.
    02  LIST-EIGHTY          PIC X(80).
    02  FILLER               PIC X(5)     VALUE SPACES.
```

Figure 4-3. Program Segment

Interpret the coding above as you answer these questions.

(a) How many files are used? _____

(b) What is the record-size for the input file? _____

(c) What is the record-size for the output file? _____

(d) What field is intended to be used as an end-of-input-file indicator?

_____

- - - - - - - - - - - - - - - - - -

(a) 2 (STUDENTS and LISTOUT); (b) 80; (c) 90; (d) END-OF-STUDENTS

19. You'll use the Divisions in Figure 4-3 in the next few frames as you complete a COBOL program that produces a listing of the input file, with a sequence number for each. Notice the Working-Storage area LIST-WORK-AREA. This is the length of the output record. It is used to name and

value its fields. You can use it to set up the output record. VALUE clauses can't be used in the FILE SECTION except in special circumstances you'll learn about later. You'll be able to use both the INTO option of READ and the FROM option of WRITE. Here is a pseudocode for the program.

```
Main-logic
        Set-up files
        Get input record
        PERFORM UNTIL end-of-input file
            Process file
        ENDPERFORM
        Terminate program
Process file
        Add 1 to counter
        Put record to output file
        Get input record
```

First write a GET-INPUT-RECORD paragraph.

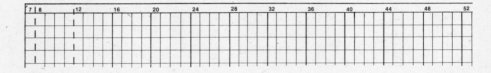

```
GET-INPUT-RECORD.
    READ STUDENTS INTO LIST-EIGHTY
        AT END MOVE 'Y' TO END-OF-STUDENTS.
```

(Notice that you READ the record into a field within LIST-WORK-AREA.)

20. Now write a MAIN-LOGIC paragraph, referring to Figure 4-3 as needed.

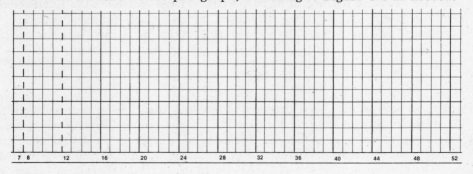

```
PROCEDURE DIVISION.
MAIN-LOGIC.
    OPEN INPUT STUDENTS
        OUTPUT LISTOUT.
    PERFORM GET-INPUT-RECORD.
    PERFORM PROCESS-FILE
        UNTIL END-OF-STUDENTS = 'Y'.
    CLOSE STUDENTS
        LISTOUT.
    STOP RUN.
```

21. To complete the COBOL program, now write a PROCESS-FILE paragraph.

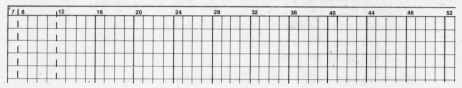

- -

```
PROCESS-FILE.
    ADD 1 TO LIST-COUNT.
    WRITE LIST-REC FROM LIST-WORK-AREA.
    PERFORM GET-INPUT-RECORD.
```

(Notice that we WRITE the output record from the complete LIST-WORK-AREA.)

SUMMARY

In this chapter, you have started using card files as input and printer files as output. You learned to use the INTO option of READ and the FROM option of WRITE. You have learned to interpret file-related entries in the Environment and Data Divisions, and to code file handling statements for the Procedure Division. You have written the Procedure Division for a card-to-print program.

SELF-TEST

After you have written your answers to the Self-Test, check your answers in the Answer Key that follows. Be sure you understand any differences between your answers and ours before you begin the next chapter. Following each suggested answer is a frame reference in parentheses, in case you need to review.

The questions in this Self-Test refer to the partial program in Figure 4-4.

```
IDENTIFICATION DIVISION.
PROGRAM-ID.
    FINAL4.
ENVIRONMENT DIVISION.
INPUT-OUTPUT SECTION.
FILE-CONTROL.
    SELECT PEOPLE-FILE
        ASSIGN TO UR-S-CARDS.
    SELECT REPORT-FILE
        ASSIGN TO UR-S-PRINTER.
DATA DIVISION.
FILE SECTION.
FD  PEOPLE-FILE
    LABEL RECORDS ARE OMITTED.
01  PEOPLE-RECORD.
    02  P-NAME.
        03  P-N-LAST          PIC X(15).
        03  P-N-FIRST         PIC X(10).
        03  P-N-MID           PIC X(10).
    02  P-ADDRESS.
        03  P-A-STREET        PIC X(15).
        03  P-A-CITY          PIC X(10).
        03  P-A-STATE         PIC XX.
        03  P-A-ZIP           PIC 9(5).
    02  P-SSNO                PIC 9(9).
    02  FILLER                PIC X(4).
FD  REPORT-FILE
    LABEL RECORDS ARE OMITTED.
01  LISTING-RECORDS           PIC X(133).
WORKING-STORAGE SECTION.
01  NO-MORE-CARDS             PIC X(3)        VALUE ' NO'.
01  WS-LIST-FORM.
    02  WS-LINE               PIC X           VALUE SPACE.
    02  WS-NAME.
        03  WS-N-FIRST        PIC X(10).
        03  FILLER            PIC X           VALUE SPACE.
        03  WS-N-LAST         PIC X(15).
    02  FILLER                PIC X(5)        VALUE SPACES.
    02  WS-LOCATION.
        03  WS-L-CITY         PIC X(10).
        03  FILLER            PIC X           VALUE ','.
        03  WS-L-STATE        PIC XX.
    02  FILLER                PIC X(88)       VALUE SPACES.
```

Figure 4-4. Partial Program

1. What position in the input record contains the initial of the middle name?

    _____

2. Write COBOL statement(s) to prepare the files for use in the program.

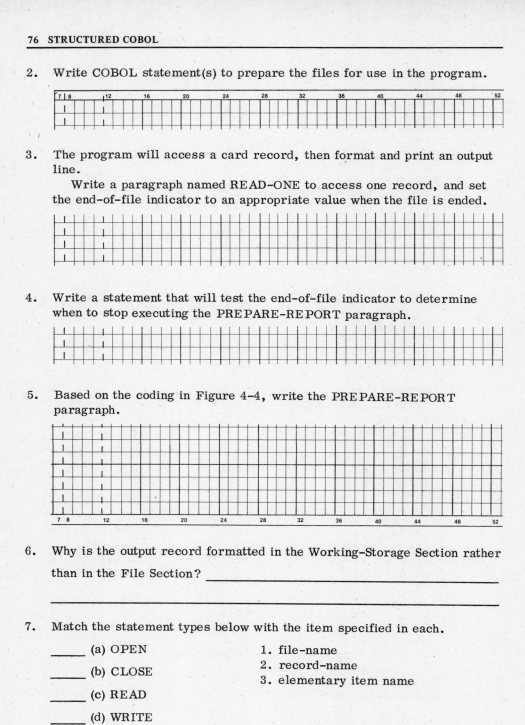

3. The program will access a card record, then format and print an output line.
    Write a paragraph named READ-ONE to access one record, and set the end-of-file indicator to an appropriate value when the file is ended.

4. Write a statement that will test the end-of-file indicator to determine when to stop executing the PREPARE-REPORT paragraph.

5. Based on the coding in Figure 4-4, write the PREPARE-REPORT paragraph.

6. Why is the output record formatted in the Working-Storage Section rather than in the File Section? _____

_____

7. Match the statement types below with the item specified in each.

    _____ (a) OPEN   1. file-name
    _____ (b) CLOSE   2. record-name
                            3. elementary item name
    _____ (c) READ
    _____ (d) WRITE

Answer Key

1. position 26   (6)

2. OPEN INPUT PEOPLE-FILE
        OUTPUT REPORT-FILE.   (8)

   (You could have used two OPEN statements.)

3. READ-ONE.
        READ PEOPLE-FILE
            AT END MOVE 'YES' TO NO-MORE-CARDS.   (12)

4. PERFORM PREPARE-REPORT
        UNTIL NO-MORE-CARDS = 'YES'.   (20)

5. PREPARE-REPORT.
        MOVE P-N-LAST   TO WS-N-LAST.
        MOVE P-N-FIRST TO WS-N-FIRST.
        MOVE P-A-CITY   TO WS-L-CITY.
        MOVE P-A-STATE TO WS-L-STATE.
        WRITE LISTING-RECORDS FROM WS-LIST-FORM.
        PERFORM READ-ONE.   (15, 16)

6. Because VALUE clauses can't be used in the File Section.   (5)

7. (a) 1; (b) 1; (c) 1; (d) 2   (11, 13)

CHAPTER FIVE
COBOL Arithmetic

Virtually every COBOL program includes some arithmetic. You've already used the ADD statement to count records. In this chapter, you'll learn to use the rest of the COBOL arithmetic statements and options. You'll learn to specify error handling, and to round results as needed. By the end of the chapter, you'll be able to use any of the COBOL arithmetic statements in programs.

When you complete this chapter, you will be able to:

- code separate ADD, SUBTRACT, MULTIPLY, and DIVIDE statements;

- use a GIVING option with ADD, SUBTRACT, MULTIPLY, or DIVIDE;

- code a COMPUTE statement to calculate a value;

- specify that an arithmetic result field be ROUNDED; and

- use the ON SIZE ERROR option to specify error processing in any COBOL arithmetic statement.

This section will introduce you to the arithmetic statements available in COBOL. We will start with a few Data Division entries that make arithmetic more efficient or effective.

ARITHMETIC STATEMENTS

1. You already know that data items must have 9's in their PICTURE clauses if any arithmetic is to be done. Most arithmetic also requires some recognition of where a decimal point belongs. Here are three ways you can give the computer this information in a PICTURE clause.

(1)	999	three digits	123$_\wedge$	(decimal position at right)
(2)	99V9	three digits	12$_\wedge$3	(assumed decimal where indicated)
(3)	99.9	three digits	12.3	(actual decimal where indicated)

Example (1) is assumed to have a decimal place at the far right; any picture of all 9's is considered an integer. Example (2) is assumed to have a decimal place where the V occurs in the picture. If you were to ADD the values in the first two examples, the result would be equivalent to 135.3

—COBOL will line up assumed decimal places! The third example can't be used in arithmetic at all—fields to be used in arithmetic can include only 9's and one V in their PICTURES. Example (3) <u>can</u> be used for output, though. The picture character '.' is printed in the position of the assumed decimal point.

Which of the data items below can be used for arithmetic?

_____ (a) HOURS   PIC   99

_____ (b) WEEK   PIC   XX

_____ (c) WAGE   PIC   9V99

_____ (d) GROSS-PAY   PIC   999V99

_____ (e) GROSS   PIC   999.99

- - - - - - - - - - - - - - - - - - -

a, c, d

2. Sometimes data is negative—but if a picture doesn't allow for it, the data will be treated as positive. The S picture character allows for a sign. It is the first character in a PICTURE but, along with V, doesn't represent a character position. Internally, though, the system will keep track of the sign and the decimal. If there is any chance a numeric field may be negative, its picture should have an S. Many programmers include an S in the picture of every numeric data item.

(a) Which of the pictures below represent valid numeric fields?

_____ 99VS   _____ SV99   _____ 99V99S   _____ S99V9

(b) How many character positions are represented by S999? _____

(c) How is a negative number stored if the data item did not include an S in its picture? _____

- - - - - - - - - - - - - - - - - - -

(a) SV99 and S99V9; (b) 3; (c) as a positive number (absolute value)

3. Neither a V nor an S represents a character position. A picture of S9(5)V9 represents six character positions. However, a decimal point or actual sign does represent a character position.

How many positions are represented by each picture listed below?

(a) S999V99 _____   (c) S9(5)V99 _____

(b) 99999 _____   (d) S9(6) _____

- - - - - - - - - - - - - - - - - - -

(a) 5; (b) 5; (c) 7; (d) 6

4. The simplest forms of the four COBOL arithmetic statements are given below:

ADD $\left\{ \begin{array}{l} \text{data-name} \\ \text{literal} \end{array} \right\}$ TO   data-name

SUBTRACT $\left\{ \begin{array}{l} \text{data-name} \\ \text{literal} \end{array} \right\}$ FROM   data-name

MULTIPLY $\left\{ \begin{array}{l} \text{data-name} \\ \text{literal} \end{array} \right\}$ BY   data-name

DIVIDE $\left\{ \begin{array}{l} \text{data-name} \\ \text{literal} \end{array} \right\}$ INTO   data-name

In each case, after the operation takes place, the last-named data-name contains the result. Suppose the data-name is ANSFIELD (PIC 999), and it has a beginning value of 12 for each statement below. What is the value after execution of each?

(a) ADD 4 TO ANSFIELD. _____

(b) SUBTRACT 4 FROM ANSFIELD. _____

(c) MULTIPLY 4 BY ANSFIELD. _____

(d) DIVIDE 4 INTO ANSFIELD. _____

- - - - - - - - - - - - - - - - - - -

(a) 16; (b) 8; (c) 48;   (d) 3

5. Numeric literals, even in arithmetic statements, may contain an actual decimal point. The system aligns it as needed for the operation. Remember that the decimal is assumed to be at the far right if no other location is given.

Suppose ANSFIELD has been described as PIC 99V9 and FIELDA has been described as PIC 99. Assume that ANSFIELD has a value of 012 and FIELDA has a value of 4 for each statement below. What is the value of ANSFIELD after each?

(a) ADD 4 TO ANSFIELD. _____

(b) SUBTRACT .4 FROM ANSFIELD. _____

(c) MULTIPLY FIELDA BY ANSFIELD. _____

- - - - - - - - - - - - - - - - -

(a) 5$\wedge$2;   (b) 0$\wedge$8;   (c) 04$\wedge$8;   (d) 00$\wedge$3

6. In the course of aligning decimal places, some digit positions may be lost, or truncated. Other times, padding with zeros may take place. For example, suppose one of the statements in frame 5 had read ADD 4.25 TO

ANSFIELD. The resulting value would have been 054, as the extra "5" won't fit in the result field. If we had said MULTIPLY 4.1 BY ANSFIELD, the resulting value of 492 would be stored as 049. MULTIPLY 4.4 BY ANSFIELD would have the resulting value of 528 stored as 052. You'll see a bit later how to specify rounding, rather than truncation, be done. That would allow this last result to be stored as 053 instead.

Assume we have fields as shown below.

```
FIELDX    PIC 999     VALUE 122
FIELDY    PIC 99V9    VALUE 033
FIELDZ    PIC 99V9    VALUE 100
```

Give the result after each statement below. State what digits, if any, are truncated.

(a) ADD 2.5 TO FIELDX _____

(b) SUBTRACT FIELDY FROM FIELDZ _____

(c) MULTIPLY FIELDZ BY FIELDX _____

(d) DIVIDE 11 INTO FIELDY _____

- - - - - - - - - - - - - - - - - -

(a) 124—"5" is truncated; (b) 067; (c) 220—"1" is truncated on the left; (d) 003

7. Write COBOL statements to accomplish the following:

(a) Double the value in FIELDX.

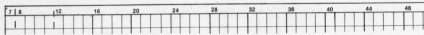

(b) Divide the value in FIELDY by 3.

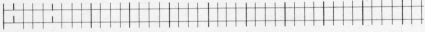

(c) Subtract the value in FIELDY from the value in FIELDX.

(d) Multiply the values in FIELDX and FIELDY and store the result in FIELDX.

- - - - - - - - - - - - - - - - - -

```
(a)  MULTIPLY 2 BY FIELDX   (or ADD FIELDX TO FIELDX)
(b)  DIVIDE 3 INTO FIELDY
(c)  SUBTRACT FIELDY FROM FIELDX.
(d)  MULTIPLY FIELDY BY FIELDX
```

(Remember, the last-named field will contain the result.)

GIVING Option

8.   Another option of COBOL arithmetic statements is "GIVING data-name". GIVING specifies a field in which the result will be stored. When GIVING is used, no other field in the statement is changed as a result of the arithmetic operation.

   When the GIVING option is added to a statement, the original statement doesn't change, except in the case of ADD. The word TO is omitted when GIVING is used. A comma and space may be used to separate items; at least one space must be used, as in this example.

   ADD 2, FIELDX GIVING FIELDZ.

   Assume you have data items as shown below.

```
HOURS    PIC  99V9
WAGE     PIC  9V99
GROSS    PIC  999V99
COUNTR   PIC  999
COUNTT   PIC  999
```

(a) Write a statement to multiply the WAGE field by 1.5 and store the result in WAGE.

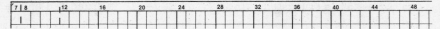

(b) Write a statement to multiply HOURS and WAGE and store the result in GROSS.

(c) Assume the value of HOURS is 40,0 and WAGE is 7,50 at question (b). What are the values of all three fields after the statement you wrote

   for (b) is executed? _____

(d) Write a statement to add 1 to COUNTR and store the result in COUNTT.

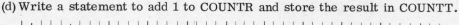

- - - - - - - - - - - - - - - - - - - -

(a)   MULTIPLY 1.5 BY WAGE.
(b)   MULTIPLY HOURS BY WAGE GIVING GROSS.
(c)   HOURS 40,0;   7,50;   GROSS: 300,00
(d)   ADD 1 COUNTR GIVING COUNTT.

9.   The data-name named in the GIVING option isn't really used in the arithmetic operations; it's just used to hold the result. Therefore, it doesn't have to be a numeric field. You may include editing features such as an actual decimal point or sign. Assume you have data items as described on the next page.

```
BALANCE        PIC  999V99
CHARGE         PIC  99V99
CREDIT         PIC  99V99
OUT-BALANCE    PIC  999.99
```

(a) Which fields can be used in arithmetic statements without the GIVING
option? _____

(b) Which fields could be used in the GIVING option?

_____

(c) Write a statement to subtract CREDIT from BALANCE so you can use
the result in an ADD statement later on.

(d) Write a statement to add CHARGE to BALANCE and store the result
so it has an actual decimal point.

- - - - - - - - - - - - - - - - - - - -

(a) BALANCE, CHARGE, and CREDIT
(b) all of them
(c) SUBTRACT CREDIT FROM BALANCE.
(d) ADD CHARGE BALANCE GIVING OUT-BALANCE.

(You might have used a comma between CHARGE and BALANCE as well
as a space.)

ROUNDED Option

10. Another option that may be specified in any arithmetic statement is
ROUNDED. ROUNDED is written immediately after the result field.
The effect is to round the result, rather than simply truncate, if there
are extra digits to the right of the decimal point. Thus, if we have a result field defined as 99V9, the value 77.78 would be rounded to 77.8.

(a) Write a statement to multiply HOURS by WAGE and store the rounded
result in SALARY.

(b) Write a statement to divide SALARY by 40 and store the rounded result in FAIR-SHARE.

(c) Write a statement to add FIELDX to FIELDY and round it to fit.

```
7 8    12    16    20    24    28    32    36    40    44    48
 |
```

- -

```
(a)  MULTIPLY HOURS BY WAGE GIVING SALARY ROUNDED.
(b)  DIVIDE 40 INTO SALARY GIVING FAIR-SHARE ROUNDED.
(c)  ADD FIELDX TO FIELDY ROUNDED.
```

ON SIZE ERROR Option

11. The ROUNDED option is used when you expect extra digits to the right of the decimal position. Another option, ON SIZE ERROR, is used when the field could have extra digits to the left of the decimal position. Truncation of digits on the left causes significant errors in arithmetic. When you use ON SIZE ERROR, it must be the last clause in an arithmetic statement, and it must be followed by a period. It includes one or more statements to be executed only if the result is too large (on the left) to fit in the result field. For example, any result with a value of 100 or more would create a size error if the result field were defined as 99, 99V99, or V9999. Here are some examples. Notice we write each clause on a separate line. This isn't a COBOL rule but a structured convention.

```
MULTIPLY HOURS BY WAGE
     GIVING GROSS
     ON SIZE ERROR PERFORM OVER-GROSS.
ADD HOURS TO TOTAL-HOURS
     ON SIZE ERROR DISPLAY "CHECK-HOURS",
        EMPLOYEE-NUMBER.
```

(a) Write a statement to divide SALARY by 40 resulting in FAIRSHARE. If the result field has too many positions to the right of the decimal, round it. If there are too many positions to the left of the decimal, perform DIVIDE-RESULT-TOO-LARGE.

(b) Write a statement to find the product of FIELDX and FIELDY, and store the result in FIELDY. If the result is too large, "execute PARAGRAPH-XY."

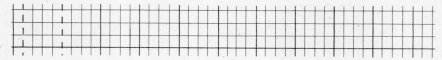

- -

(a) DIVIDE 40 INTO SALARY
        GIVING FAIRSHARE ROUNDED
          ON SIZE ERROR PERFORM DIVIDE-RESULT-TOO-LARGE.
(b) MULTIPLY FIELDX BY FIELDY
          ON SIZE ERROR PERFORM PARAGRAPH-XY.

The <u>COMPUTE</u> Statement

12. COBOL offers a fifth arithmetic statement, the COMPUTE statement, that allows you to write more "arithmetic-like" statements.

> format: COMPUTE data-name = expression

> example: COMPUTE X = Y + 3

> example: COMPUTE X = 9 * Y / 5 + 32

In a COMPUTE statement, the data-name on the left of the equal sign holds the result of the expression on the right. Suppose X = 2 and Y = 3. Give the value of Z in each COMPUTE statement below.

(a) COMPUTE Z = X.   _____

(b) COMPUTE Z = X + Y.   _____

(c) COMPUTE Z = Y - X.   _____

(d) COMPUTE Z = 2.   _____

- - - - - - - - - - - - - - - - - -

(a) 2; (b) 5; (c) 1; (d) 2

13. The expression on the right in a COMPUTE statement can be a numeric literal, a data-name, or an arithmetic expression using arithmetic operators, as shown below. Notice that a double asterisk represents raising to a power (3^2) while a single asterisk represents multiplication.

Arithmetic Operators

Symbol	Meaning	Example
**	exponentiation	3 ** 2
/	division	10 / 5
*	multiplication	2 * 5
-	subtraction	3 - 1
+	addition	2 + 3

An expression can be quite complex. Whenever more than one operator appears in an expression, they are evaluated in order of priority—first **, then * and /, and finally + and -. When operators are of equal priority, the evaluation is from left to right. Parentheses can modify the order of evaluation; inner parentheses are evaluated first.

For example, examine the expressions below:

    7 + 8 - 3 * 2 becomes 9
    7 + (8 - 3) * 2 becomes 17
    (7 + 8 - 3) * 2 becomes 24.

When in doubt, use parentheses. Extra ones never hurt, as long as you have as many open parentheses [(] as close parentheses [)].

Assume FIELDX = 4, FIELDY = 3, and FIELDZ = 5. What is the value of each expression below?

(a) FIELDY + FIELDX * FIELDZ _____

(b) FIELDX * (FIELDZ - FIELDY) _____

(c) FIELDX ** 2 + FIELDZ * FIELDY _____

(d) (FIELDX ** 2 + FIELDZ) * FIELDY _____

(e) FIELDX + FIELDZ + FIELDY / 3 _____

(f) (FIELDX + FIELDZ + FIELDY) / 3 _____

- - - - - - - - - - - - - - - - - - -

(a) 23; (b) 8; (c) 16 x 15 = 240; (d) 21 x 3 = 63; (e) 10; (f) 4

14. Each arithmetic operator, including the equal sign, must be preceded and followed by a space. A sign indicating a positive or negative value, however, should not be followed by a space. No two operators can occur next to each other. You may use parentheses to separate them. Correct any spacing errors in the COMPUTE statements below.

(a) COMPUTE C = A+B

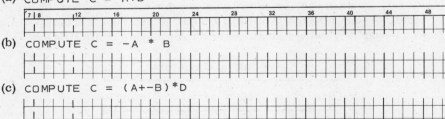

(b) COMPUTE C = -A * B

(c) COMPUTE C = (A+-B)*D

- - - - - - - - - - - - - - - - - - -

(a) COMPUTE C = A + B
(b) COMPUTE C = (-A) * B
(c) COMPUTE C = (A + (-B)) * D

15. The statements below calculate the area of a triangle:

    MULTIPLY BASE BY HEIGHT GIVING TRIANGLE-AREA.
    MULTIPLY 0.5 BY TRIANGLE-AREA.

Write a COMPUTE statement to accomplish the same result.

- - - - - - - - - - - - - - - - - -

```
COMPUTE TRIANGLE-AREA = BASE * HEIGHT * 0.5.
```

16. ROUNDED and ON SIZE ERROR can both be specified in a COMPUTE statement. As in the other arithmetic statements, ROUNDED is included directly following the name of the result field, and ON SIZE ERROR is the last clause in the statement.

The formula for converting FAHRENHEIT to CELSIUS degrees is (5/9 FAHRENHEIT) - 32. Write a COMPUTE statement to accomplish this, rounding the result and executing RESULT-FIELD-SIZE if digits on the left are truncated.

- - - - - - - - - - - - - - - - - -

```
COMPUTE CELSIUS ROUNDED = (5 * FAHRENHEIT / 9) - 32
       ON SIZE ERROR PERFORM RESULT-FIELD-SIZE.
```

17. You recall that any field used in an arithmetic statement must be a numeric variable or a numeric literal. A numeric variable has a PICTURE that includes 9's, perhaps one V, and perhaps an S. A numeric literal includes digits, perhaps a decimal point, perhaps a sign, but no quotes. A variable named in the GIVING option (or on the left of the equal sign in COMPUTE) need not be numeric, and often includes an actual decimal point for editing. You'll learn more about the variable descriptions in the next chapter. For now, just assume that all given are appropriately described.

Suppose you need to calculate an estimated price for fencing. You know two dimensions of the field (FIELD-LENGTH and FIELD-WIDTH), and you know the average price per foot (FIELD-PRICE).

(a) Write a COMPUTE statement to find FENCE-ESTIMATE, round it, and, in case of SIZE ERROR, display the dimensions on the console.

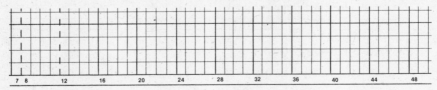

(b) Write statements to accomplish the same thing without using COMPUTE. A form is provided on the next page.

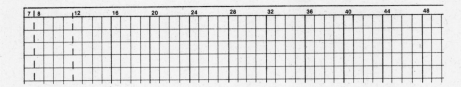

- - - - - - - - - - - - - - - - - - - -

```
(a) COMPUTE FENCE-ESTIMATE ROUNDED =
        (FIELD-LENGTH + FIELD-WIDTH) * 2 * FIELD-PRICE
        ON SIZE ERROR
            DISPLAY FIELD-LENGTH, FIELD-WIDTH UPON CONSOLE.


(b) ADD FIELD-LENGTH FIELD-WIDTH GIVING FENCE-ESTIMATE.
    MULTIPLY 2 BY FENCE-ESTIMATE.
    MULTIPLY FIELD-PRICE BY FENCE-ESTIMATE ROUNDED
        ON SIZE ERROR
            DISPLAY FIELD-LENGTH, FIELD-WIDTH UPON CONSOLE.
```

18. Suppose you have a deck of cards, each containing one field named QUANTITY. You want to add up all these QUANTITY's, to get TOTAL-QUANTITY. Finally, you want to move TOTAL-QUANTITY to TOTAL-OUT in OUT-RECORD and print it in the output file. Part of the Procedure Division is shown below.

```
MAIN-LOGIC.
    OPEN INPUT IN-FILE
         OUTPUT OUT-FILE.
    MOVE ZEROS TO TOTAL-QUANTITY.
    READ IN-FILE
        AT END MOVE 'Y' TO EOF-CARD.
    PERFORM SUM-UP-QUANTITY
        UNTIL EOF-CARD = 'Y'.
    PERFORM PUT-OUT-LINE.
    CLOSE IN-FILE, OUT-FILE.
    STOP RUN.
```

(a) Write a paragraph SUM-UP-QUANTITY. Include a SIZE ERROR option to DISPLAY a message if the value gets too large.

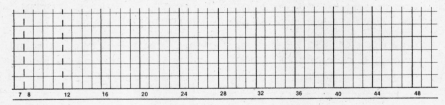

(b) Write PUT-OUT-LINE.

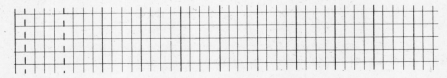

- - - - - - - - - - - - - - - - - - - -

(a) SUM-UP-QUANTITY.
        ADD QUANTITY TO TOTAL-QUANTITY
            ON SIZE ERROR DISPLAY 'TOO BIG'.
        READ IN-FILE
            AT END MOVE 'Y' TO EOF-CARD.

(b) PUT-OUT-LINE.
        MOVE TOTAL-QUANTITY TO TOTAL-OUT.
        WRITE OUT-RECORD.

SUMMARY

You have learned how to use arithmetic statements in COBOL, both as separate statements and COMPUTE. You've learned to specify that a result field
is to be rounded, and what to do if the value is too large to fit in the result
field.

In the summary exercise for this chapter, you'll have a chance to pull
all this together as you write a Procedure Division that involves arithmetic
on individual records as well as summary information.

Summary Exercise

19. This program will calculate and print gross pay for each employee who
    has a record in the input card file. Then it will print the total of all the
    gross pay calculated. The first three divisions (shown in Figure 5-1)
    include the record layouts, as well as working storage records for set-
    ting up two different output lines. Additional working-storage variables
    are defined for the end-of-file marker, as well as fields for calculating
    GROSS for an individual employee and TOTAL-GROSS for all employees.

```
IDENTIFICATION DIVISION.
PROGRAM-ID.
    SALARY.
ENVIRONMENT DIVISION.
INPUT-OUTPUT SECTION.
FILE-CONTROL.
    SELECT CARD-FILE
        ASSIGN TO UR-S-INONE.
    SELECT PRINT-FILE
        ASSIGN TO UR-S-OUTONE.
DATA DIVISION.
FILE SECTION.
FD  CARD-FILE
    LABEL RECORDS ARE OMITTED.
01  CARD-RECORD.
    02  C-NUMBER          PIC 9(9).
    02  C-NAME            PIC X(28).
    02  FILLER            PIC XXX.
    02  C-HOURS           PIC 99V9.
    02  FILLER            PIC XX.
    02  C-WAGE            PIC 99V99.
    02  FILLER            PIC X(31).
```
(continued on the next page)

```
FD   PRINT-FILE
     LABEL RECORDS ARE OMITTED.
01   PRINT-LINE               PIC X(121).
WORKING-STORAGE SECTION.
01   EOF-CARD                 PIC X              VALUE 'N'.
01   GROSS-VALUES.
     02   GROSS               PIC S999V99        VALUE ZERO.
     02   TOTAL-GROSS         PIC S9(6)V99       VALUE ZERO.
01   EMPLOYEE-LINE.
     02   FILLER              PIC X(10)          VALUE SPACES.
     02   E-NAME              PIC X(28).
     02   FILLER              PIC X(12)          VALUE SPACES.
     02   E-GROSS             PIC 999.99.
     02   FILLER              PIC X(65)          VALUE SPACES.
01   SUMM-LINE.
     02   FILLER              PIC X(20)          VALUE SPACES.
     02   OUT-GROSS           PIC 9(6).99.
     02   FILLER              PIC X(92)          VALUE SPACES.
```

Figure 5-1

The pseudocode in Figure 5-2 shows the program logic. Notice that if the GROSS for an individual is more than $1000, the employee name should be displayed on the printer.

Pseudocode

Main Logic
        Set up files
        Read an input record
        PERFORM UNTIL no more input records
                Calculate-output
        ENDPERFORM
        Set up summary line
        Print summary line
        End program
Calculate-output
        Find gross pay
        If gross pay > 1000
        DISPLAY name
        ELSE
        ENDIF
        Move fields to record for printing
        Write line
        Accumulate total-gross
        Read an input record

Figure 5-2

Examine the first three divisions and the pseudocode carefully. Then write the control logic paragraph for the program.

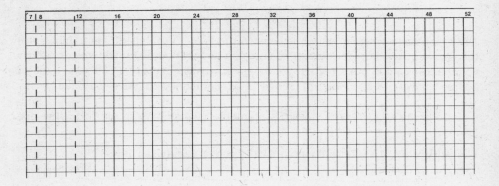

```
PROCEDURE DIVISION.
MAIN-LOGIC.
    OPEN INPUT CARD-FILE
        OUTPUT PRINT-FILE.
    READ CARD-FILE
        AT END MOVE 'Y' TO EOF-CARD.
    PERFORM CALCULATE-OUTPUT
        UNTIL EOF-CARD = 'Y'.
    MOVE TOTAL-GROSS TO OUT-GROSS.
    WRITE PRINT-LINE FROM SUMM-LINE.
    CLOSE CARD-FILE, PRINT-FILE.
    STOP RUN.
```

20. Now code the paragraph CALCULATE-OUTPUT.

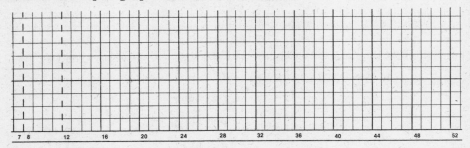

```
CALCULATE-OUTPUT.
    COMPUTE GROSS ROUNDED = C-HOURS * C-WAGE
        ON SIZE ERROR DISPLAY C-NAME.
    MOVE GROSS TO E-GROSS.
    MOVE C-NAME TO E-NAME.
    WRITE PRINT-LINE FROM EMPLOYEE-LINE.
    ADD GROSS TO TOTAL-GROSS.
    READ CARD-FILE
        AT END MOVE 'Y' TO EOF-CARD.
```

SELF-TEST

After you have written your answers to the Self-Test, check your answers in the Answer Key that follows. Be sure you understand any differences between your answers and ours before you begin the next chapter. Following each suggested answer is a frame reference in parentheses, in case you need to review.

Code the COBOL arithmetic statements to accomplish the following operations:

1. Multiply QUANTITY times PRICE. Store result in GROSS.

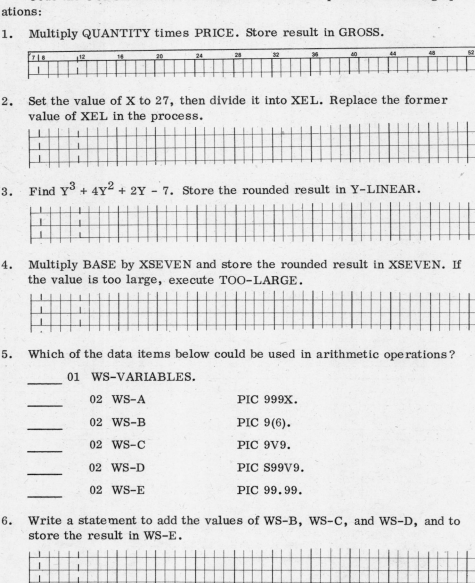

2. Set the value of X to 27, then divide it into XEL. Replace the former value of XEL in the process.

3. Find $Y^3 + 4Y^2 + 2Y - 7$. Store the rounded result in Y-LINEAR.

4. Multiply BASE by XSEVEN and store the rounded result in XSEVEN. If the value is too large, execute TOO-LARGE.

5. Which of the data items below could be used in arithmetic operations?

   _____ 01 WS-VARIABLES.

   _____   02 WS-A   PIC 999X.

   _____   02 WS-B   PIC 9(6).

   _____   02 WS-C   PIC 9V9.

   _____   02 WS-D   PIC S99V9.

   _____   02 WS-E   PIC 99.99.

6. Write a statement to add the values of WS-B, WS-C, and WS-D, and to store the result in WS-E.

Answer Key

1. MULTIPLY QUANTITY BY PRICE GIVING GROSS.   (8)
    or
   COMPUTE GROSS = QUANTITY * PRICE.   (12)

2. MOVE 27 TO X.
   DIVIDE X INTO XEL.   (4)
    or
   COMPUTE X = 27.
   COMPUTE XEL = XEL/X.   (12)

3. COMPUTE Y-LINEAR ROUNDED = (Y**3) + (4 * Y**2) + (2 * Y) - 7.
   (all parentheses could have been omitted.)   (10, 12)

4. MULTIPLY BASE BY XSEVEN ROUNDED
     ON SIZE ERROR PERFORM TOO-LARGE.   (10, 11)

5. WS-B, WS-C, and WS-D
   (WS-A contains an X, WS-E contains a decimal point.)   (1, 2)

6. ADD WS-B WS-C WS-D GIVING WS-E.   (8)
    or
   COMPUTE WS-E = WS-B + WS-C + WS-D.   (12)

CHAPTER SIX
The First Three Divisions

You have learned to code Procedure Division statements to solve problems involving card and printer files. Before we get into more complicated programming we need to look more closely at the entries in the first three divisions of a COBOL program.

In this chapter, you'll learn to code the required entries for the Identification Division and Environment Division as well as some of the optional entries. You'll also learn to describe files and their associated records in the Data Division. You'll learn to use edit characters to format data by creating the appropriate PICTURE clauses in the Data Division. And you'll learn to control horizontal and vertical spacing in printouts.

When you have completed this chapter, you will be able to:

- code a complete COBOL program;

- code required and optional paragraphs for the Identification Division;

- code two sections in the Environment Division;

- code two sections in the Data Division;

- use the following edit characters in printer record descriptions; and

Z	B	+
*	O	-
$		DB
		CR

- arrange vertical spacing in a report.

Identification Division

1. The Identification Division has one required paragraph and several optional ones. In the layout on the next page, the paragraph names are written on separate lines. The appropriate entry may be coded on the same line, if you prefer.

```
    IDENTIFICATION DIVISION.
    PROGRAM-ID.
        program-name.
    [AUTHOR.
        comment-entry.]
    [INSTALLATION.
        comment-entry.]
    [DATE-WRITTEN.
        comment-entry.]
    [DATE-COMPILED.
        comment-entry.]
    [SECURITY.
        comment-entry.]
    [REMARKS.
        comment-entry.]
```

When used, the paragraphs must be in this order, but the comment-entries can include anything you wish, even periods. The next paragraph-name marks the end of a comment-entry. The paragraph-names must begin in area A. The comment must be entirely contained in the B area. Most installations have conventions as to which of the Identification Division paragraphs are to be used. At least AUTHOR and DATE-COMPILED are usually needed. REMARKS here can be used as an alternative to * comments.

Suppose you are going to write a program to prepare a report on student attendance. Code the Identification Division using at least three optional paragraphs and creating meaningful comment-entries.

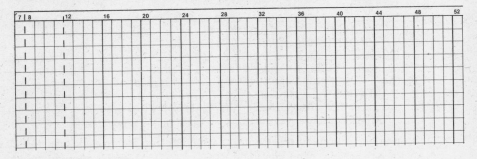

```
7 |8     |12    16     20     24     28     32     36     40     44     48     52
|IDENTIFICATION DIVISION.
|PROGRAM-ID.
|       |ATTENDANCE.
|AUTHOR.
|       |RUTH ASHLEY.
|INSTALLATION.
|        |DUOTECH, INC.
|        |4590 CLAIREMONT DR.
|        |SAN DIEGO, CA 92117
|DATE-WRITTEN.
|        |JANUARY 1980.
|DATE-COMPILED.
|        |FEBRUARY 28, 1980.
|SECURITY.
|        |NONE.
|REMARKS.
|        |THIS IS A TEST.
```

These are samples only. The DATE-COMPILED entry will generally be replaced with the actual date at compilation.

You may have used any three of the optional paragraphs. You must have included the division header and the PROGRAM-ID paragraph.

ENVIRONMENT DIVISION

2.   The Environment Division describes the hardware the program needs and relates that to the files. Here is the general framework for the Environment Division.

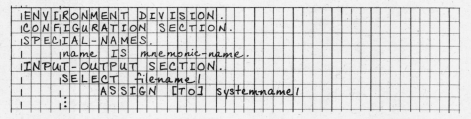

```
|ENVIRONMENT DIVISION.
|CONFIGURATION SECTION.
|SPECIAL-NAMES.
|       |name IS mnemonic-name.
|INPUT-OUTPUT SECTION.
|       |SELECT filename1
|       |.  ASSIGN [TO] systemname1
|       |.:
```

You need to include the Configuration Section if you need the SPECIAL-NAMES paragraph. And you need SPECIAL-NAMES for several things— you may want to set a top-of-page indicator, or assign a DISPLAY to print on a particular unit. The "name" is determined by the computer system. The "mnemonic-name" is created by you and used in the program. You'll learn more about SPECIAL-NAMES and some other Configuration Section paragraphs later.

As we mentioned earlier, you need the Input-Output Section whenever the program uses files. And you need a SELECT entry with an ASSIGN clause for each file you use. The file-name is the name you call the file when you OPEN or CLOSE it. The system-name depends on the installation, and it relates, or assigns, the named file to the device indicated. We used a typical system-name for a card file earlier, UR-S-CARDS, to indicate a unit-record, sequential file. The format is decreed by the system—for some systems just CARDS is fine. We'll give you a system-name whenever you need one in this book. Notice in the Environment Division framework that the FILE-CONTROL paragraph-name starts in the A area. SELECT and ASSIGN are both in the B area.

Suppose your ATTENDANCE program uses two files, STUDENT-FILE and LISTING-FILE. The system-names will be UR-S-CARDS and UR-S-PRINTER. Write a complete Environment Division for the program. (You won't need SPECIAL-NAMES.)

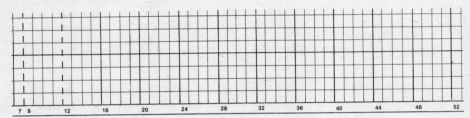

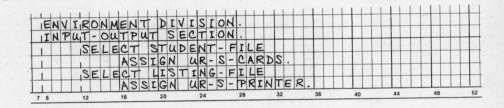

(The SELECT and ASSIGN clause for each file could be on a single line. The sequence of SELECT entries is not important. You could have included TO in your ASSIGN clause.)

DATA DIVISION

3. As you know by now, the Data Division includes the File Section and the Working-Storage Section. The File Section includes an FD entry for each file selected in the Environment Division followed by the description of the record associated with each. On the next page is the Data Division framework.

```
|DATA| DIVISION.
|FILE| SECTION.
|FD   |file-name|
|     |LABEL RECORDS clause.
|01  |record-name|.
|    |02    record description.
|    |:
|FD  |file-name2
|    |LABEL RECORDS clause.
|01  |record-name2.
|    |02   record description.
|    |:
|WORKING-STORAGE SECTION.
|01  |record-description
|    |:
```

The File Section always comes first. The FD entries can be in any sequence, but each must be immediately followed by its record description. As indicated earlier you must specify LABEL RECORDS ARE OMITTED for all card and printer files. Notice that FD and 01 are in area A.

Write an FD entry for the card file you selected in frame 2.

```
|
|
```

- - - - - - - - - - - - - - - - - -

```
|FD  |STUDENT-FILE
|    |LABEL RECORDS ARE OMITTED.
```

4. Both sections of the Data Division describe data. Before we get into the details of either, we are going to look more closely at the picture characters. Figure 6-1 shows some of the picture characters you saw in earlier chapters.

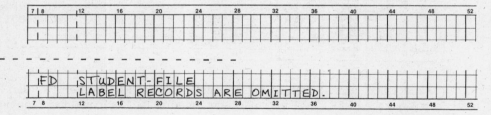

X	any character
9	any digit
V	decimal point position (no character)
S	sign indicator (no character)
.	decimal point, actual

Figure 6-1

You know, for example, that 9(6) means an item contains 6 digits, and X(25) means it contains 25 characters. The assumed decimal point (V) marks a decimal point position. Suppose we have a picture 999V99. If the digits in the field were 12345, the value would be 123.45. If we add 1 to that, we get 124.45, since 1 is an integer. As you learned in Chapter 5, the system keeps track of the decimal point position, and aligns and adjusts as needed. The S, like the V, does not represent a character position, but is maintained by the system. A numeric item may have only one S and one V, and may be used in arithmetic. A field whose picture contains anything other than 9, S, or V can't be used in arithmetic. But it can contain an actual decimal point. This is aligned with assumed point, but unlike V, the . does represent a character position.

Write a picture for each of the following:

(a) An item that will contain four digits. _____

(b) A social security number. _____

(c) A price that may be as high as 1999.95. This value will be used in

arithmetic. _____

(d) An item to print out (c) with a decimal point. _____

(e) A description of 20 characters. _____

- - - - - - - - - - - - - - - - - - - -

(a) 9999 or 9(4); (b) 9(9); (c) 9999V99 or 9(4)V9(2); (d) 9999.99 or 9(4).99; (e) X(20)

5. Records are described with a level 01 item to name the complete record. Other level numbers are used to name fields within the record.

```
7│8    │12    16    20    24    28    32    36    40    44    48    52
 │01   │INPUT-RECORD.
 │      02    IN-NAME                PIC  X(25).
 │      02    IN-ADDRESS             PIC  X(35).
 │      02    IN-PHONE               PIC  9(10).
 │      02    FILLER                 PIC  X(10).
```

In this example INPUT-RECORD is a level 01 item, which is then subdivided into four elementary items. The elementary items each have a picture that gives the type of characters and the item length. INPUT-RECORD refers to the entire 80 characters of an input record. We can define the same record another way, using three levels.

```
 7 8   12    16    20    24    28    32    36    40    44    48    52
01    INPUT-RECORD.
       02    IN-NAME.
              03    IN-FIRST      PIC  X(12).
              03    IN-MID        PIC  X.
              03    IN-LAST       PIC  X(12).
       02    IN-ADDRESS.
              03    IN-MOST       PIC  X(30).
              03    IN-ZIP        PIC  X(5).
       02    IN-PHONE            PIC  9(10).
       02    FILLER             PIC  X(10).
```

In this example, the 01 level is still the record level. Items intermediate between record and elementary items (such as IN-NAME) are group items. Any item that is not subdivided further is an elementary item and thus requires a picture clause.

(a) Is IN-ADDRESS an elementary or a group item? _____

(b) Is IN-PHONE an elementary or a group item? _____

(c) Is IN-ZIP an elementary or group item? _____

(d) How many character positions are represented by the elementary items? _____

(e) Suppose IN-PHONE were to be subdivided so the first three positions were IN-AREA, and the rest IN-LOCAL. Rewrite that part of the record description.

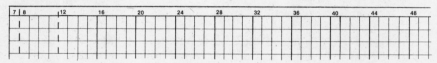

- - - - - - - - - - - - - - - - - - - -

(a) group; (b) elementary; (c) elementary; (d) 80;

(e)

```
       02    IN-PHONE.
              03    IN-AREA       PIC  999.
              03    IN-LOCAL      PIC  9(7).
```

6. In coding record descriptions, the 01 level number appears in area A. The record-name and the rest of its description appear in area B. In structured COBOL, we indent and line up the levels so the structure of the record is obvious. (Some programmers like to use levels 05 and 10 instead of 02 and 03. You may, if you prefer.) The record structure on the next page represents an 80-column card.

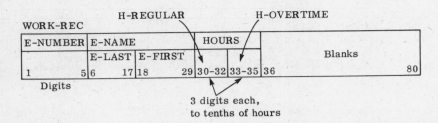

Write a record description entry for this record. Remember that the V is not a character position.

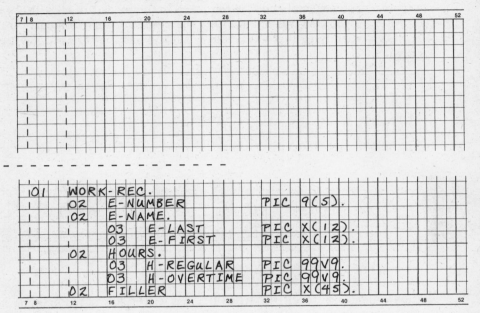

```
01   WORK-REC.
     02    E-NUMBER          PIC  9(5).
     02    E-NAME.
           03    E-LAST      PIC  X(12).
           03    E-FIRST     PIC  X(12).
     02    HOURS.
           03    H-REGULAR   PIC  99V9.
           03    H-OVERTIME  PIC  99V9.
     02    FILLER            PIC  X(45).
```

7. All the character positions in a record must be accounted for in a record description entry. FILLER can be used to refer to parts of a record you don't use. Write a record description entry for a record called MAKE-DO, which is to contain a five-digit number (CODE-NR) beginning in position 10. Account for 133 positions in a print line, with blanks in all unused positions.

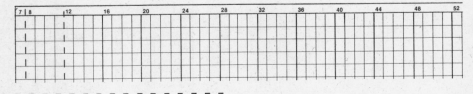

```
7 | 8    12      16      20      24      28      32      36      40      44      48      52
 01     MAKE-DO.
        02   FILLER   PIC  X(10)  VALUE  SPACES.
        02   CODE-NR  PIC  9(5).
        02   FILLER   PIC  X(118)  VALUE  SPACES.
```

8. The very first character position in a printer file is not usually a print
    position; it is saved for a carriage-control character. This carriage-
    control position can be used to adjust the spacing, signal the end of a
    page, or generally control vertical spacing on the printer. You will not
    use the carriage-control position too much in this book but we will always
    keep the first position unused. Rewrite the record description entry for
    MAKE-DO, specifying that CODE-NR will be printed in the first available
    position.

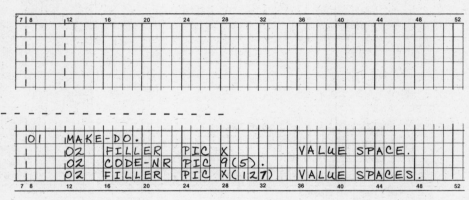

```
 01     MAKE-DO.
        02   FILLER   PIC  X        VALUE  SPACE.
        02   CODE-NR  PIC  9(5).
        02   FILLER   PIC  X(127)   VALUE  SPACES.
```

9. Write a description of PRINT-RECORD that will result in the printing of
    ID-NO (all digits) in print positions 2 through 7 and PRICE (up to 87.63
    maximum) in positions 10 through 14. Use a 133 character record.

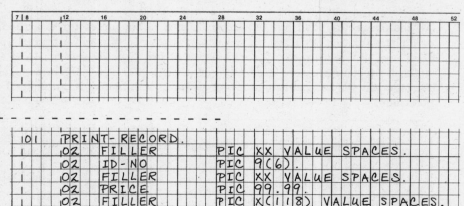

```
 01     PRINT-RECORD.
        02   FILLER        PIC  XX   VALUE  SPACES.
        02   ID-NO         PIC  9(6).
        02   FILLER        PIC  XX   VALUE  SPACES.
        02   PRICE         PIC  99.99.
        02   FILLER        PIC  X(118)  VALUE  SPACES.
```

10. Data to be printed must be placed in a print record in some way, usually by a MOVE statement or a GIVING option. A numeric edited item, such as one containing a decimal point, may receive a numeric value. Here are some examples of what happens. Notice that the system can add zeros at either end, and that digits can be lost. Neither a decimal point nor a V can appear at the far right of the picture.

Sending Field	Receiving Field	
VALUE	PICTURE	RESULT
34ʌ56	999.999	034.560
34ʌ56	99.9	34.5
ʌ0056	99.99	00.00
100ʌ	999.99	100.00

Fill in expected results for the sample values below.

19ʌ98	999.9	(a) _____
173ʌ1	999.99	(b) _____
ʌ1731	99.999	(c) _____
173ʌ1	.999	(d) _____
17ʌ31	99999.99	(e) _____

- - - - - - - - - - - - - - - - - -

(a) 019.9; (b) 173.10; (c) 00.173; (d) .100; (e) 00017.31

11. We often want to eliminate leading zeros from an edited item. We can accomplish "zero suppression" by replacing leading zeros with blanks. The edit character Z does this for us. Whenever Z is used instead of a 9 in a picture, a leading zero in that position will be replaced with a blank, or suppressed. If the picture contains all Z's, and the value happens to be zero, nothing will be printed at all! Z's must begin on the left end of the data item, and extend toward the right. As soon as a 9 appears, no more Z's are allowed. In the examples below, notice the effect of zero suppression on the actual decimal point. Remember that ƀ indicates blank.

Sending Field	Receiving Field	
VALUE	PICTURE	RESULT
7321	ZZZZ	7321
0732	ZZZZ	ƀ732
0001	ZZZZ	ƀƀƀ1
0000	ZZZZ	ƀƀƀƀ
07ʌ21	ZZ.ZZ	ƀ7.21
00ʌ01	ZZ.ZZ	ƀƀƀƀ1
00ʌ01	Z9.99	ƀ0.01

Notice that the last example provides a more readable printout than the one before it. You have to decide how you want data to be printed when a value is less than one, because the decimal point will be suppressed if the character before it is. For practice, give the result field for each sample value and picture below.

10ᐱ98	ZZZ.99	(a)	_____
00ᐱ17	ZZZ.ZZ	(b)	_____
00ᐱ17	ZZ9.99	(c)	_____
0023ᐱ973	ZZZ.ZZ	(d)	_____
000003	ZZZZZZ	(e)	_____

- - - - - - - - - - - - - - - - - -

(a) ᵦ10.98; (b) ᵦᵦᵦᵦ17; (c) ᵦᵦ0.17; (d) ᵦ23.97; (e) ᵦᵦᵦᵦᵦ3

12. The asterisk (*) edit character works much like Z, but it replaces leading zeros with asterisks rather than blanks. The * is often used as a check protection symbol. When it is used, asterisks will appear in leading zero positions. Any padding on the right is with zeros, however. Thus a picture of ****, would cause the value 0012 to be printed as **12. A picture of **.** would cause the value 2ᐱ6 to be printed as *2.60. What will be the result of each of the following moves?

	Sending Field VALUE	Receiving Field PICTURE	RESULT
(a)	00006	***99	_____
(b)	0000	****	_____
(c)	001ᐱ6	***.**	_____
(d)	011ᐱ34	****.*	_____

- - - - - - - - - - - - - - - - - -

(a) ***06; (b) ****; (c) **1.60; (d) **11.3

13. The comma is another useful edit character. When a comma (,) appears in an edit pattern, a comma is inserted in the result field in the corresponding position in the result. If a comma is included in a string of * or Z edit characters, it is printed only if a digit is printed to the immediate left. Otherwise the comma is replaced with asterisk or blank, depending on whether you used * or Z in the picture. On the next page are some examples. Notice that the comma is printed if neither Z nor * is used.

Sending Field	Receiving Field	
VALUE	PICTURE	RESULT
00123	ZZ,ZZZ	b̸b̸b̸123
01234	ZZ,ZZZ	b̸1,234
00123	**,***	***123
01234	**,***	*1,234
00123	99,999	00,123

Give the result field for each of the following:

	Sending Field	Receiving Field	
	VALUE	PICTURE	RESULT
(a)	0000432	Z,ZZZ,ZZZ	_____
(b)	0234567	Z,ZZZ,ZZZ	_____
(c)	0000432	**,***.**	_____
(d)	1234567	**,***.**	_____

- - - - - - - - - - - - - - - - -

(a) b̸b̸b̸b̸b̸b̸432; (b) b̸b̸234,567; (c) *****4.32; (d) *1,234.56

14. A dollar sign can be inserted in an edited field. If you put a single $ at the left of an edited field, a $ is inserted there, no matter whether the digit positions are filled with 9, Z, or *.
     Give the edited result of each of the following:

	Sending Field	Receiving Field	
	VALUE	PICTURE	RESULT
(a)	298	$999.99	_____
(b)	298	$ZZZ.99	_____
(c)	298	$***.99	_____

- - - - - - - - - - - - - - - - -

(a) $002.98; (b) $b̸b̸2.98; (c) $**2.98

15. The dollar sign can be used to suppress leading zeros and place a $ just to the left of the leftmost digit. The dollar sign "floats" to a position adjacent to the first significant (non-zero) digit. A picture of $$$$.99 would cause a value of 298 to be printed as b̸b̸$2.98. A value of 098 would be printed as $.98. Commas in a string of $'s are suppressed just as in a string of Z's.

Give the edited result of each of the following.

	VALUE	PICTURE	RESULT
(a)	0̸12	$$$.99	_____
(b)	0̸05	$$$.$$	_____
(c)	0	$$$.$$	_____
(d)	1298	$$,$$$.$$	_____

- - - - - - - - - - - - - - - - -

(a) ƀƀ$.12; (b) ƀƀ$.05; (c) all blanks; (d) $1,298.00

16. Combine the picture characters you've learned so far as you write pictures to edit the following:

(a) A price that will have up to seven digits. Include a decimal point and comma where appropriate. Use a dollar sign on the far left, and print all leading zeros. _____

(b) Rewrite the picture to use asterisks to replace the leading zeros, and use no dollar sign. _____

(c) Rewrite the picture again, to float the dollar sign so it appears just to the left of the first non-zero digit. _____

- - - - - - - - - - - - - - - - -

(a) $99,999.99; (b) **,***.**; (c) $$$,$$$.$$

17. Suppose you wish to have printed a CUSTOMER-NUMBER beginning in position 20 (print position 19) and a CREDIT-LIMIT beginning in column 35 on the printer page. PRESENT-BALANCE is to begin in column 45. Write a record description to specify the following:

- CUSTOMER-NUMBER is eight digits long, with commas at appropriate points (every three digits from the right).
- CREDIT-LIMIT has three digits and is preceded by a dollar sign. No decimal point is necessary, and all digits are printed.
- PRESENT-BALANCE has up to three digits preceding the decimal point and two digits after. The dollar sign is printed immediately before the first non-zero digit to the left of the decimal point.

In writing your record description be sure to count the character positions and add FILLER items to make up 133 positions.

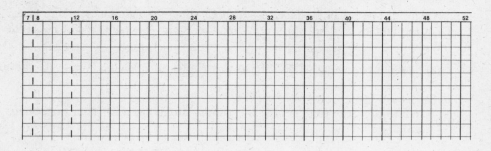

```
7│8    │12    16    20    24    28    32    36    40    44    48    52
│01  │RECORD-DESCRIPTION.
│      │02  FILLER                    PIC X(19).
│      │02  CUSTOMER-NUMBER  PIC 99,999,999.
│      │02  FILLER                    PIC X(5).
│      │02  CREDIT-LIMIT        PIC $999.
│      │02  FILLER                    PIC X(6).
│      │02  PRESENT-BALANCE PIC $$$$.99.
│      │02  FILLER                    PIC X(82).
```

18. The editing symbols 0 (insert zero) and B (insert blank) can be used to
edit both numeric and non-numeric data. The picture XXBXX would cause
a source value 1015 to be printed as 10ꞵ15. The picture XXXB99B99 would
cause the value JAN1340 to be printed as JAN 13 40.

Here are several examples of edited data items.

SENDING VALUE	PICTURE	RESULT
ABL3	XX0XX	AB0L3
1234	99099	12034
'-1'	XBBX	-ꞵꞵ1
10	90B9	10ꞵ0

Refer back to these examples as necessary to complete the following:

SENDING VALUE	PICTURE	RESULT
DAY	XXXB	(a) _____
DAY	X0XBX	(b) _____
57	99B00	(c) _____
57	900B9	(d) _____

- - - - - - - - - - - - - - - - - - - -

(a) DAYꞵ; (b) D0AꞵY; (c) 57ꞵ00; (d) 500ꞵ7

19. Again, B and 0 can be used to edit both numeric and non-numeric data, but the editing symbols Z, *, $, and . can only be used to edit numeric items.

(a) The source value of ZYX is to be printed as Z0ɫY0X. Write its picture.

_____

(b) Write pictures to describe the report items derived from the source value below:

RESULT	SENDING VALUE	PICTURE OF RESULT
Nɫɫ300ɫ7	N37	(1) _____
$00193.20	193₂	(2) _____
5700	57	(3) _____

- - - - - - - - - - - - - - - - - -

(a) X0BX0X
(b) (1) XBBX00BX, or XBB900B9
    (2) $00999.90, or $99999.99
    (3) XX00 or 9900

20. We can use editing symbols to indicate the sign (positive or negative) of a value in a printed report. We can do this only if the source value was originally described with an S, which gives it an operational sign. Which types of data items could be edited with a plus or minus sign?

_____

- - - - - - - - - - - - - - - - - -

numeric only

21. The editing sign indicators are shown below. You may use + and - at either end of a picture. The last two must be at the far right, however.

Numeric Edit Symbol	Location in Picture	Effect on Report Item
+	rightmost or leftmost	+ inserted in symbol location if value positive - inserted if value negative
-	rightmost or leftmost	- inserted if value negative; otherwise blank inserted
DB	rightmost	DB inserted if value negative; otherwise two blanks inserted
CR	leftmost	CR inserted if value negative; otherwise two blanks inserted

Examine the editing table on the previous page.

(a) Which editing symbol would result in the printing of a minus sign if the value were negative? _____

(b) Which editing symbol would result in the printing of a plus sign if the value were positive? _____

- - - - - - - - - - - - - - - - - - -

(a) + or –; (b) +

22. Which of the pictures below seem correct, based on the information given in the table in frame 21?

_____ (a) 99–99   _____ (e) 99BCR

_____ (b) –9999   _____ (f) XXCR

_____ (c) –99.99   _____ (g) –XX

_____ (d) DB99   _____ (h) +09

- - - - - - - - - - - - - - - - - - -

b, c, e, h (In a, – is neither rightmost nor leftmost; in d, DB is not rightmost; in f and g, the data item is not numeric, even though the editing symbols are correctly placed.)

23. A data item with a sending value of –292 is described with PIC S999. As you know, S is not a character position, but the computer will remember the sign. This item could be edited to show the sign in many different ways. Some of these various editing pictures are shown below. What is the result for each picture, based on the sending value above?

Picture	Report Item
999+	(a) _____
999–	(b) _____
999DB	(c) _____
999BCR	(d) _____

- - - - - - - - - - - - - - - - - - -

(a) 292–; (b) 292–; (c) 292DB; (d) 292ⱡCR

24. Now assume the source value is +292. Refer to the table in frame 21 and supply the results for the pictures on the following page.

Picture	Report Item
999BCR	(a) _____
+999	(b) _____
-999	(c) _____

- - - - - - - - - - - - - - - - - -

(a) 292ƀƀƀ (one ƀ for the B, and two for the CR); (b) +292; (c) ƀ292

25. Complete the values of report items below.

Picture	Sending Value	Result
99.99+	+28̭75	(a) _____
999DB	+123	(b) _____
$9.99BCR	+1̭23	(c) _____
-9(4)	+4438	(d) _____

- - - - - - - - - - - - - - - - - -

(a) 28.75+; (b) 123ƀƀ; (c) $1.23ƀƀƀ; (d) ƀ4438

26. The + and - editing symbols can be floated, much as the $ is floated. The result of ++++,+99, with various sending values, is shown below.

Sending	Printed
+ 75	+75
+0003	+03
-7231	-7,231

The floating minus sign works in much the same way, with the same effect as a single minus.

(a) Write a picture that will allow a balance of up to seven digits, with comma and decimal point for cents. If the value is negative, a sign should appear just to the left of the first non-zero digit.

_____

(b) What would be the result with that picture if the sending field were 17̭98? _____

(c) If the sending field were 192̭85? _____

- - - - - - - - - - - - - - - - - -

(a) ---,---.--; (b) ƀƀƀƀ-17.98; (c) ƀƀ1,928.50

27. As you know, most of the characters in the picture of a data item represent positions. And the lengths of pictures of all the data items in a record make up the total length of the record. Card records are 80 characters long, while a print record may be any length up to the limit of the printer. Many printers have a 133-character limit, some 121, and some smaller printers may have even fewer available positions. As a review, give the length of each item below.

(a) 02 IN-PRICE   PIC 9(3)V99. _____

(b) 02 OUT-PRICE PIC $$$$.99. _____

(c) 01   IN-RECORD.
```
        02   FILLER      PIC   X(10).
        02   IN-ITEM     PIC   X(20).
        02   FILLER      PIC   X(5).
        02   IN-PRICE    PIC   X(3)V99.
        02   FILLER      PIC   X(40).

             (IN-RECORD)  _____
```

- - - - - - - - - - - - - - - - - - - -

(a) 5; (b) 7; (c) 80

28. When you describe an input or output record, you need to add FILLER positions to fill out the complete record length. Using the format below, write a complete input record description. Use appropriate names (be sure they're valid), and remember to have pictures only for the elementary items.

STUDENT-RECORD

ID	NAME			Blanks
	LAST	FIRST	MID	
1 9	10 24	25 39	40 50	51 80

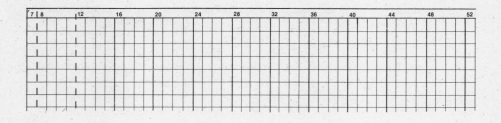

- - - - - - - - - - - - - - - - - - -

```
01   STUDENT-RECORD.
     02   STUDENT-ID      PIC X(9).
     02   STUDENT-NAME.
          03  ST-LAST     PIC X(13).
          03  ST-FIRST    PIC X(15).
          03  ST-MID      PIC X(11).
     02   FILLER          PIC X(30).
```

(You should be comfortable with areas and columns as used in the Data Division now.)

29. You will often need to print several different types of lines in an output print file. You may have a regular output information line (called a detail line) as well as heading lines and perhaps a summary line. For this reason, many programmers like to describe the output record in the File Section as a single field, then use a WRITE ... FROM statement to print each line, as you saw in Chapter 5. You can then describe the layout of the different lines in the Working-Storage Section.

    Describe an output record for a 133-character line printer (call it LINE-RECORD) as a single field.

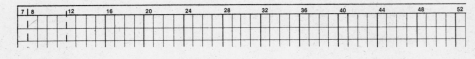

```
01   LINE-RECORD   PIC X(133).
```

30. The File Section for a card-to-print program will include an FD for one file, followed by the record description for that file, then an FD and record description for the other file. Using the information below, code a File Section for the Data Division.

Input file: INVENTORY

Part-num	Description	Quantities (up to 9999)			Price (up to $100)		
		ON HAND	ON ORDER	SOLD	WHSL	RETAIL	Blank
6 char	24 char						

dollars and cents, assumed decimal

Output file: LISTOUT   You have a 121-character line printer available.

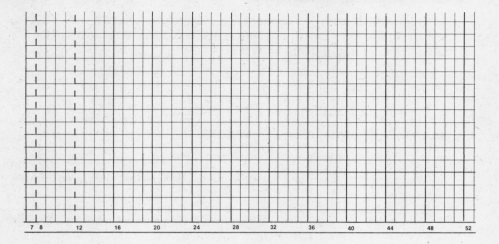

```
FD   INVENTORY
     LABEL RECORDS ARE OMITTED.
01   IN-RECORD.
     02   PART-NUM              PIC X(6).
     02   DESCRIPTION           PIC X(24).
     02   QUANTITIES.
          03   ON-HAND          PIC 9(4).
          03   ON-ORDER         PIC 9(4).
          03   SOLD             PIC 9(4).
     02   PRICE.
          03   WHOLESALE        PIC 999V99.
          03   RETAIL           PIC 999V99.
     02   FILLER               PIC X(28).
FD   LISTOUT
     LABEL RECORDS ARE OMITTED.
01   OUT-RECORD               PIC X(121).
```

> If you have to stop soon, this is a good break point.

WORKING-STORAGE SECTION

31. You must describe all data items that aren't associated with an input or
    output file in the Working-Storage Section. Indicators, such as end-of-
    file switches, extra fields needed for arithmetic, constant values, and
    line formats can all be described in Working-Storage. You'll see how
    these and other data are used as you continue in this book.

    As you know, the Working-Storage Section is similar to the File Sec-
    tion in that it includes record descriptions. But there are some differ-
    ences. In Working-Storage, we are allowed to use VALUE clauses to
    assign values to data items. And we can describe independent data items
    —using level 77. Since level 77 is similar to level 01 without subdivisions,

we'll stick with level 01. Many programmers use level 77, however, so it's good to be familiar with it. Here are some examples that assign initial values. One of them uses level 77.

```
77  PACKED-PRICE  PIC 9(5)V99   VALUE ZERO.
01  END-OF-CARDS  PIC X          VALUE   'N'.
```

(a) What is the initial value of END-OF-CARDS? _____

(b) What is the initial value of PACKED-PRICE? _____

(c) Which item could be used for arithmetic? _____

(d) Write a description of a level 02 FILLER item that will have 20 blank positions.

- - - - - - - - - - - - - - - - - -

(a) 'N'; (b) zero; (c) PACKED-PRICE;
(d) 02 FILLER PIC X(20) VALUE SPACES.

32. In structured COBOL, we like to group separate items with similar functions into a record as you can see below.

```
01  END-OF-FILE-SWITCHES.
    02  EOF-CARD1   PIC X   VALUE 'N'.
    02  EOF-CARD2   PIC X   VALUE 'N'.
```

While the items might never be referred to as a record, they are grouped and easy to find in the Working-Storage Section.

Suppose you need to describe three numeric items called N-PRICE, N-QUANTITY, and N-RESULT. Write a record description of NUMERIC-ITEMS to include them, using a picture of five 9's for each. Include an assumed decimal point in the price and result fields.

- - - - - - - - - - - - - - - - - -

```
01  NUMERIC-ITEMS.
    02  N-PRICE     PIC 999V99.
    02  N-QUANTITY  PIC 9(5).
    02  N-RESULT    PIC 999V99.
```

33. The form on the next page shows the Working-Storage coding for a heading record and a WORKING record.

```
  7|8     |12    16    20    24    28    32    36    40    44    48    52
 |01  |HEADING-RECORD.
 |     |02  FILLER PIC X(10) VALUE IS SPACES.
 |     |02  HEADING-1 PIC A(6) VALUE IS 'NUMBER'.
 |     |02  FILLER PIC X(12) VALUE IS SPACES.
 |     |02  HEADING-2 PIC A(4) VALUE IS 'NAME'.
 |     |02  FILLER PIC X(26) VALUE IS SPACES.
 |     |02  HEADING-3 PIC A(3) VALUE IS 'AGE'.
 |     |02  FILLER PIC X(72) VALUE IS SPACES.
 |01  |WORKING-RECORD.
 |     |02  FILLER PIC X(10) VALUE IS SPACES.
 |     |02  SYMBOL PIC 9(4).
 |     |02  FILLER PIC X(14) VALUE IS SPACES.
 |     |02  NAME PIC A(20).
 |     |02  FILLER PIC X(10) VALUE IS SPACES.
 |     |02  AGE PIC 99.
 |     |02  FILLER PIC X(73) VALUE IS SPACES.
```

(a) How will HEADING-RECORD appear on the page?

_____

(b) Where will the values of the items in WORKING-RECORD appear on

the listing? _____

- - - - - - - - - - - - - - - - - - -

(a) Printed words separated by spaces; (b) Values will be printed under
headings

34. Suppose your FD entry for the print file used in frame 33 had included:

```
FD  PRINT-FILE
    LABEL-RECORDS ARE OMITTED.
 01  PRINT-RECORD    PIC X(133).
```

(a) Write a statement to print the heading line from frame 33.

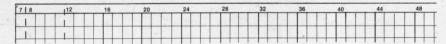

(b) Write a statement to print the working line (after values are moved in)
from frame 33.

- - - - - - - - - - - - - - - - -

(a) WRITE PRINT-RECORD FROM HEADING-RECORD.
(b) WRITE PRINT-RECORD FROM WORKING-RECORD.

35. Write the necessary Working-Storage Section entries to describe the heading and data records diagrammed below.

HEADING

4 blanks	NAME	34 blanks	ADDRESS	47 blanks	BALANCE	30 blanks

(includes
carriage
position)

DATA-LINE

4 blanks	C-NAME 30 char	10 blanks	C-ADDR 40 char	10 blanks	C-BAL	Remainder blanks

appear as: 7 digits, 2 to right of actual decimal point, with floating dollar sign and comma

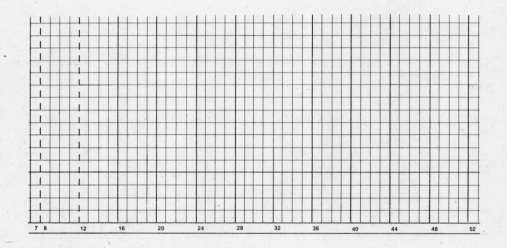

- - - - - - - - - - - - - - - - - - - -

```
01   HEADING-RECORD.
     02   FILLER       PIC  X(4)         VALUE  SPACES.
     02   H-NAME       PIC  X(4)         VALUE  'NAME'.
     02   FILLER       PIC  X(34)        VALUE  SPACES.
     02   H-ADDRESS    PIC  X(7)         VALUE  'ADDRESS'.
     02   FILLER       PIC  X(47)        VALUE  SPACES.
     02   H-BALANCE    PIC  X(7)         VALUE  'BALANCE'.
     02   FILLER       PIC  X(30)        VALUE  SPACES.
```

(answer continued on the next page)

```
01    DATA-LINE.
      02  FILLER      PIC X(4)            VALUE SPACES.
      02  C-NAME      PIC X(30).
      02  FILLER      PIC X(10)           VALUE SPACES.
      02  C-ADDR      PIC X(40).
      02  FILLER      PIC X(10)           VALUE SPACES.
      02  C-BAL       PIC $$$,$$$.$$.
      02  FILLER      PIC X(29).
```

VERTICAL SPACING

You have seen in previous frames how to arrange horizontal spacing on a printer page, by using FILLER items with VALUE SPACES. Now let's see how to arrange vertical spacing. To do this, you need to use the Configuration Section in the Environment Division and a new option on the WRITE statement.

36. The WRITE statement format we will use is shown below.

WRITE record-name [FROM identifier]

$$\left[\text{AFTER ADVANCING} \quad \left\{ \begin{array}{l} \text{n LINES} \\ \text{mnemonic-name} \end{array} \right\} \right]$$

We'll focus on the LINES option first. You can use an integer, such as 2, or a data-name with an integer (whole number) picture and value, for n. Thus you could specify WRITE PRINT-RECORD AFTER ADVANCING 2 LINES to create double spacing—one blank line between records—in your report. One caution—single spacing is the default, so if you don't use the AFTER ADVANCING option, you'll get single spacing. But if you use ADVANCING in one WRITE statement for a file, you must specify it in every WRITE statement for that file, even if you want single spacing for the rest of the lines.

In the example above, the printer will advance two lines, then print the output record named in the WRITE statement. Write a statement that will cause the printer to advance five lines, then print a record.

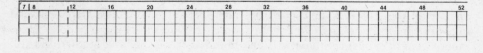

WRITE PRINT-RECORD AFTER ADVANCING 5 LINES.

37. When we design a report, we generally want the heading to be printed at the top of a page. We can specify an advance to the top of the next printer page if we define a mnemonic (meaningful) name in the SPECIAL-NAMES paragraph of the Environment Division. The mnemonic-name sets up a term we will use in the program for a special purpose.

```
ENVIRONMENT DIVISION.
CONFIGURATION SECTION.
SPECIAL-NAMES.
     C01 IS TO-TOP.
```

In this example, the required section header and paragraph name are coded. "C01" is the system symbol for channel 1—the standard top-of-page indicator. (Actually there may be up to twelve channels, depending on the system, but we are considering only one in this book.)

Once channel 1 is defined as TO-TOP, you can specify the mnemonic name in the ADVANCING option. Refer back to the questions in frame 34.

(a) Write a statement to print the heading at the top of the next page.

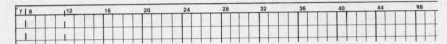

(b) Write a statement to put 3 blank lines between the heading and the first working line.

- - - - - - - - - - - - - - - - - -

```
(a) WRITE PRINT-RECORD FROM HEADING-RECORD
         AFTER ADVANCING TO-TOP.
(b) WRITE PRINT-RECORD FROM WORKING-RECORD
         AFTER ADVANCING 4 LINES.
```

You have seen how to control vertical spacing in a report. In the next chapter you'll learn to count lines on a page and thus print headings on later pages.

Summary Exercise

All the information you will need to write a program called PRINT-A-REPORT is contained in the group of diagrams on the next two pages. This program will read an input card file and prepare and print a triple-spaced report containing some of the data from cards on which the pay code is less than 5. In this program you will use many of the items you studied in this chapter. Write your program on the coding sheet provided, beginning on page 120 with frame 38. The next several frames will guide you, and allow you to check your progress.

    Input: Use CARD-FILE. system-name UR-S-CARDS
       (see next page)

    Output: Use PRINT-FILE. system-name UR-S-PRINTER
       (see next page)

CARD-RECORD							
C-CODE	C-PERSONAL-DATA			C-CREDIT-DATA			
	C-NAME	C-ADDRESS	C-PHONE	C-YR-OPENED	C-MAX-CREDIT	C-PRESENT-DUE	C-PAY-CODE
9 digits	21 char	25 char	10 char	2 digits	6 digits, 2 rt. of dec.	6 digits, 2 rt. of dec.	1 digit

PRINT-LINE	133 character positions

HEADING-LINE						
FILLER	H1 "CUSTOMER CODE"	FILLER	H2 "PAYMENT HISTORY"	FILLER	H3 "CURRENT BALANCE"	FILLER
10 spaces		10 spaces		10 spaces		to fill line

INFO-LINE						
FILLER	O-CODE	FILLER	O-PAYCODE	FILLER	O-PRESENT-DUE print 6 digits, float $, print decimal	FILLER
12 spaces	9 digits	19 spaces	1 char	21 spaces		to fill line

Pseudocode

```
Main paragraph:
    Print heading
    Read card
    PERFORM UNTIL no more cards
        Process records
    ENDPERFORM
    End program
Process records:
    IF    paycode less than 5
        Move input fields to output records
        Write line
    ELSE
        Do nothing
    ENDIF
    Read card
```

Structure Chart

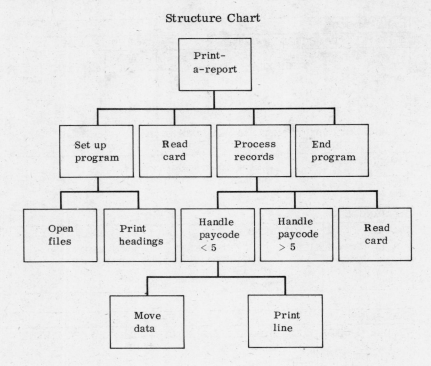

38. Code the Identification and Environment Divisions. Be sure to code two sections in the Environment Division.

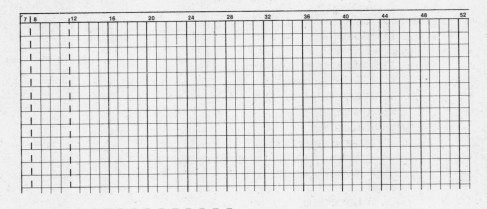

```
IDENTIFICATION DIVISION.
PROGRAM-ID. PRINT-A-REPORT.
ENVIRONMENT DIVISION.
CONFIGURATION SECTION.
SPECIAL-NAMES.
    C01 IS TO-TOP.
INPUT-OUTPUT SECTION.
FILE-CONTROL.
    SELECT CARD-FILE
        ASSIGN TO UR-S-CARDS.
    SELECT PRINT-FILE
        ASSIGN TO UR-S-PRINTER.
```

39. Now code the File Section of the Data Division.

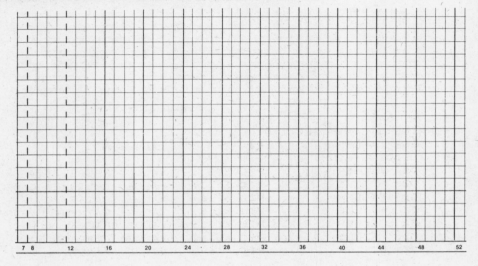

- - - - - - - - - - - - - - - - - - -

```
DATA DIVISION.
FILE SECTION.
FD   CARD-FILE
     LABEL RECORDS ARE OMITTED.
01   CARD-RECORD.
     02   C-CODE             PIC 9(9).
     02   C-PERSONAL-DATA.
          03   C-NAME        PIC X(21).
          03   C-ADDRESS     PIC X(25).
          03   C-PHONE       PIC X(10).
     02   C-CREDIT-DATA.
          03   C-YR-OPENED   PIC 99.
          03   C-MAX-CREDIT  PIC 9(4)V99.
          03   C-PRESENT-DUE PIC 9(4)V99.
          03   C-PAYCODE     PIC 9.
     02   FILLER             PIC X(25).
FD   PRINT-FILE
     LABEL RECORDS ARE OMITTED.
01   PRINT-LINE              PIC X(133).
```

40. Code the Working-Storage Section of the Data Division. You will need an end-of-file indicator and record descriptions for two print lines.

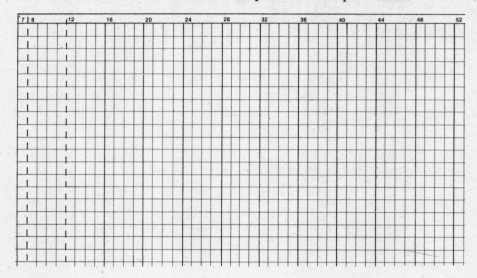

```
WORKING-STORAGE SECTION.
01   EOF-CARD              PIC X          VALUE 'N'.
01   HEADING-LINE.
     02   FILLER           PIC X(10)      VALUE SPACES.
     02   HFILL1           PIC X(13)      VALUE 'CUSTOMER CODE'.
     02   FILLER           PIC X(10)      VALUE SPACES.
     02   HFILL2           PIC X(15)      VALUE 'PAYMENT HISTORY'.
     02   FILLER           PIC X(10)      VALUE SPACES.
     02   HFILL3           PIC X(15)      VALUE 'CURRENT BALANCE'.
     02   FILLER           PIC X(60)      VALUE SPACES.
01   INFO-LINE.
     02   FILLER           PIC X(12)      VALUE SPACES.
     02   O-CODE           PIC X(9).
     02   FILLER           PIC X(19)      VALUE SPACES.
     02   O-PAYCODE        PIC X.
     02   FILLER           PIC X(21)      VALUE SPACES.
     02   O-PRESENT-DUE    PIC $$$$$.99.
     02   FILLER           PIC X(63)      VALUE SPACES.
```

41. Refer to the pseudocode now, and code the main control paragraph for the Procedure Division.

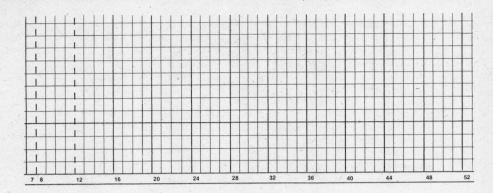

```
PROCEDURE DIVISION.
MAIN-PARAGRAPH.
    OPEN INPUT CARD-FILE
        OUTPUT PRINT-FILE.
    WRITE PRINT-LINE FROM HEADING-LINE
        AFTER ADVANCING TO-TOP.
    PERFORM READ-CARD.
    PERFORM PROCESS-RECORDS
        UNTIL EOF-CARD = 'Y'.
    CLOSE PRINT-FILE, CARD-FILE.
    STOP RUN.
```

(Be sure the name you used in AFTER ADVANCING is the same name
you used in the SPECIAL-NAMES paragraph.)

42. Now code the processing paragraph and the input paragraph.

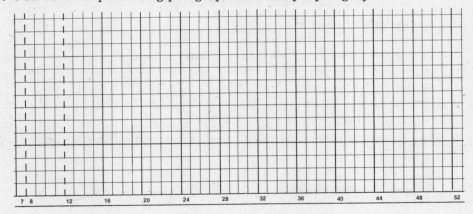

```
PROCESS-RECORDS.
    IF C-PAYCODE LESS THAN 5
        MOVE C-CODE TO O-CODE
        MOVE C-PAYCODE TO O-PAYCODE
        MOVE C-PRESENT-DUE TO O-PRESENT-DUE
        WRITE PRINT-LINE FROM INFO-LINE
            AFTER ADVANCING 3 LINES
    ELSE
        NEXT SENTENCE.
    PERFORM READ-CARD.
READ-CARD.
    READ CARD-FILE
        AT END MOVE 'Y' TO EOF-CARD.
```

(ELSE NEXT SENTENCE could have been omitted.)

SELF-TEST

After you have written your answers to the Self-Test, check them in the Answer Key that follows. Be sure you understand any differences between your answers and ours before you begin the next chapter. Following each suggested answer is a frame reference in parentheses, in case you need to review.

1. Which paragraph in the Identification Division can be used for each of these functions:

    (a) Name the program _____

    (b) Name the writer _____

    (c) Identify when the program was written _____

    (d) Describe the program _____

2. Code a required paragraph for the Identification Division.

7	8			12			16			20			24			28			32			36			40			44			48			52

3. Name (in order) the two sections used in the Environment Division.

    (a) _____

    (b) _____

4. Name (in order) the two sections used in the Data Division.

    (a) _____

    (b) _____

5. Which paragraph of which section of which division is used to specify a name to refer to the top of a page? _____

_____

6. Code Environment Division entries (including section header) for a card file named PERSONNEL, with system-name UR-S-INCOMING.

7. Code Data Division entries (including section headers) for the file in question 6. It is associated with a record that contains the following:

Columns

1-8	employee ID	(digits)
9-30	name	(characters)
31-50	address	(characters)
51-65	status	
51-66	salary	(up to 2000.00—assumed decimal)
57-60	insurance	(characters)
61-65	attendance	(digits)
rest	blank	

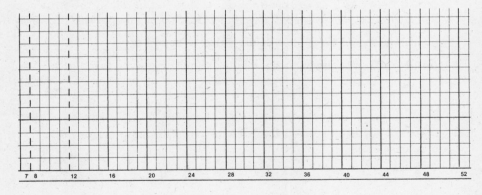

8. A report containing some of the data from PERSONNEL will be prepared on a 133-character line printer. A heading line will appear as follows, with the data beginning in column 30.

SALARY REPORT, CLASS B EMPLOYEES

Code the record description for the Working-Storage Section, using the form below.

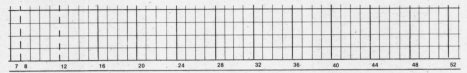

9. Suppose you defined NEXT-PAGE to refer to C01, and defined OUT-LINE as your 133-position output record. Write a statement to print the heading line you just described in frame 8.

10. Write picture clauses for the following items moved from EMPLOYEE-RECORD.

(a) OUT-SALARY is to appear with a $ just to the left of the first non-zero digit. Print a comma and decimal point as appropriate. Two zeros should be printed if the value is zero. _____

(b) OUT-ID is to appear with a blank separating each two digits.

_____

11. Show what will be printed for each of the following picture-value combinations.

Picture	Value		
$****.**	97₂	(a)	_____
----,999	-4000	(b)	_____
ZZZ.ZZ	0	(c)	_____

Answer Key

1. (a) PROGRAM-ID
   (b) AUTHOR
   (c) DATE-WRITTEN
   (d) REMARKS   (1)

2. PROGRAM-ID.
      NAME-PROG.   (Could be coded on one line.)   (1)

3. CONFIGURATION SECTION
  INPUT-OUTPUT SECTION   (2)

4. FILE SECTION
  WORKING-STORAGE SECTION   (3)

5. SPECIAL-NAMES paragraph
  CONFIGURATION SECTION
  ENVIRONMENT DIVISION   (37)

6.
```
   INPUT-OUTPUT SECTION.
        SELECT PERSONNEL
            ASSIGN TO UR-S-INCOMING.
```
  (SELECT and ASSIGN could be on one line.)   (2)

7.
```
   FILE SECTION.
   FD   PERSONNEL
        LABEL RECORDS ARE OMITTED.
   01   EMPLOYEE-RECORD.
        02   EMPLOYEE-ID          PIC 9(8).
        02   EMPLOYEE-NAME        PIC X(22).
        02   EMPLOYEE-ADDRESS     PIC X(20).
        02   EMPLOYEE-STATUS.
             03   EMP-SALARY       PIC 9(4)V99.
             03   EMP-INSURANCE    PIC 9(4).
             03   EMP-ATTENDANCE   PIC 9(5).
        02   FILLER               PIC X(15).
```

8.
```
   01   HEAD-REPORT.
        02   FILLER    PIC X(29)   VALUE SPACES.         (35)
        02   FILLER    PIC X(104)  VALUE
                       'SALARY REPORT, CLASS B EMPLOYEES'.
```

9.
```
   WRITE OUT-LINE FROM HEAD-REPORT.
        AFTER ADVANCING NEXT-PAGE.         (37)
```

10. (a) $$,$$$.99   (15)
   (b) 99B99B99B99   (18)

11. (a) $**97.20   (12)
   (b) ƀƀ-4,000   (21,26)
   (c) ƀƀƀƀƀƀ   (11)

CHAPTER SEVEN
COBOL Conditions

You have been using one type of condition, the relation condition, in IF and PERFORM statements. This chapter will cover several other ways to express conditions in COBOL. IF statements can be nested to allow more flexibility in selection of actions. You can combine conditions using two logical operators, AND and OR. You'll learn to use these as well in this chapter. The various ways of specifying conditions in COBOL give you much more control over sequence of execution than you have seen up to now.

When you finish this chapter, you will be able to:

- code relation conditions for algebraic (numeric) and non-numeric variables;

- code conditions using NUMERIC and ALPHABETIC class conditions;

- code condition-name conditions using level 88 data-names;

- use the NOT, AND, and OR logical operators; and

- code nested IFs.

RELATION CONDITIONS

1. As you recall, a relation condition is expressed in this way:

$$\left\{ \begin{array}{l} \text{data-name-1} \\ \text{literal-1} \\ \text{expression-1} \end{array} \right\} \quad \text{operator} \quad \left\{ \begin{array}{l} \text{data-name-2} \\ \text{literal-2} \\ \text{expression-2} \end{array} \right\}$$

Restrictions:
- Two literals may not be compared (related) at once.
- Both elements must be numeric or both must be non-numeric.
- The relational operator may be GREATER THAN, LESS THAN, or EQUAL TO; any of these may be preceded by NOT.
- The mathematical symbols $>$, $<$, and $=$ may be used.

The format above explains the most commonly used condition, the relation condition. Two elements are related to each other in the specified way. If the relation is true, then the action-statement of the IF is executed. If false, control passes to the item following the ELSE clause, or the next period (this is usually the next statement). In the example below, what would be the next statement executed if NR = 7, and CODX = 6?

```
IF CODX NOT GREATER THAN NR - 3
    ADD 1 TO SUMX
    PERFORM REVIEW-P.
PERFORM HELP.
```

_____

- - - - - - - - - - - - - - - - - -

PERFORM HELP. (Recall that more than one statement can be included in an IF. The location of the period marks the end of IF. In this example, data-name CODX is compared to an expression.)

2. An algebraic comparison considers the sign (positive or negative) of the value represented. Indicate whether each of the following would be true or false if A = -7, B = +4, and C = -1.

    (a) C GREATER THAN A + B _____

    (b) A EQUAL TO 2 * B - C _____

    (c) B NOT LESS THAN 7 * C _____

- - - - - - - - - - - - - - - - - -

    (a) true (-1 is larger than -3)
    (b) false (-7 does not equal 8 + 1)
    (c) true (+4 is greater than 7 * -1)

3. Non-numeric items can also be specified in a relation condition. Two names can be compared to find out if they are identical, or which is "greater." They are not, however, compared algebraically. Non-numeric items are compared according to the official collating sequence of ANS COBOL, as shown in Appendix B. In the alphabetic part of this sequence, you will see that Z has a higher value; it is greater than A. When two names are compared, the name that appears earlier in an alphabetic listing would be considered:

    _____ (a) greater than the other.   _____ (c) equal to the other.

    _____ (b) less than the other.   _____ (d) algebraically.

- - - - - - - - - - - - - - - - - -

    b

4. Refer to the collating sequence in Appendix B. A data item beginning 0 through 9 would be considered:

_____ (a) greater than one beginning with a letter.

_____ (b) less than one beginning with a letter.

_____ (c) greater than one beginning with a blank.

_____ (d) less than one beginning with a blank.

- - - - - - - - - - - - - - - - - - - -

a, c (The blank is the lowest item in the collating sequence.)

5. Examine the data descriptions and values below.

	Variables		Values
01	PURCHASE-RECORD.		
02	CUS-NO	PIC X(5).	54570
02	ITEM-ID	PIC X(5).	XXXQP
02	PRICE-EA	PIC 999V99.	00763
02	TOTAL-NR	PIC 999.	342
02	ITEM-EXP	PIC X(62).	
01	DEALINGS.		
02	CUST-ID	PIC X(5).	42381
02	PART-ID	PIC X(5).	PRSTU
02	COST-EA	PIC S999V99.	+07500
02	ORDERED	PIC 999.	047
02	PART-DESC	PIC X(62).	

For each comparison below, specify the type of comparison (algebraic or collating sequence) and truth value (true or false) of the condition.

	Comparison	Truth Value
(a) ORDERED LESS THAN TOTAL-NR	_____	_____
(b) PRICE-EA GREATER THAN COST-EA	_____	_____
(c) CUS-NO NOT GREATER THAN CUST-ID	_____	_____
(d) CUST-ID LESS THAN PART-ID	_____	_____

- - - - - - - - - - - - - - - - - - -

(a) algebraic/true; (b) algebraic/false; (c) collating sequence/false; (d) collating sequence/false

6. A non-numeric comparison is carried out character by character, beginning at the left. The shorter item is padded on the right with blanks. Refer to the collating sequence to determine which of each pair on the next page is greater. (The comparison stops as soon as one character is greater.)

(a) 123XYZ   (c) CAN-GO
    XYZ123 _____   CANADA _____

(b) FARR
    FARWELL _____

- - - - - - - - - - - - - - - - - -

(a) 123XYZ; (b) FARWELL (W is greater than R); (c) CANADA (A is greater than -)

CONDITION-NAME CONDITIONS

7. Another type of COBOL condition is the condition-name condition, which is set up in the Data Division. Level 88 is coded in area B.

```
02   PAYSCALE PIC 9.
         88 OFFICE-TECH VALUE IS 1.
         88 PROF-ADMIN  VALUE IS 2.
         88 ACADEMIC    VALUE IS 3.
```

In this example, the conditional variable PAYSCALE is an elementary data item, and thus has a PICTURE clause. Level 88 specifies not a subdivision but different values that may be assigned to the conditional variable. A statement could be IF OFFICE-TECH PERFORM HOURLY-PARA.

HOURLY-PARA would be executed if the value of PAYSCALE were _____.

- - - - - - - - - - - - - - - - - -

1

8. Write a statement that would execute YEARLY-PARA if the value of PAYSCALE were 3.

| 7 | 8 | | 12 | | 16 | | 20 | | 24 | | 28 | | 32 | | 36 | | 40 | | 44 | | 48 | | 52 |

- - - - - - - - - - - - - - - - - -

IF ACADEMIC PERFORM YEARLY-PARA.

9. Refer to the condition description below.

```
03   MARITAL-STATUS  PIC X.
         88  MARRIED      VALUE 'M'.
         88  SINGLE       VALUE 'S'.
```

(a) The elementary data item here is _____

(b) The conditional variable is _____

(c) Conditional-names have level number _____

(d) Write a statement to cause 1 to be added to SUM-S if the record indicates the person is single.

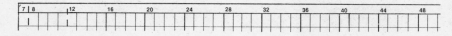

(a) MARITAL-STATUS; (b) MARITAL-STATUS; (c) 88;
(d) IF SINGLE, ADD 1 TO SUM-S.

Every condition-name (level 88 item) must contain a VALUE clause. This is the one place VALUE may be specified in the File Section. VALUE clauses may be used as needed in the Working-Storage Section, of course.

10. CLASS-LIST is a level 03 elementary data item that will contain a three-digit number. For the program under consideration it will contain 102 (FRESHMAN), 202 (SOPHOMORE), 302 (JUNIOR), or 402 (SENIOR). Write the entries to set CLASS-LIST up as a conditional variable.

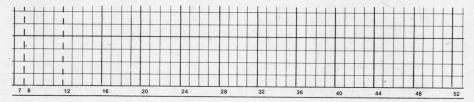

```
03   CLASS-LIST PIC 999.    (or XXX)
     88 FRESHMAN   VALUE IS 102.
     88 SOPHOMORE  VALUE IS 202.
     88 JUNIOR     VALUE IS 302.
     88 SENIOR     VALUE IS 402.
```

CLASS CONDITION

11. COBOL provides another condition called the class condition, which allows you to determine whether a variable is numeric or alphabetic. The class condition is used in an IF statement to determine the contents of a variable. The format is:

$$\text{IF data-name [NOT]} \begin{Bmatrix} \text{NUMERIC} \\ \text{ALPHABETIC} \end{Bmatrix}$$

We generally use the class condition to test input data. The most common use is to verify that values are numeric before attempting arithmetic. Write a COBOL statement to execute a paragraph called NON-NUMERIC-DATA if IN-PRICE isn't a numeric value.

```
  7 |8    |12    16    20    24    28    32    36    40    44    48    52
  |      |
  |      |
```

- - - - - - - - - - - - - - - - - -

IF IN-PRICE NOT NUMERIC PERFORM NON-NUMERIC-DATA.

12. The class condition has a few restrictions. You can't test data-names
described with all 9's for numeric class. And you can't test any data
described with all A's for alphabetic. (A is a special-purpose picture
character we haven't discussed. It is little used in practice.) Data-
names described with X's, or combinations of characters, can be tested
for either condition.

   Refer back to frame 5. Which of these data-names could be tested for

NUMERIC status? _____

_____

- - - - - - - - - - - - - - - - - -

CUS-NO, ITEM-ID, ITEM-EXP, CUST-ID, PART-ID, PART-DESC

13. NOT is a logical operator that can precede any operator, and it has the
effect of changing the result. Thus, we can code

   PART-ID NUMERIC or PART-ID NOT NUMERIC
   PART-ID = 0   or PART-ID NOT = 0

   Give the value (true or false) of each condition below. Assume the
   values of the data-names (all described with X's) are as shown:

   PART-ID   8972B
   INVENTORY-CODE   873

   (a) PART-ID NUMERIC _____

   (b) PART-ID NOT NUMERIC _____

   (c) INVENTORY-CODE NUMERIC _____

   (d) INVENTORY-CODE NOT > 900 _____

- - - - - - - - - - - - - - - - - -

(a) false; (b) true; (c) true; (d) true

COMPOUND CONDITIONS

We can combine conditions to create a compound condition using the logical
operators AND and OR. We'll show you the basic combinations here, although

much more complex ones are legal in COBOL. In structured COBOL, we try to keep our programs understandable to human readers, so only readily understood compound conditions should be used in most instances.

14. A compound condition made up of several simple conditions connected with OR is true if any one of the simple conditions is true. Look at this example:

```
IF HOURS-WORKED < ZERO OR
    HOURS WORKED > 40
        PERFORM BAD-HOURS.
```

Here the paragraph BAD-HOURS will be performed if either condition is true. If HOURS-WORKED has a negative value or is greater than 40, the compound condition is true. Examine the example below:

```
IF PRICE > 20.0 OR
    MANUFACTURER = 'DUOTECH' OR
    QUANTITY-SOLD < 6
        PERFORM SPECIAL-DEAL
ELSE
    PERFORM READ-NEXT.
```

Which paragraph will be executed for each set of values?

(a) PRICE = 21.00, MANUFACTURER = 'TEKNICON', QUANTITY-SOLD = 9 _____

(b) PRICE = 18.00, MANUFACTURER = 'TEKNICON', QUANTITY-SOLD = 9 _____

(c) PRICE = 20.00, MANUFACTURER = 'DUOTECH', QUANTITY-SOLD = 5 _____

- - - - - - - - - - - - - - - - - -

(a) SPECIAL-DEAL (the first condition is true)
(b) READ-NEXT (none of the conditions is true)
(c) SPECIAL-DEAL (the second and third conditions are true)

15. A compound condition made up of several simple conditions connected with AND is true only if all the simple conditions are true.

```
IF HOURS-WORKED > 0 AND
    HOURS-WORKED < 41
        PERFORM NORMAL-HOURS
ELSE
        PERFORM BAD-HOURS.
```

In this example, NORMAL-HOURS will be executed only if both conditions are true—that is, if the value of HOURS-WORKED is between 0 and 41

(1 to 40 inclusive). If the value is negative, zero, or more than 41, BAD-HOURS will be performed. Examine the example below:

```
IF PRICE > 20.0 AND
    MANUFACTURER = 'DUOTECH' AND
    QUANTITY-SOLD < 6
        PERFORM SPECIAL-DEAL
ELSE
        PERFORM READ-NEXT.
```

Which paragraph will be executed for each set of values:

(a) PRICE = 20.00, MANUFACTURER = 'DUOTECH', QUANTITY-SOLD

= 5 _____

(b) PRICE = 21.00, MANUFACTURER = 'DUOTECH', QUANTITY-SOLD

= 4 _____

- - - - - - - - - - - - - - - - - -

(a) READ-NEXT (The first condition is false.)
(b) SPECIAL-DEAL (All conditions are true.)

16. Compound conditions may be used in PERFORM statements as well. Here is an example.

```
PERFORM PROCESS-INPUT
        UNTIL EOF-INDICATOR = 'Y' OR
            RECORD-COUNTER > 600.
```

Under what condition will PROCESS-INPUT not be executed?

_____

_____

- - - - - - - - - - - - - - - - - -

Either at the end of the input file or when the RECORD-COUNTER passes 600

17. Suppose you want a program to execute paragraph MAX-INCOME if the value of G-INCOME is greater than SS-MAX and if the value of SS-MAX is less than 20 thousand. Otherwise you want to execute MEDIUM-INCOME. Write an IF statement that accomplishes this with a compound condition.

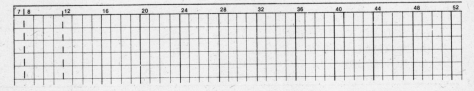

- - - - - - - - - - - - - - - - - -

```
IF   G-INCOME > SS-MAX AND
        SS-MAX < 20000
     PERFORM MAX-INCOME
ELSE
     PERFORM MEDIUM-INCOME.
```

NESTED IF STATEMENTS

The statement following IF or ELSE can be another IF statement. The logic of nested IFs can generally be accomplished using a series of IFs or a compound condition. Many times, however, a nested IF, which is an IF within an IF, provides a clearer and more effective way to solve a selection problem. This section will cover the logic and coding of nested IFs in structured COBOL.

18. The coding below shows a nested IF in which the ELSE clauses are omitted.

```
IF   HOURS-WORKED > 0
     IF HOURS-WORKED < 41
        PERFORM NORMAL-HOURS.
```

In this example, the action will be performed only if both conditions are true. It is functionally identical to a compound condition. Examine the coding below:

```
IF   HOURS-WORKED > 0
     IF HOURS-WORKED < 41
        PERFORM NORMAL-HOURS
     ELSE
        PERFORM TOO-MANY-HOURS
ELSE
     PERFORM NO-HOURS.
```

In this example, an IF is nested in the true portion of the outer IF. The indentation reflects structure; the system simply pairs each ELSE with the most recent unpaired IF. Notice a period follows the last ELSE action.

Trace the nested IF to determine what action would be performed for each value of HOURS-WORKED?

(a) 60 _____

(b) 39 _____

(c) 0 _____

- - - - - - - - - - - - - - - - - -

(a) TOO-MANY-HOURS
(b) NORMAL-HOURS
(c) NO-HOURS

19. The coding below shows another example of an IF nested within another
    IF as the action statement.

```
IF   SEX-CODE = 'F'
     IF   BIRTH-DATE < 1940
          MOVE 'X' TO INS-CODE
     ELSE
          MOVE 'Y' TO INS-CODE
ELSE
     NEXT SENTENCE.
```

    Each ELSE clause is paired with the most recent unpaired IF. Although
we use indentation is Structured COBOL to show the pairing, the system
ignores indentation and just pairs them up. In this example, a record with
SEX-CODE of M would fall through to the last ELSE, no matter what the
BIRTH-DATE is. ELSE NEXT SENTENCE can still be omitted if it is
terminated with a period.

    For each set of values below, indicate whether the INS-CODE will be
left unchanged, changed to 'X' or changed to 'Y'.

(a) SEX-CODE = F, BIRTH-DATE = 1939 _____

(b) SEX-CODE = F, BIRTH-DATE = 1940 _____

(c) SEX-CODE = F, BIRTH-DATE = 1941 _____

(d) SEX-CODE = M, BIRTH-DATE = 1940 _____

- - - - - - - - - - - - - - - - - - -

(a) changed to 'X'; (b) changed to 'Y'; (c) changed to 'Y'; (d) unchanged

20. Suppose you want a program to execute one of two paragraphs if the value
    of G-INCOME is greater than SS-MAX. If SS-MAX is greater than (or
    equal to) 20,000 you want to execute MIN-MAX. If SS-MAX is less than
    that amount, you want to execute MAX-INCOME. If G-INCOME isn't
    greater than SS-MAX, you will execute MEDIUM-INCOME.

    Write a nested IF to accomplish this.

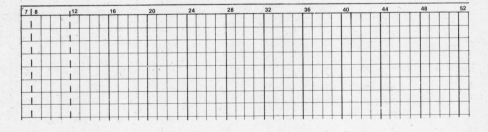

- - - - - - - - - - - - - - - - - -

```
IF  G-INCOME > SS-MAX
    IF  SS-MAX < 20000
        PERFORM MAX-INCOME
    ELSE
        PERFORM MIN-MAX
ELSE
    PERFORM MEDIUM-INCOME.
```

21. Each IF and ELSE can include more than one statement. Consider the nested IF example in frame 19. You need to use WRITE-FILE-RECORD as the output statement.

    (a) Where would you insert the WRITE if each record is to be written out?

    _____

    (b) Where would you insert the WRITE if only changed records are written

    out? _____

- - - - - - - - - - - - - - - - - - -

    (a) after the nested IF; (b) after each MOVE statement

22. An IF can be nested within an ELSE as well. Suppose you want to select one of three actions, depending on the value of EMP-DEPARTMENT. For a value of 111, you need to PERFORM MARKET-TYPE; for a value of 222, you need to PERFORM ADMIN-TYPE; for any other value you need to PERFORM REGULAR-TYPE. For the ADMIN-TYPE only you need to display the value of EMP-NAME on the system device. Code a nested IF to solve the problem.

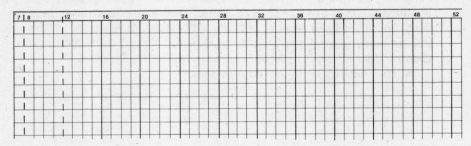

- - - - - - - - - - - - - - - - - - -

```
IF   EMP-DEPARTMENT = 111
     PERFORM MARKET-TYPE
ELSE
    IF  EMP-DEPARTMENT = 222
        PERFORM ADMIN-TYPE
        DISPLAY EMP-NAME
    ELSE
        PERFORM REGULAR-TYPE.
```

SUMMARY

In this chapter we have looked at several ways conditions can be used in a COBOL program. You've seen how relation conditions apply to non-numeric data. You've learned to use the NUMERIC and ALPHABETIC class conditions. You can use level 88 to code condition-name conditions in the Data Division. Finally, you learned to code compound conditions and nested IFs. You'll use all of them as you work through the rest of this book, and as you continue in programming, you will find many applications for all these conditional expressions.

SELF-TEST

After you have written your answers to the Self-Test, check your answers in the Answer Key that follows. Be sure you understand any differences between your answers and ours before you begin the next chapter. Following each suggested answer is a frame reference in parentheses, in case you need to review.

1.   Suppose the values of variables are as follows:

A	'ABC'	D	123
B	'123'	E	456
C	'DEF'	F	-90

What is the value (true or false) of each relational condition below?

(a) A GREATER THAN C _____

(b) C LESS THAN B   _____

(c) D GREATER THAN F _____

(d) F NOT LESS THAN E _____

2.   Complete the Data Division entry below so that a value of 1 refers to READ-IN, 2 refers to WRITE-OUT, and 3 refers to PUNCH-UP.

       02   ACTION-PLAN   PIC 9.

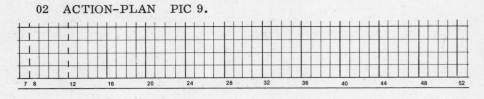

3.   Suppose you need to execute PUNCH-ROUTINE if the value of ACTION-PLAN is 3. Write the appropriate selection statement using a condition-name condition.

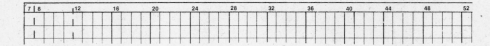

4. Write a statement to execute BAD-DATA if the value of ACTION-PLAN contains a letter instead of a digit.

5. Write a statement that will cause PRETEND to be executed repeatedly until both CREDIT-BALANCE is positive and DEBT-RATIO is higher than 20.

6. Modify your answer to question 5 so that PRETEND will be executed until just one condition is true—either one.

7. A nested IF can accomplish the following based on the value of a variable COIN. The value of COIN will be 05 or 10. Any other error rates a message (PERFORM HANDLE-ERROR). If the value is 05, you will add 1 to NICKELS, if 10, add 1 to DIMES. Code the nested IF.

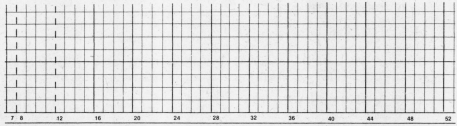

Answer Key

1. (a) false   (4)
   (b) true   (4)
   (c) true   (2)
   (d) false   (2)

```
2.  02  ACTION-PLAN      PIC 9.
        88   READ-IN              VALUE 1.
        88   WRITE-OUT            VALUE 2.
        88   PUNCH-UP             VALUE 3.        (10)

3.  IF   PUNCH-UP
        PERFORM PUNCH-ROUTINE.        (9)

4.  IF   ACTION-PLAN ALPHABETIC
        PERFORM BAD-DATA.            (12)
```
(You can't test NUMERIC directly, since ACTION-PLAN has a picture of 9.)

```
5.  PERFORM PRETEND
        UNTIL CREDIT-BALANCE > 0 AND
            DEBT-RATIO     > 20.        (15)

6.  PERFORM PRETEND
        UNTIL CREDIT-BALANCE > 0 OR
            DEBT-RATIO     > 20.        (14)

7.  IF   COIN = 05
        ADD 1 TO NICKELS
    ELSE
        IF   COIN = 10
            ADD 1 TO DIMES
        ELSE
            PERFORM HANDLE-ERRORS.        (20)
```

CHAPTER EIGHT
Sequential Files I

Virtually all computer installations store data on sequential files. Magnetic tape and disk applications are part of all realistic programs. These files store the data more compactly than do cards, and the data is much easier for the computer to access.

In this chapter you will begin to code simple applications that use tape and disk files. You'll learn to account for the functional differences between the two in your coding. We'll deal with one input file per program in this chapter, as we learn to create and update tape and disk files. Then in Chapter 9 you'll learn to handle multiple input files.

When you complete this chapter, you will be able to:

- code Environment and Data Division entries to describe sequential disk or tape files;

- code COBOL programs to create a sequential disk or tape file; and

- code a COBOL program to update a sequential disk or tape file.

The basic coding you have learned to use for card and printer files is applicable to sequential tape and disk files as well. Of course, we don't have to worry about page formatting or line counting when the output file is on disk or tape. The tape or disk file also is much more flexible in terms of record size. And the records may be blocked, which permits more efficient input and output (I/O) operations.

Now let's look at some of the major features of tape and disk sequential files.

BLOCKED RECORDS

1. Each record on magnetic tape or disk takes up space. A gap is normally left between records, to allow the tape to get up to the speed expected for the READ or WRITE. These gaps take up space on the device. When records are blocked, several of them are stored end-to-end with no gaps between. And an entire block, made up of several records, is read or written at a time. In the program, you still deal with one record at a time; the computer takes care of the details. When the records are

blocked, one physical record equals several logical records, and there are fewer gaps. So we save space on the tape or disk, as well as time in doing input and output (I/O) operations. If a blocking factor of ten is used, ten records are placed in one block. Then only one-tenth the space is taken up with gaps, and only one-tenth the number of I/O operations are needed.

When records on an input file are blocked, a block is read as a unit into an input area. The records are still accessed by the programmer at a rate of one for each READ statement executed. If records are in blocks of eight, the first READ statement would place one block of eight records in the input area, and the first record would be available to the programmer. On execution of a second READ statement, which of the following would happen?

_____ (a) Another block of records would be placed in the input area.

_____ (b) Eight records would be available to the programmer.

_____ (c) Record number two would be available to the programmer.

_____ (d) No records would be placed in the input area.

- - - - - - - - - - - - - - - - - -

c, d (After all the records in the block have been accessed, the next READ places the next block in the input area.)

2. These two advantages—conserving storage space and saving physical I/O operations—make blocking very desirable. Together they help to minimize run time, and hence costs. For example, an amount of disk or tape that can hold 60 unblocked 80-byte records can hold about 140 records when they are blocked by twenty. (A byte is the amount of computer space needed to store one character.) In this case each block is 1600 bytes long, and will hold 1600 characters. But only 5% (1/20) as many physical I/O operations are performed. When an output tape file is being created, blocking could be used to:

_____ (a) conserve space on the device.

_____ (b) cause fewer physical output operations to take place.

_____ (c) place several records on tape after an output area is filled.

- - - - - - - - - - - - - - - - - -

all of these

ENVIRONMENT DIVISION ENTRIES

3. As you recall, you need to code SELECT and ASSIGN entries in the Environment Division for all files. The ASSIGN format we have been using for card and printer files is: UR-S-*dd*name. The system-name

is similar for magnetic tape and sequential disk files. A magnetic tape unit is considered a utility device and the symbol UT is used. A disk drive is a direct-access device and the symbol DA is used. Both types of file require S-ddname in their ASSIGN clause. Code Environment Division entries for the following files.

(a) A card file to be called IN-FILE in the program identified by the system as CARDIN.

(b) A magnetic tape file to be called LIB-FILE in the program, identified by the system as TAPEIN.

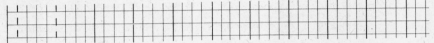

(c) A sequential disk file to be called TRAN-FILE in the program, identified by the system as DISKIN.

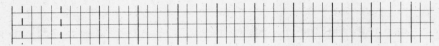

- - - - - - - - - - - - - - - - - - -

(a) SELECT IN-FILE   ASSIGN TO UR-S-CARDIN.
(b) SELECT LIB-FILE   ASSIGN TO UT-S-TAPEIN.
(c) SELECT TRAN-FILE ASSIGN TO DA-S-DISKIN.

4. Read the program I/O descriptions below, and determine how many SELECT and ASSIGN clauses would be needed for each.

(a) The program uses a single disk file, a card file for input, and prints a report at the end. _____

(b) A program needs a tape file for input, another for output, a printed report of the processing, and a disk file to hold error records.

_____

- - - - - - - - - - - - - - - - - - -

(a) 3 (disk, card, and printer); (b) 4 (2 tapes, printer, and disk)

DATA DIVISION ENTRIES

5. Just as each file used in a program requires Environment Division entries, so each one requires an FD entry in the Data Division. As you learned in Chapter 4, every FD entry must include at least the file-name

(as in SELECT) and a LABEL RECORDS clause. We use LABEL REC-
ORDS ARE OMITTED for all card and printer files. Tape files may
omit labels as well, but disk files are required to include them, and
tape files may include labels. While header and trailer labels may be
created in a program, most programmers use standard ones. In fact,
many systems require standard labels. The useful alternative to LABEL
RECORDS ARE OMITTED is LABEL RECORDS ARE STANDARD. When
STANDARD labels are specified, the header and trailer labels are created or processed automatically by the system.

(a) Which type(s) of file (card, printer, tape, disk) can use standard

   labels? _____

(b) Which type(s) of file (card, printer, tape, disk) can skip labels?

   _____

(c) When a disk file is being created, who is responsible for putting in

   standard labels—the program or the system? _____

- -

(a) tape or disk; (b) card, printer, or tape; (c) the system (it is done
automatically)

6. You may include several additional clauses in an FD entry. Figure 8-1
    summarizes the commonly used FD entries. You can see that FD and
    LABEL RECORDS are required for all files. RECORD CONTAINS and
    DATA RECORD are optional for all files.

FD Entries   file types

		card	printer	tape	disk
FD	file-name	R	R	R	R
	LABEL RECORDS	R	R	R	R
	BLOCK CONTAINS	N	N	P	P
	RECORD CONTAINS	P	P	P	P
	DATA RECORD	P	P	P	P

R = = = = = > Required
N = = = = = > Never permitted
P = = = = = > Permitted

Figure 8-1

RECORD CONTAINS n CHARACTERS can be used to make clear to
readers the record length for any file. Since we are only concerned
with fixed length records in this book, we'll generally omit this clause.
Some installations may require it, however.

The DATA RECORD clause is used to name the record or records associated with a file. It, too, is for documentation only. Since the record description must directly follow the FD entry, the DATA RECORD clause is not needed.

The BLOCK CONTAINS clause is required if records are blocked. BLOCK CONTAINS 5 RECORDS specifies a blocking factor of five.

The FD entry below shows the format of the clauses. Examine it, then answer the questions that follow.

```
FD   INVENTORY
     LABEL RECORDS ARE OMITTED
     BLOCK CONTAINS 10 RECORDS
     RECORD CONTAINS 120 CHARACTERS
     DATA RECORD IS PARTS-RECORD.
```

(a) On what device might the INVENTORY file be located?

_____

(b) What is the blocking factor for this file? _____

(c) How many character positions make up the block? _____

(d) Will standard labels be processed automatically for this file? _____

(e) What coding would be on the line following the FD entry?

_____

- - - - - - - - - - - - - - - - - - - -

(a) magnetic tape (Since labels are omitted, this cannot be on disk. Since records aren't 80 characters long, and are blocked, it cannot be cards.)
(b) 10; (c) 1200 (120 times 10); (d) no (labels are omitted);
(e) 01   PARTS-RECORD.

7.   The RECORD CONTAINS and DATA RECORD clauses are primarily for documentation. Most computer systems ignore them, except for format. The BLOCK CONTAINS clause, however, must be correct or zero if used. One way most installations handle this is to code BLOCK CONTAINS 0 RECORDS, and specify the actual blocksize in the control language of the system. If you aren't sure which method your installation uses, just code the correct blocking factor in the BLOCK CONTAINS clause.

The example in frame 6 was coded in correct format. The FD must be in area A, and the file-name and clauses must be entirely contained in area B. We place each clause on a separate line for clarity. Notice that a period follows only the last of the FD clauses.

For each file described below, code the FD entry.

(a) SELECT LIB-FILE ASSIGN TO UT-S-TAPEIN. This file has eight 100-byte records in a block. It has no labels. The 01 level is LIB-RECORD. Write as complete an FD entry as possible, using the form on the next page.

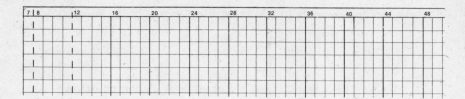

(b) SELECT TRAN-FILE ASSIGN TO DA-S-DISKIN. This file has eight 120-byte records to a block, but blocksize will be specified in the control language. Write as complete an FD entry as possible.

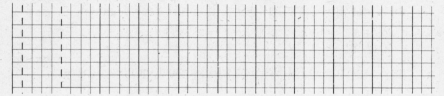

(c) Code a minimum FD entry for an unblocked disk file named DISKF that has 320-byte records named OUTREC.

- - - - - - - - - - - - - - - - - - - -

```
(a)   FD   LIB-FILE
           LABEL RECORDS ARE OMITTED
           BLOCK CONTAINS 8 RECORDS
           RECORD CONTAINS 100 CHARACTERS
           DATA RECORD IS LIB-RECORD.

(b)   FD   TRAN-FILE
           LABEL RECORDS ARE STANDARD
           BLOCK CONTAINS 0 RECORDS
           RECORD CONTAINS 120 CHARACTERS.

(c)   FD   DISKF
           LABEL RECORDS ARE STANDARD.
```

OPENING AND CLOSING FILES

8.   All files used in a program must first be OPENed with the appropriate I/O option, and they must be CLOSEd before the program ends. When we create a file, we first OPEN it as OUTPUT; we'll be putting data out to a tape or disk to build the file. After it is created, the file can be OPENed as INPUT and processed. Disk files have an additional option. They can be opened as I-O and used for input and output in the same program. You'll see later in this chapter how to update disk files by reading

and writing records to the same file. Here are the formats:

$$\text{OPEN} \left\{ \begin{array}{l} \text{INPUT} \\ \text{OUTPUT} \\ \text{I-O} \end{array} \right\} \text{file-name,}\ldots \quad \text{CLOSE file-name,}\ldots$$

Write OPEN and CLOSE statements as indicated below.

(a) A tape file (TFILE1) that will be created by the program.

OPEN
CLOSE

(b) A disk file (DFILE1) that will be used for read only.

OPEN
CLOSE
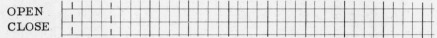

(c) A tape file (TFILE2) that will be read into the program.

OPEN
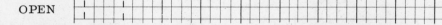

(d) A disk file (DFILE2) that will be used as input and output during the program.

OPEN

(e) Write single OPEN and CLOSE statements to handle (a) and (c).

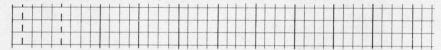

- -

(a) OPEN   OUTPUT TFILE1.
    CLOSE   TFILE1.
(b) OPEN   INPUT DFILE1.
    CLOSE DFILE1.
(c) OPEN   INPUT TFILE2.
(d) OPEN   I-O DFILE2.
(e) OPEN   INPUT TFILE2
          OUTPUT TFILE1.
    CLOSE TFILE2 TFILE1.

CARD-TRANSFER PROCEDURE

9. A very common need in many companies is to transfer card decks to magnetic tape or disk. A basic card-to-tape procedure is shown in Figure 8-2. Notice that the WRITE statement for this program is no different from what you have been using. The ADVANCING options are used only with printer files, of course.

Examine the program in Figure 8-2. Suppose the program must be modified to put the card images on disk.

```
      IDENTIFICATION DIVISION.
      PROGRAM-ID.  CARD-TO-TAPE.
      AUTHOR.   RUTH ASHLEY.
      ENVIRONMENT DIVISION.
      INPUT-OUTPUT SECTION.
      FILE-CONTROL.
          SELECT CARD-FILE
              ASSIGN TO UR-S-INCARDS.
          SELECT MASTER-FILE
              ASSIGN TO UT-S-OUTAPE.
      DATA DIVISION.
      FILE SECTION.
      FD  CARD-FILE
      LABEL RECORDS ARE OMITTED.
      01  CARD-RECORD             PIC X(80).
      FD  MASTER-FILE
          BLOCK CONTAINS 10 RECORDS
          LABEL RECORDS ARE OMITTED.
      01  MASTER-RECORD           PIC X(80).
      WORKING-STORAGE SECTION.
      01  CARD-EOF                PIC X
                                  VALUE 'N'.
      PROCEDURE DIVISION.
      MAIN-LOGIC.
          OPEN INPUT CARD-FILE
              OUTPUT MASTER-FILE.
          READ CARD-FILE
              AT END MOVE 'Y' TO CARD-EOF.
          PERFORM TRANSFER-RECORDS
              UNTIL CARD-EOF = 'Y'.
          CLOSE CARD-FILE
              MASTER-FILE.
          STOP RUN.
      TRANSFER-RECORDS.
          WRITE MASTER-RECORD FROM CARD-RECORD.
          READ CARD-FILE
              AT END MOVE 'Y' TO CARD-EOF.
```

Figure 8-2

(a) What entries in the Environment Division must be changed?

_____

(b) What entries in the Data Division must be changed?

_____

(c) What entries in the Procedure Division must be changed?

_____

- - - - - - - - - - - - - - - - - -

(a) MASTER–FILE ASSIGN (to DA–S–system–name)

(b) MASTER–FILE FD (need STANDARD labels)

(c) no changes needed

MICROCOMPUTER DISKS

Many small computer systems have COBOL compilers, but few include card readers or tape drives. You can, however, build disk files directly from the terminal; this section will show you how to build a disk file without cards.

10. When records are ACCEPTed to be put on disk, only one file need be selected and defined. Figure 8–3 shows how a disk file may be created from a terminal. Examine the program.

   (a) What statement(s) in Figure 8–3 replace(s) the READ for a card file?

   _____

   (b) What is used as the equivalent of an end-of-file indicator in the program of Figure 8–3? _____

   (c) Suppose the WORKING-STORAGE Section includes COUNT-RECORDS PIC 999 VALUE ZERO, and the statement before STOP RUN is DISPLAY COUNT-RECORDS. Where could you insert ADD 1 TO COUNT-RECORDS to result in a count of the records written to the disk file? _____

- - - - - - - - - - - - - - - - - - - -

   (a) the statements in GET–INPUT—DISPLAYs and ACCEPTs

   (b) an entry of all 9's in TERM–NUM

   (c) in BUILD–DISK—anywhere before GET–INPUT

11. Suppose you are building a "dummy" master file that is to contain only employee numbers, with blanks for the name and address fields.

   (a) What changes will you need in the Working-Storage Section of Figure 8–3? _____

   (b) Recode GET–INPUT to build the record needed.

   (c) What changes will you need to BUILD–DISK? _____

- - - - - - - - - - - - - - - - - - - -

```
IDENTIFICATION DIVISION.
      PROGRAM-ID. BUILDIT.
ENVIRONMENT DIVISION.
FILE-CONTROL.
      SELECT MASTER-FILE
          ASSIGN TO DISK.
DATA DIVISION.
FILE SECTION.
FD   MASTER-FILE
      LABEL RECORDS ARE STANDARD.
01   MASTER-RECORD.
      02   MASTER-NUM        PIC X(4).
      02   MASTER-NAME       PIC X(30).
      02   MASTER-ADDRESS    PIC X(40).
      02   FILLER            PIC X(6).
WORKING-STORAGE SECTION.
01   TERMINAL-RECORD.
      02   TERM-NUM          PIC X(4).
      02   TERM-NAME         PIC X(30).
      02   TERM-ADDRESS      PIC X(46).
PROCEDURE DIVISION.
MAIN-LOGIC.
      OPEN   OUTPUT MASTER-FILE.
      PERFORM GET-INPUT.
      PERFORM BUILD-DISK
          UNTIL TERM-NUM = 9999.
      CLOSE MASTER-FILE.
      STOP RUN.
BUILD-DISK.
      WRITE MASTER-RECORD FROM TERMINAL-RECORD.
      PERFORM GET-INPUT.
GET-INPUT.
      DISPLAY 'ENTER EMPLOYEE NUMBER (4 DIGITS)'.
      ACCEPT TERM-NUM.
      DISPLAY 'ENTER THE EMPLOYEE NAME'.
      ACCEPT TERM-NAME.
      DISPLAY 'NOW ENTER THE COMPLETE ADDRESS'.
      ACCEPT TERM-ADDRESS.
```

Figure 8-3

Answers to frame 11

(a) add VALUE SPACES to TERM-NAME and TERM-ADDRESS

(b)
```
GET-INPUT.
      DISPLAY 'ENTER EMPLOYEE NUMBER'.
      ACCEPT TERM-NUM.
```

(c) none; the TERMINAL-RECORD contains the appropriate values

SEQUENCE CHECKING

12. When you are creating a file, you usually want to do more than just write records. You may want to count them, for example. Another very frequent step is to check the sequence numbers to make sure they are in order.

    This pseudocode shows the structure of sequence checking.

    ```
    Get input record
    IF   new sequence number > last sequence number
         build record for new file
    ELSE
         record is out of sequence
    ENDIF
    ```

    In order to accomplish sequence checking, the program must save the key value from the current record before the next record is accessed. Suppose the program in Figure 8-3 includes SAVE-NUMBER PIC 9(6).

    (a) Code a statement to save the sequence number.

    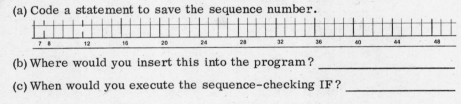

    (b) Where would you insert this into the program? _____

    (c) When would you execute the sequence-checking IF? _____

    _____

    - - - - - - - - - - - - - - - - - - -

    (a) MOVE TERM-NUM TO SAVE-NUMBER.
    (b) just before the WRITE statement
    (c) just after the GET-INPUT paragraph

13. Code a sequence-checking routine named SEQUENCE-CHECK for the program in Figure 8-3. Any time a record is out of sequence, you want to put the record number on the printer terminal (DIABLO). Be sure to adhere to the structured coding conventions.

    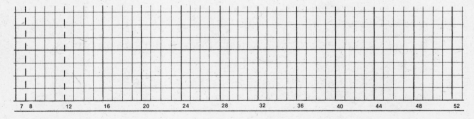

    - - - - - - - - - - - - - - - - - - -

```
SEQUENCE-CHECK.
    IF   TERM-NUM > SAVE-NUMBER
         NEXT SENTENCE
    ELSE
         DISPLAY TERM-NUM UPON DIABLO
         PERFORM GET-INPUT.
```

(Your indentation and layout should be similar to this. Only one major statement part should be on one line. The NEXT SENTENCE is required when it is the IF (THEN) action.)

14. Where in the program of Figure 8-3 would you code PERFORM SEQUENCE-CHECK to ensure that the disk file resulting from the program is in ascending sequence by employee number? _____

_____

- - - - - - - - - - - - - - - - - - -

after each PERFORM GET-INPUT

You have seen how you can use either cards or terminal input to create a disk or tape sequential file. You have seen how to check sequence and count records while creating a sequential file.

In the next section, we will look at how to update or change data in a tape or disk file. Here, we'll use only one input file, but in the next chapter, you'll learn to use a separate input transaction file to update a tape or disk file.

15. We mentioned earlier that disk files can be opened as I-O to allow to read and write to the same file, while tape files can be used only as input or output—one at a time.

In order to make changes to a tape file—to update it—we have to create a complete new file. The existing file is read in, one record at a time. Changes can be made to any or all records. But each record, whether changed or not, must be written to the output tape or it is lost. A program reads one record, perhaps changes it, then writes it to a different (new) tape file. The process is repeated for each record in the input file.

Suppose we have a master-tape file with records of information about employees. We need to change an insurance-coverage code (INS-CODE) on the records of all women employees. If SEX-CODE equals 'F', we will need to set INS-CODE equal to 'X' (for extensive).

The main logic for the program is shown on the next page. Code the UPDATE-FILE routine. Be sure that each record (call them OLDREC and NEWREC) is written to the new file, whether changed or not.

```
PROCEDURE DIVISION.
MAIN-LOGIC.
    OPEN INPUT OLDFILE
        OUTPUT NEWFILE.
    READ OLDFILE
        AT END MOVE 'Y' TO FILE-EOF.
    PERFORM UPDATE-FILE
        UNTIL FILE-EOF = 'Y'.
    CLOSE OLDFILE, NEWFILE.
    STOP RUN.
```

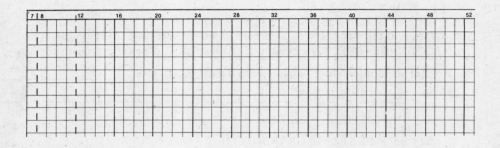

- - - - - - - - - - - - - - - - - -

```
UPDATE-FILE.
    IF  SEX-CODE = 'F'
        MOVE 'X' TO INS-CODE
    ELSE
        NEXT SENTENCE.
    WRITE NEWREC FROM OLDREC.
    READ OLD FILE
        AT END MOVE 'Y' TO FILE-EOF.
```

16. When a disk file is being updated, it can be opened as I-O. Every record in the sequential file must still be read. But only the changed records must be rewritten in place. Only one file is needed. Refer back to the preceding frame.

   (a) How would you recode the OPEN statement if you were updating a disk (UPFILE) instead of a tape?

   (b) Recode UPDATE-FILE so that only changed records are rewritten.

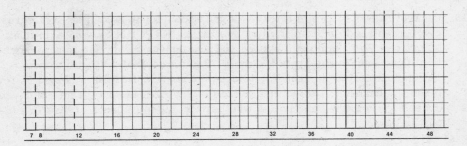

- - - - - - - - - - - - - - - - - - -

```
(a) OPEN I-O UPFILE.
(b) UPDATE-FILE.
        IF SEX-CODE = 'F'
            MOVE 'X' TO INS-CODE
        ELSE
            NEXT SENTENCE.
        READ UPFILE
            AT END MOVE 'Y' TO FILE-EOF.
```

17. Sequence checking is often done using a nested IF. When separate messages are required for duplicate records (new number = old number), a nested IF can be used. Which nested IF below would perform sequence checking correctly?

```
_____ (a) IF NEW-NUMBER > OLD-NUMBER
            NEXT SENTENCE
        ELSE
            IF NEW-NUMBER = OLD-NUMBER
                PERFORM DUP-RECORD
            ELSE
                PERFORM SEQUENCE-ERROR.

_____ (b) IF NEW-NUMBER < OLD-NUMBER
            PERFORM SEQUENCE-ERROR
        ELSE
            IF NEW-NUMBER = OLD-NUMBER
                PERFORM DUP-RECORD
            ELSE
                NEXT SENTENCE.

_____ (c) IF NEW-NUMBER = OLD-NUMBER
            PERFORM DUP-RECORD.
        IF NEW-NUMBER < OLD-NUMBER
            PERFORM SEQUENCE-ERROR.
```

- - - - - - - - - - - - - - - - - - -

a, b (c uses separate IFs. This could work under certain circumstances, but it isn't efficient.)

18. Control in nested IFs is tricky, as you know. Many nested IF structures
can be replaced or simplified by nesting a PERFORM to handle an inner
selection. For example, suppose you are updating salaries in a personnel
file. Only employees hired before 1979 get a cost-of-living increase.
Permanent employees get 5%, temporary get 3%. Here is a nested IF to
make the changes. Notice that we're displaying messages if an employee
doesn't get a raise, and noting whether the reason is date of hire or employee type.

```
IF YR-HIRED < 1979
    IF TYPE-EMPLOYEE = 'PERM'
        MULTIPLY SALARY BY 1.05
    ELSE
        IF TYPE-EMPLOYEE = 'TEMP'
            MULTIPLY SALARY BY 1.03
        ELSE
            DISPLAY EMP-NUMBER 'NOT PERM OR TEMP'
ELSE
    DISPLAY EMP-NUMBER 'RECENT HIRE'.
```

This is a fairly complex nested IF. It could have been coded in several
different ways. Rewrite it now so that the outer IF above PERFORMs a
paragraph that contains a nested IF. Code the PERFORMed paragraph
as well.

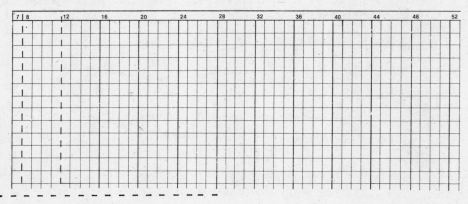

```
IF  YR-HIRED < 1979
    PERFORM FIX-SALARY
ELSE
    DISPLAY EMP-NUMBER 'RECENT HIRE'.
  .
  .
  .
    FIX-SALARY.
        IF TYPE-EMPLOYEE = 'PERM'
            MULTIPLY SALARY BY 1.05
        ELSE
            IF TYPE-EMPLOYEE = 'TEMP'
                MULTIPLY SALARY BY 1.03
            ELSE
                DISPLAY EMP-NUMBER 'NOT PERM OR TEMP'.
```

SUMMARY

In this chapter you have learned to handle sequential disk and magnetic tape files. You have learned to code the appropriate Environment and Data Division entries. You can code a program to create a disk or tape file from cards or a terminal, with counting or sequence checking as needed.

You have also learned the basic difference between disk and tape update programs. In the following exercise you will write a program to update a tape file.

Summary Exercise

Assume you are going to update a tape file. This is an inventory file; it contains item number, description, quantity, and price for all the stock. The item number is made up of five digits and one letter—the letter indicates manufacturer. The manufacturer whose code is P has raised its prices and you need to modify the file to increase the selling price of items that cost more than $5.00 by 10% (.10), and the rest by 5% (.05). The input file (INVENTORY) record description is shown below. You won't have to recode it—just use its data-names.

```
01    STOCK-RECORD.
      02   ITEM-NUMBER.
           03   ITEM-NO-MOST      PIC 9(5).
           03   ITEM-NO-LAST      PIC X.
      02   DESCRIPTION            PIC X(24).
      02   QUANTITY-ON-HAND       PIC 9999.
      02   QUANTITY-ON-ORDER      PIC 9999.
      02   COST-PRICE             PIC 999V99.
      02   SELLING-PRICE          PIC 999V99.
```

Frame 20 shows pseudocode for the logic to update this tape file. During the next several frames, you'll write the complete program.

19. Code the first three divisions for the update program. Here is some information you will need.

    - If you plan to use WRITE ... FROM, you won't need to detail your output record.

    - Define Working-Storage items for the end-of-file switch and a counter to keep count of how many records are updated.

    - The system will find the existing tape file as "UT-S-INVNT1".

    - Use standard labels.

    - The inventory file (old and new) is blocked by 20.

    A form for your coding appears on the next page.

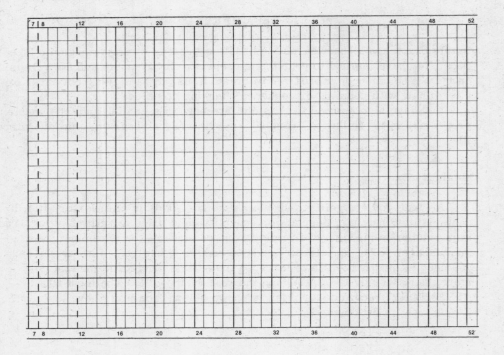

- - - - - - - - - - - - - - - - - -

```
     IDENTIFICATION DIVISION.
     PROGRAM-ID.
         FIX-INVENTORY.
     AUTHOR.
         YOUR NAME.
     ENVIRONMENT DIVISION.
     INPUT-OUTPUT SECTION.
     FILE-CONTROL.
         SELECT OLD-INVENTORY
             ASSIGN TO UT-S-INVNT1.
         SELECT NEW-INVENTORY
             ASSIGN TO UT-S-INVNT2.
     DATA DIVISION.
     FILE SECTION.
     FD   OLD-INVENTORY
         BLOCK CONTAINS 20 RECORDS
         LABEL RECORDS ARE STANDARD.
     01   STOCK-RECORD.
         02   ITEM-NUMBER.
             03   ITEM-NO-MOST         PIC 9(5).
             03   ITEM-NO-LAST         PIC X.
         02   DESCRIPTION              PIC X(24).
         02   QUANTITY-ON-HAND         PIC 9999.
         02   QUANTITY-ON-ORDER        PIC 9999.
         02   COST-PRICE               PIC 999V99.
         02   SELLING-PRICE            PIC 999V99.
```

(continued on the next page)

```
FD  NEW-INVENTORY
    BLOCK CONTAINS 20 RECORDS
    LABEL RECORDS ARE STANDARD.
01  NEW-RECORD                   PIC X(48).
WORKING-STORAGE SECTION.
01  EOF-SWITCH                   PIC X        VALUE 'N'.
01  UPDATE-COUNTER               PIC 999      VALUE ZERO.
```

20. The pseudocode for the program is shown below.

```
Main logic
        Get input record
        PERFORM UNTIL no more records
                Update file
        ENDPERFORM
        Display count
        Terminate program
Update file
        IF code=P
           increment counter
           IF cost>5.00
                    multiply price by 1.10
           ELSE
                    multiply price by 1.05
           ENDIF
        ELSE
        ENDIF
           Put output record
        Get input record
```

Code the Procedure Division in structured COBOL.

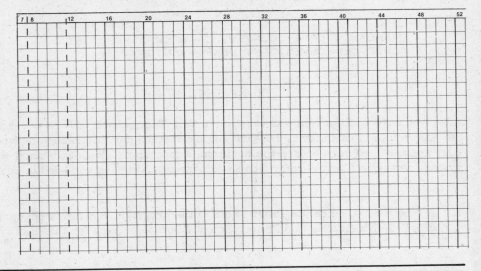

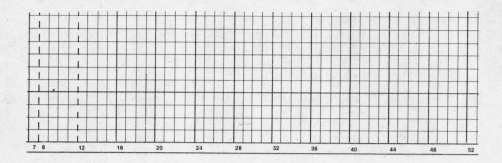

```
PROCEDURE DIVISION.
MAIN-LOGIC.
    OPEN INPUT OLD-INVENTORY
        OUTPUT NEW-INVENTORY.
    PERFORM GET-INPUT.
    PERFORM UPDATE-FILE
        UNTIL EOF-SWITCH = 'Y'.
    PERFORM WRAPUP.
    STOP RUN.
UPDATE-FILE.
    IF ITEM-NO-LAST = 'P'
        ADD 1 TO UPDATE-COUNTER
        IF COST-PRICE > 5.00
            MULTIPLY 1.10 BY SELLING-PRICE ROUNDED
        ELSE
            MULTIPLY 1.05 BY SELLING-PRICE ROUNDED
    ELSE
        NEXT SENTENCE.
    WRITE NEW-RECORD FROM STOCK-RECORD.
    PERFORM GET-INPUT.
GET-INPUT.
    READ OLD-INVENTORY
        AT END MOVE 'Y' TO EOF-SWITCH.
WRAPUP.
    DISPLAY UPDATE-COUNTER, '  RECORDS UPDATED'.
    CLOSE OLD-INVENTORY, NEW-INVENTORY.
```

SELF-TEST

After you have written your answers to the Self-Test, check your answers in the Answer Key that follows. Be sure you understand any differences between your answers and ours before you begin the next chapter. Following each suggested answer is a frame reference in parentheses, in case you need to review.

1. A tape file, to be called PROBLEMS in the program, has a system name of UT-S-PROBCOB. Code Environment Division entries for this file.

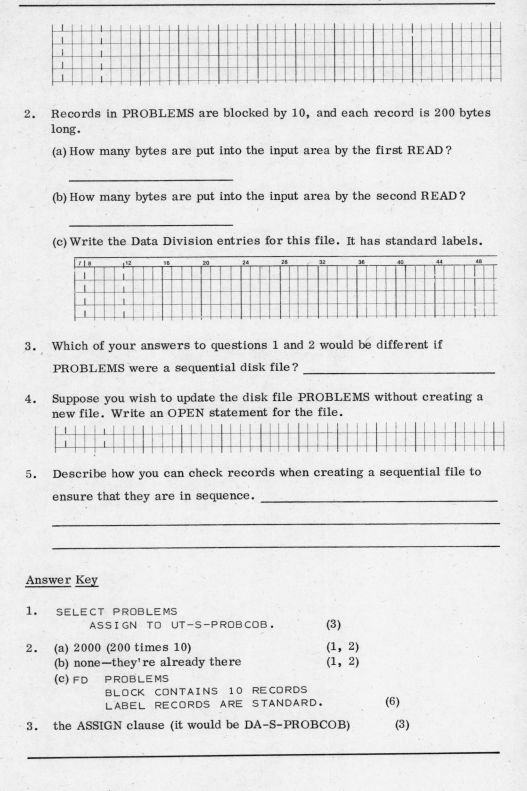

2. Records in PROBLEMS are blocked by 10, and each record is 200 bytes long.

   (a) How many bytes are put into the input area by the first READ?

   _____

   (b) How many bytes are put into the input area by the second READ?

   _____

   (c) Write the Data Division entries for this file. It has standard labels.

3. Which of your answers to questions 1 and 2 would be different if PROBLEMS were a sequential disk file? _____

4. Suppose you wish to update the disk file PROBLEMS without creating a new file. Write an OPEN statement for the file.

5. Describe how you can check records when creating a sequential file to ensure that they are in sequence. _____

   _____

   _____

Answer Key

1.   ```
     SELECT PROBLEMS
          ASSIGN TO UT-S-PROBCOB.          (3)
     ```

2.   (a) 2000 (200 times 10)   (1, 2)
     (b) none—they're already there   (1, 2)
     (c) ```
         FD   PROBLEMS
              BLOCK CONTAINS 10 RECORDS
              LABEL RECORDS ARE STANDARD.   (6)
         ```

3.   the ASSIGN clause (it would be DA-S-PROBCOB)   (3)

4. `OPEN I-O PROBLEMS.`   (8)

5. Save the key value. Compare the new key value to the saved one. If the new one is higher, the record is in sequence.   (12)

CHAPTER NINE
Sequential Files II

In the last chapter you learned to define a sequential tape or disk file, to create such a file from cards or terminal input, and to update a file. We discussed updating sequential files when that was the only input file. In the business world, most tape and disk applications use at least two input files. One is the master file, which contains all the records of a given type for an organization. The other is the transaction file, which is usually smaller and has record numbers corresponding to the records in the master file that are to be accessed, updated, or deleted. Other transaction files may contain numbers and information on records to be added to the master file.

Regular processing of master files with transaction records is called maintaining the master file. A payroll master file may be updated with various types of transaction files. New employees may be added, salaries may be updated, and employees may leave. Information on any (or all) of these may make up a transaction file for maintaining the master payroll file. As you work through this chapter, you will learn how to maintain sequential tape and disk files.

When you complete this chapter, you will be able to:

- code a structured COBOL Procedure Division to access records from a master file based on a transaction file;

- code a structured COBOL Procedure Division to update a sequential master file based on a transaction file;

- code a structured COBOL Procedure Division to add records to a master file;

- code a segment to delete records from a master file; and

- code appropriate end-of-file processing for a two-input-file program.

A master file on tape or disk doesn't just store data. It is used regularly, as programs look up information, and add, delete, or modify records. Most of the information about what is to be done with which records comes in through a second input file—a transaction file. Whether the transaction file is on cards, tape, or disk makes no difference to the Procedure Division. We'll look first at techniques for accessing records from an input master file when no changes are to be made.

ACCESSING RECORDS

1. Each record in a master file contains an identifying field that we call a key field. This can be a number, a name, or anything that is unique in each record. The records in a sequential disk or tape file are arranged in sequence according to this key. Each record in a transaction file also contains a key. The transaction file usually has fewer records than the master file, and these must be sorted in the same key sequence as the master file.

   (a) If the master file is sequenced in ascending order by social security number, how must the transaction file be sequenced?

   _____

   (b) Which file will generally contain more records: master or

   transaction? _____

   (c) From which file will you read the largest number of records?

   _____

- - - - - - - - - - - - - - - - - -

   (a) the same way; (b) master; (c) master

2. To access a given record from a sequential file, you need to read every preceding record in the file, comparing key sequence numbers after each READ. When the two are equal, you have accessed the matching record, and can output a message or print some information from the record.

   Suppose we have a master file sequenced by part number. We also have a transaction list. We want to check if each number in the transaction list is one we carry in our file and print a report of YES or NOT IN FILE for each. Here are some entries from the files.

Transaction	Master
10800	10789
10863	10800
10870	10863
10873	10872
	10873

   What output (YES or NOT IN FILE) would you expect for each of these transaction records?

   (a) 10800 _____

   (b) 10863 _____

   (c) 10870 _____

- - - - - - - - - - - - - - - - - - -

(a) YES; (b) YES; (c) NOT IN FILE

3.   Figure 9-1 shows a hierarchy for any program that uses keys in a transaction file to access records from another sequential file. Study the chart,
then answer the questions that follow. (> means greater than; < means
less than).

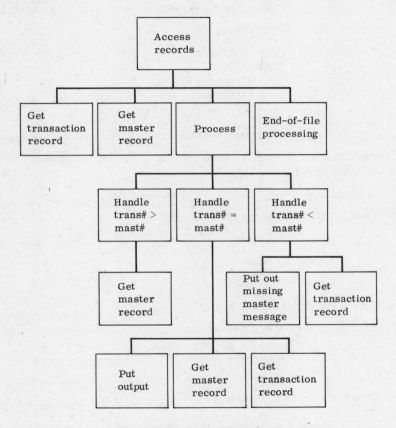

Figure 9-1.   Accessing Records Structure

(a) What must the program accomplish before it enters the main processing portion of the program?

_____

(b) Under what condition is the matching record accessed?

_____

(c) Under what condition is it clear that the key indicated by the transaction record is not in the master file?

_____

(a) read a record from each file; (b) if the two keys are equal (trans# = mast#); (c) if the transaction key is less than the master key (trans < mast)

4. Processing any record-matching structure involves comparing key numbers on records from both files. At each comparison, the pair must include one of each. These are the first few records from sample files.

Transaction	Master
10800	10789
10863	10800
10870	10863
10873	10872
	10872

Let's trace these through the chart in Figure 9-1.

(a) What two records are compared as soon as the program enters the process loop?

Transaction: _____ Master: _____

(b) Which of the three conditions is true?

_____ trans# > mast#

_____ trans# = mast#

_____ trans# < mast#

(c) What does the program do next?_____

(d) What pair is compared next?

Transaction: _____ Master: _____

(e) Which condition is true? _____

(f) What does the program do next? _____

_____

(g) What pair is compared next?

Transaction: _____ Master: _____

- - - - - - - - - - - - - - - - - - -

(a) transaction: 10800   Master: 10789
(b) trans# > mast#
(c) gets another master record
(d) transaction: 10800   Master: 10800
(e) trans# = mast#
(f) puts out yes for accessed record; gets a record from each file
(g) transaction: 10863   Master: 10863

5. At this point, the current pair is equal, so after the necessary output, the next record from each file is read.

   Transaction: 10870   Master: 10872

   (a) What condition is true?_____

   (b) What action is taken? _____

   _____

   (c) What is the next pair compared?

   Transaction: _____   Master: _____

- - - - - - - - - - - - - - - - - - -

   (a) trans# < mast#
   (b) a missing master message (NOT IN FILE) is written, and a new transaction record read
   (c) transaction: 10873   Master: 10872

6. The PROCESS-RECORDS loop can include a nested IF to test for the various conditions. Here is a pseudocode:

```
IF    trans-key greater than master-key
      get new master record
ELSE
      IF    trans-key equals master-key
            handle match achieved
      ELSE
            handle no-match
      ENDIF
ENDIF
```

   Write a nested IF for this pseudocode, using TRANS-KEY and MAST-KEY as the fields being compared. Create any other names as needed.

- - - - - - - - - - - - - - - - - - -

```
IF TRANS-KEY > MASTER-KEY
    PERFORM GET-MASTER
ELSE
    IF TRANS-KEY = MASTER-KEY
        PERFORM MATCH-ACHIEVED
    ELSE
        PERFORM NO-MATCH.
```

7. Refer to the answer in frame 6. What types of COBOL statements would be included in each of the following paragraphs:

    (a) GET-MASTER _____

    (b) MATCH-ACHIEVED _____

    (c) NO-MATCH _____

- - - - - - - - - - - - - - - - - - -

    (a) READ—master
    (b) MOVE, WRITE, 2 READS
    (c) MOVE, WRITE, 1 READ—transaction

8. Write the three PERFORMed paragraphs. Recall that YES or NOT IN FILE is printed with the key as appropriate. Relevant file and data-names are shown below:

    MASTER-FILE, MASTER-RECORD, MASTER-KEY, MASTER-EOF
    TRANS-FILE, TRANS-RECORD, TRANS-KEY, TRANS-EOF
    OUTPUT-FILE, OUTPUT-RECORD, OUTPUT-KEY, OUTPUT-COMMENT.

    (a) GET-MASTER.

    (b) MATCH-ACHIEVED.

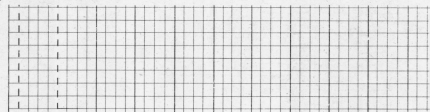

    (c) NO-MATCH.

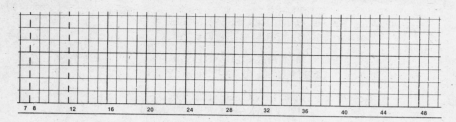

- - - - - - - - - - - - - - - - - -

```
(a)  GET-MASTER.
         READ MASTER-FILE
             AT END MOVE 'Y' TO MASTER-EOF.

(b)  MATCH-ACHIEVED.
         MOVE MASTER-KEY TO OUTPUT-KEY.      (or MOVE
         MOVE 'YES' TO OUTPUT-COMMENT.       TRANS-KEY...)
         WRITE OUTPUT-RECORD.
         READ TRANS-FILE
             AT END MOVE 'Y' TO TRANS-EOF.
         PERFORM GET-MASTER.                 (or READ...)

(c)  NO-MATCH.
         MOVE TRANS-KEY TO OUTPUT-KEY.          (definitely
         MOVE 'NOT IN FILE' TO OUTPUT-COMMENT.  not MOVE
         WRITE OUTPUT-RECORD.                   MASTER-
         READ TRANS-FILE                        KEY)
             AT END MOVE 'Y' TO TRANS-EOF.
```

(The READ TRANS-FILE could also be coded as a separate paragraph.)

9.   You have now written the major part of the Procedure Division of a
     sequential record accessing program. Whenever two input files are used,
     however, the end-of-file processing can get complicated, since you can
     seldom know in advance which file will end first.

     (a) Suppose the transaction file reaches its end before the master file

         does. What action might the program take? _____

     (b) Suppose the master file reaches its end before the transaction file
         does. What action might be appropriate for the program?

         _____

- - - - - - - - - - - - - - - - - -

     (a) stop the program (There are no more records to access.)
     (b) print NOT IN FILE for each remaining transaction

10. In a record-matching situation you generally want to perform the com-
     parison routine until either file has reached the end. Which PERFORM
     statement on the next page would accomplish this in our example?

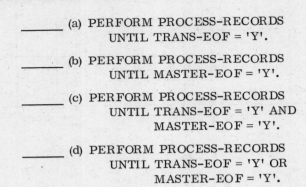

_____ (a) PERFORM PROCESS-RECORDS
        UNTIL TRANS-EOF = 'Y'.

_____ (b) PERFORM PROCESS-RECORDS
        UNTIL MASTER-EOF = 'Y'.

_____ (c) PERFORM PROCESS-RECORDS
        UNTIL TRANS-EOF = 'Y' AND
        MASTER-EOF = 'Y'.

_____ (d) PERFORM PROCESS-RECORDS
        UNTIL TRANS-EOF = 'Y' OR
        MASTER-EOF = 'Y'.

- - - - - - - - - - - - - - - - -

d (Recall that OR means one or both, while AND means both.)

11. Most of the main logic of the program we have been developing is shown below:

```
PROCEDURE DIVISION.
MAIN-LOGIC.
    OPEN INPUT MASTER-FILE, TRANS-FILE
        OUTPUT OUTPUT-FILE.
    PERFORM GET-MASTER.
    PERFORM GET-TRANS.
    PERFORM PROCESS-RECORDS
        UNTIL TRANS-EOF = 'Y' OR
            MASTER-EOF = 'Y'
    .
    .
    .
    CLOSE MASTER-FILE, TRANS-FILE, OUTPUT-FILE.
    STOP RUN.
```

Considering what we have just been discussing about the end-of-file processing, the next step is to determine which file ended and terminated the PERFORM. This should include one of two conditions. Write either one.

- - - - - - - - - - - - - - - -

MASTER-EOF = 'Y'   or   TRANS-EOF = 'Y'

12. The coding for an end-of-file routine, to be inserted in the coding of frame 11, is shown below.

```
IF  MASTER-EOF = 'Y'
    PERFORM NO-MATCH
        UNTIL TRANS-EOF = 'Y'.
```

(a) What will happen if the transaction file ends first?

_____

(b) What will happen if the master file ends first?

_____

- - - - - - - - - - - - - - - - - - - -

(a) Control will fall to CLOSE files.
(b) Any remaining transactions will be reported as NOT IN FILE.

13. Suppose you have a large master file in which employees are sequenced by social security number. You have a transaction file containing a set of social security numbers, all for people who are supposed to be on your staff. Your task is to print out the name associated with each transaction number. Describe what the program should do in each situation described below:

(a) The master number is 376401495 and the transaction number is 500729381. _____

(b) Both numbers are 191398724. _____

_____

(c) The transaction number is 438621981 and the master number is 500729381. _____

(d) The master file terminates before the transaction file does.

_____

- - - - - - - - - - - - - - - - - - -

(a) get a master record and compare again
(b) print the number and name, get a record from each file
(c) print some error message (This shouldn't happen if all are on staff.)
(d) print error message for each remaining transaction

We have looked at accessing records is some detail because it is the first encounter you have had with a record-matching problem. Record matching takes various other forms besides access problems. Record numbers must be matched when records are added to a file to insert them correctly, when records are deleted, and when they are updated. We'll look at these applications in the following sections.

ADDING RECORDS

14. In business applications, we must often add records to a master file, as we get new customers or stock new models, and employee turnover goes on. These new records must be incorporated into the master file, in the proper sequence. Records cannot be added directly to a sequentially organized file, however, whether it be on tape or disk. The master file must be copied over, one record at a time, with the new records inserted at the appropriate locations. The transaction file contains the records to be added, arranged in key sequence as in the master file. Suppose the key numbers are these:

Transaction	Master
10801	10789
10863	10800
10864	10863
	10865
	10866

What specific action should an adding-records program take for each transaction?

(a) 10801 _____

(b) 10863 _____

(c) 10864 _____

- -

(a) insert between 10800 and 10863
(b) not insert, it's a duplicate (perhaps print an error message)
(c) insert between 10863 and 10865

15. Figure 9-2 shows a hierarchy for a program to add records to a sequential file. Notice that we are again concerned with comparing one pair of records at a time. Refer to the figure on the next page, as needed, to answer these questions.

(a) Under what condition(s) will a transaction record be written to a new

file? _____

(b) Under what condition(s) will a master record be written to a new file?

_____

(c) What happens in this example if the key of a record in the transaction file duplicates the key of a record in the master file?

_____

_____

- -

(a) trans# < mast#

(b) trans# = mast# or trans# > mast#

(c) an error message is written, the new master file is written from the old master record, and new records are obtained from each file

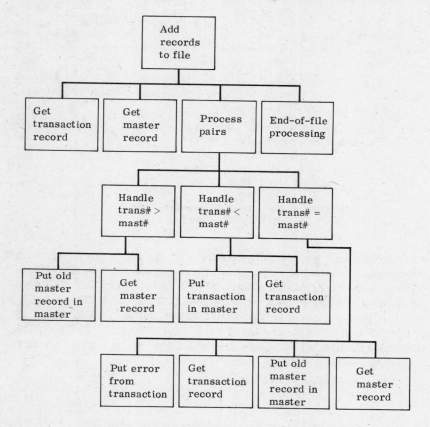

Figure 9-2. Adding-Records Structure

16. A pseudocode for the major logic of an adding records program is given below.

```
IF    transaction key greater than master key
      write new master from master
ELSE
      IF    transaction key less than master key
            write new master from transaction
      ELSE
            handle duplicate.
      ENDIF
ENDIF
```

Write a nested IF in structured COBOL to handle this. Use TRANS-KEY and MAST-KEY, and create appropriate paragraph names to perform.

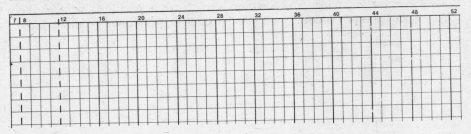

- - - - - - - - - - - - - - - - - -

```
IF  TRANS-KEY > MASTER KEY
     PERFORM PUT-FROM-MASTER
ELSE
     IF  TRANS-KEY < MASTER KEY
          PERFORM PUT-FROM-TRANSACTION
     ELSE
          PERFORM HANDLE-DUPLICATE.
```

17. In this problem, we are still working with the same files and records as we did when accessing records. In these segments, use OLD-MASTER-FILE, OLD-MASTER-RECORD, OLD-MASTER-KEY and OLD-MASTER-EOF, with similar names for the NEW-MASTER and TRANSaction files. For the actual error message on duplicate, move 'DUPLICATE' to OUTPUT-COMMENTS and the TRANS-RECORD to OUTPUT-DATA. Referring as needed to Figure 9-2 and the previous frame, write the segments below.

(a) PUT-FROM-MASTER.

(b) PUT-FROM-TRANSACTION.

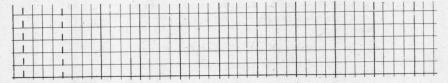

(c) HANDLE-DUPLICATE.

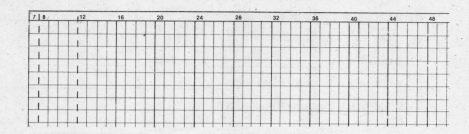

- - - - - - - - - - - - - - - - - - -

```
(a)  PUT-FROM-MASTER.
         WRITE NEW-MASTER-RECORD FROM OLD-MASTER-RECORD.
         READ OLD-MASTER-FILE
             AT END MOVE 'Y' TO OLD-MASTER-EOF.

(b)  PUT-FROM-TRANSACTION.
         WRITE NEW-MASTER-RECORD FROM TRANS-RECORD.
         READ  TRANS-FILE
             AT END MOVE 'Y' TO TRANS-EOF.

(c)  HANDLE-DUPLICATE.
         MOVE TRANS-RECORD TO OUTPUT-DATA.
         MOVE 'DUPLICATE' TO OUTPUT-COMMENT.
         WRITE OUTPUT-RECORD.
         PERFORM PUT-FROM-MASTER.
         READ TRANS-FILE
             AT END MOVE 'Y' TO TRANS-EOF.
```

18. You have just written the main processing COBOL for an adding-records problem. Refer back to them as we "walk some data through" the program.

Transaction	Master
10801	10789
10863	10800
10864	10863
	10865
	10866

(a) What pair are compared first?

Transaction: _____   Master: _____

(b) What segment from frame 17 is performed? _____

(c) What pair are compared next?

Transaction: _____   Master: _____

(d) What segment is performed? _____

(e) What pair are compared next?

Transaction: _____   Master: _____

(f) What segment is performed? _____

(g) What pair are compared next?

Transaction: _____   Master: _____

(h) What segment is performed? _____

(i) What pair are compared next?

Transaction: _____   Master: _____

(j) What segment is performed? _____

- - - - - - - - - - - - - - - - - -

(a) Transaction: 10801   Master: 10789
(b) PUT-FROM-MASTER
(c) Transaction: 10801   Master: 10800
(d) PUT-FROM-MASTER
(e) Transaction: 10801   Master: 10863
(f) PUT-FROM-TRANSACTION
(g) Transaction: 10863   Master: 10863
(h) HANDLE-DUPLICATE
(i) Transaction: 10864   Master: 10865
(j) PUT-FROM-TRANSACTION

19. The adding-records program uses two input files. You cannot know in advance which will end first. Write a PERFORM...UNTIL that will execute the ADD-RECORDS nested IF until one input file has reached its end. (Refer back to frame 17 for data-names if necessary.)

```
   7 8      12      16      20      24      28      32      36      40      44      48      52
```

- - - - - - - - - - - - - - - - -

```
PERFORM ADD-RECORDS
     UNTIL OLD-MASTER-EOF = 'Y'
           OR TRANS-EOF = 'Y'.
```

20. Consider the adding-records problem.

(a) What would the program need to do if the master file finished first?

_____

(b) What would the program have to do if the transaction file finished

first? _____

_____

- - - - - - - - - - - - - - - - - -

(a) add any remaining transactions to the new master file

(b) copy over any remaining master records to the new master file

21. Based on frames 17-20, write statements to handle the end-of-file processing in an adding-records program.

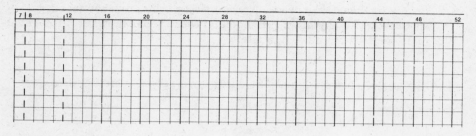

```
IF   OLD-MASTER-EOF = 'Y'
     PERFORM PUT-FROM-TRANSACTION
          UNTIL TRANS-EOF = 'Y'
ELSE
     PERFORM PUT-FROM-MASTER
          UNTIL OLD-MASTER-EOF = 'Y'.
```

You have seen in this section how records are added to a sequential file—the entire file is copied onto a new file, and records are inserted from a transaction file where they fit. The same process you have seen can be used to merge two files into one.

In the next section you'll see how to delete records from a sequential file.

DELETING RECORDS FROM A SEQUENTIAL FILE

22. Just as records cannot be added directly to a sequential file, they cannot be directly deleted. Certain records can, however, be omitted while a new master file is created from an old one. Suppose a transaction file contains the key numbers of records to be deleted from a master file. As with all record-matching problems, we are concerned with a comparison of one pair of records at a time. Describe what the program should do when each condition below is true.

(a) Transaction number is greater than master number.

_____

(b) Transaction number is less than master number. _____

_____

(c) Numbers in both files are equal. _____

_____

- - - - - - - - - - - - - - - - - - -

(a) Write the master record, and get another.
(b) This indicates that the record to be deleted isn't there, so get the next transaction record. You may also want an error message.
(c) Don't write anything; get another record from each file. The record is omitted from the new file.

23. Figure 9-3 shows a hierarchy chart for a record-deleting program.

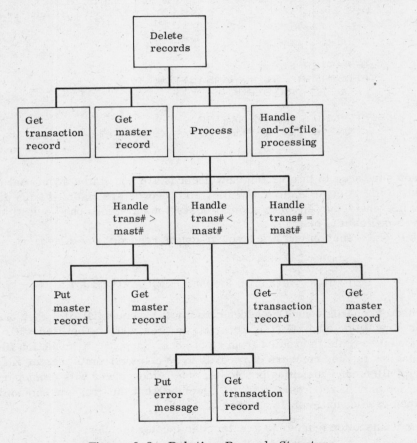

Figure 9-3. Deleting-Records Structure

Notice that the "equal" condition identifies a record to be deleted. In the record-adding program (Figure 9-2), the "equal" condition indicates an error condition. What condition indicates an error when deleting records?

_____

- - - - - - - - - - - - - - - - - - -

trans# < mast# (trans# > mast# indicates the record isn't located yet)

24. The deleting-records program, like that for adding records, requires end-of-file processing. What would the program have to accomplish in each case below?

(a) Transaction file ends first _____

_____

(b) Master file ends first _____

_____

- - - - - - - - - - - - - - - - - - - -

(a) copy over the rest of the old master records
(b) write error messages for the rest of the transaction records

25. The three condition routines for the deleting-records example are named PUT-FROM-MASTER, RECORD-MISSING, and OMIT-RECORD. Code the nested IF that would select the appropriate routine. (Use the same data-names as in previous sections.)

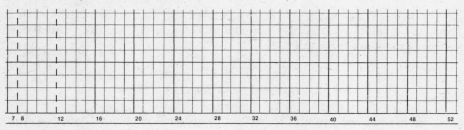

- - - - - - - - - - - - - - - - - - -

```
IF   TRANS-KEY > OLD-MASTER-KEY
     PERFORM   PUT-FROM-MASTER
ELSE
     IF   TRANS-KEY < OLD-MASTER-KEY
          PERFORM RECORD-MISSING
     ELSE
          PERFORM OMIT-RECORD.
```

26. Code a statement to transfer control to MAIN-PROCESS (which contains the nested IF you just wrote) and return control when one of the files involved reaches the end. (Create names for end-of-file indicators.)

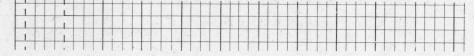

- - - - - - - - - - - - - - - - - - - -

```
PERFORM MAIN-PROCESS
    UNTIL OLD-MASTER-EOF = 'Y'
        OR TRANS-EOF = 'Y'.
```

27. Using the same procedure names as in frame 25, code a nested IF to handle end-of-file processing for a record-deleting program.

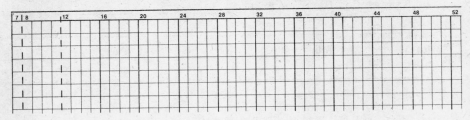

- - - - - - - - - - - - - - - - - - -

```
IF   TRANS-EOF = 'Y'
     PERFORM PUT-FROM-MASTER
         UNTIL OLD-MASTER-EOF = 'Y'
ELSE
     PERFORM RECORD-MISSING
         UNTIL TRANS-EOF = 'Y'.
```

You have seen how records are deleted from a sequential file. The records to be deleted are simply not copied to a new master file, effectively eliminating them from the file.

UPDATING SEQUENTIAL FILES

In this section you will learn how to update, or change, records in a master file. Updating is perhaps the most frequent application of matching records in business programming today. Updating is somewhat different for tape files than it is for disk. The master file on tape must be re-created to incorporate the update changes, whereas the disk file is updated in place, so only the changed records need be rewritten. You saw this difference in Chapter 8 when you learned to update a file. Here we will focus on the record-matching functions and end-of-file processing, which are similar for both tape and disk sequential files.

28. Figure 9-4, on the next page, shows a hierarchy for a program to update a master disk file. Refer to this chart as needed to answer these questions.

(a) Under what condition do you know that the transaction record does not

have a corresponding master record? _____

(b) Under what condition do you update the master record represented by the transaction number? _____

(c) Only one of the three functions requires different actions from the accessing-records problem (Figure 9-1). Which one?

_____

- - - - - - - - - - - - - - - - - - -

(a) trans# < mast#
(b) trans# = mast#
(c) trans# = mast#

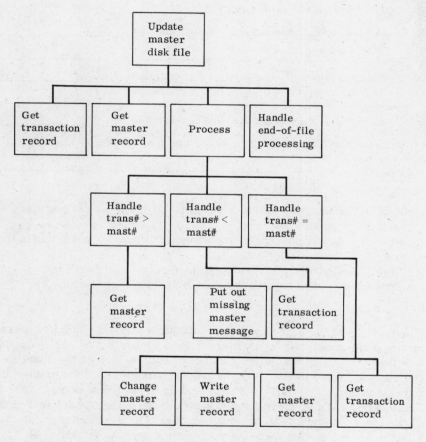

Figure 9-4. Update Disk Structure

29. If you were to modify the hierarchy in Figure 9-4 to reflect a master tape update program, only one function would be added.

(a) What additional function must be performed?

_____

(b) Under which condition would this function block be added?

_____

- - - - - - - - - - - - - - - - - - -

(a) Put master record
(b) trans# > mast#

30. Consider end-of-file processing for an update program. What is the appropriate action for each situation below?

(a) Disk master file ends before transaction file _____

_____

(b) Input tape master file ends before transaction file _____

_____

(c) Transaction file ends before disk master file _____

(d) Transaction file ends before input tape master file

_____

- - - - - - - - - - - - - - - - - - -

(a) Rest of transactions are in error; put out error messages (Handle trans# < mast#)
(b) Rest of transactions are in error; put out error messages (Handle trans# < mast#)
(c) Close files (remaining disk records need not be rewritten)
(d) Copy over rest of master records (Handle trans# > mast#)

31. Figure 9-5, on the next page, shows the first three divisions of a disk update program. Refer to the hierarchy in Figure 9-4 as necessary. You will be writing a complete Procedure Division to change the addresses in the master file as indicated in the transaction file. Use the printer file for output message "NOT IN FILE" and the transaction record. For this frame write the control logic paragraph. Include the opening and closing of files and the end-of-file processing. Use PERFORM statements for all other processing. The form for your coding appears on page 184.

```
IDENTIFICATION DIVISION.
PROGRAM-ID.
    FIX-ADDRESS.
ENVIRONMENT DIVISION.
INPUT-OUTPUT SECTION.
FILE-CONTROL.
    SELECT TRANSCARD
        ASSIGN TO UR-S-INCARD.
    SELECT MASTER-STUDENT
        ASSIGN TO DA-S-DISKMAST.
    SELECT PRINT-LIST
        ASSIGN TO UR-S-OUTGO.
DATA DIVISION.
FILE SECTION.
FD  TRANSCARD
    LABEL RECORDS ARE OMITTED.
01  TRANS-RECORD.
    02  STUDENT-NUMBER          PIC 9(9).
    02  STUDENT-ADDRESS         PIC X(31).
    02  FILLER                  PIC X(40).
FD  MASTER-STUDENT
    BLOCK CONTAINS 10 RECORDS
    LABEL RECORDS ARE STANDARD.
01  MASTER-STU-RECORD.
    02  M-NUMBER                PIC 9(9).
    02  FILLER                  PIC X(30).
    02  M-ADDRESS               PIC X(31).
    02  FILLER                  PIC X(50).
FD  PRINT-LIST
    LABEL RECORDS ARE OMITTED.
01  PRINT-LINE                  PIC X(133).
WORKING-STORAGE SECTION.
01  EOF-SWITCHES.
    02  TR-EOF-SWITCH           PIC X        VALUE 'N'.
    02  MAS-EOF-SWITCH          PIC X        VALUE 'N'.
01  MESSAGE-LINE.
    02  FILLER                  PIC X        VALUE SPACE.
    02  MESSAGE-TYPE            PIC X(11)
                                VALUE 'NOT IN FILE'.
    02  MESSAGE-DATA            PIC X(80).
    02  FILLER                  PIC X(41)    VALUE SPACES.
```

Figure 9-5

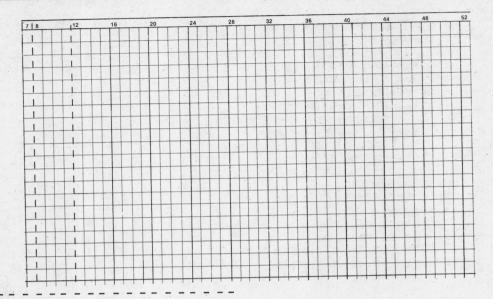

```
        PROCEDURE DIVISION.
        MAIN-PROGRAM.
            OPEN INPUT TRANSCARD
                I-O MASTER-STUDENT
                OUTPUT PRINT-LIST.
            PERFORM GET-MASTER.
            PERFORM GET-TRANS.
            PERFORM FIND-MATCH
                UNTIL TR-EOF-SWITCH = 'Y' OR
                      MAS-EOF-SWITCH = 'Y'.
            IF  TR-EOF-SWITCH = 'Y'
                NEXT SENTENCE
            ELSE
                PERFORM MISSING-MASTER
                    UNTIL TR-EOF-SWITCH = 'Y'.
            CLOSE TRANSCARD
                  MASTER-STUDENT
                  PRINT-LIST.
            STOP RUN.
```

32. Continue to refer to Figures 9-4 and 9-5 as you write these paragraphs.

(a) GET-MASTER.

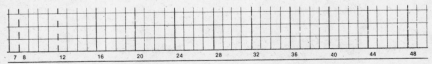

(b) GET-TRANS.

(c) FIND-MATCH.

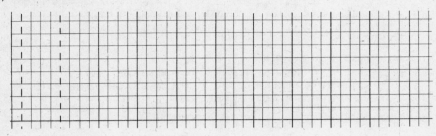

- - - - - - - - - - - - - - - - - -

```
(a)   GET-MASTER.
          READ MASTER-STUDENT
              AT END MOVE 'Y' TO MAS-EOF-SWITCH.

(b)   GET-TRANS.
          READ TRANSCARD
              AT END MOVE 'Y' TO TR-EOF-SWITCH.

(c)   FIND-MATCH.
          IF STUDENT-NUMBER > M-NUMBER
              PERFORM GET-MASTER
          ELSE
              IF STUDENT-NUMBER = M-NUMBER
                  PERFORM UPDATE-RECORD
              ELSE
                  PERFORM MISSING-MASTER.
```

33. Now to complete the disk update program, write the two remaining paragraphs.

(a) MISSING-MASTER.

(b) UPDATE-RECORD.

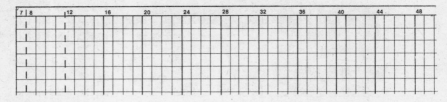

- - - - - - - - - - - - - - - - - -

(a) MISSING-MASTER.
        MOVE TRANS-RECORD TO MESSAGE-DATA.
        WRITE PRINT-LINE FROM MESSAGE-LINE.
        PERFORM GET-TRANS.

(b) UPDATE-RECORD.
        MOVE STUDENT-ADDRESS TO M-ADDRESS.
        WRITE MASTER-STU-RECORD.
        PERFORM GET-MASTER.
        PERFORM GET-TRANS.

You have just written a complete Procedure Division for a disk update program. In the next few frames you will convert it to a tape update program.

34. In Figure 9-6 the Environment and Data Division entries that would be different if this were a tape update program are marked. As you can see, they involve using two files where one file sufficed for disk. The remainder of the first three divisions are unchanged.
   Look at Figure 9-6 and refer back to the MAIN-PROGRAM in frame 31.

(a) How must the end-of-file processing be changed for tape update?

_____

(b) What other statement(s) must be changed to do a tape update as in
   Figure 9-6? _____

(c) Code the revised statements identified in (b).

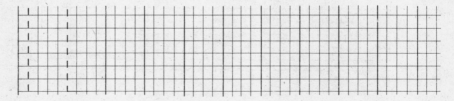

- - - - - - - - - - - - - - - - - -

(a) Change NEXT SENTENCE to COPY-MASTER
   (or other words. The point is that remaining masters must be copied
   to the new file)

(b) OPEN and CLOSE

(c)
```
OPEN INPUT TRANSCARD OLD-MASTER-STUDENT
     OUTPUT NEW-MASTER-STUDENT PRINT-LIST.
  CLOSE TRANSCARD OLD-MASTER-STUDENT
     NEW-MASTER-STUDENT PRINT-LIST.


      :
      :
    ENVIRONMENT DIVISION.
    INPUT-OUTPUT SECTION.
    FILE-CONTROL.
        SELECT TRANSCARD
            ASSIGN TO UR-S-INCARD.
        SELECT OLD-MASTER-STUDENT
            ASSIGN TO UT-S-TAPEIN.
        SELECT NEW-MASTER-STUDENT
            ASSIGN TO UT-S-TAPEOUT.
        SELECT PRINT-LIST
            ASSIGN TO UR-S-OUTGO.
    DATA DIVISION.
    FILE SECTION.
    FD  TRANSCARD
        LABEL RECORDS ARE OMITTED.
    01  TRANS-RECORD.
        02   STUDENT-NUMBER        PIC 9(9).
        02   STUDENT-ADDRESS       PIC X(31).
        02   FILLER                PIC X(40).
    FD  OLD-MASTER-STUDENT
        BLOCK CONTAINS 10 RECORDS
        LABEL RECORDS ARE STANDARD.
    01  OLD-MASTER-STU-RECORD      PIC X(120).
    FD  NEW-MASTER-STUDENT
        BLOCK CONTAINS 10 RECORDS
        LABEL RECORDS ARE STANDARD.
    01  MASTER-STU-RECORD.
        02   M-NUMBER              PIC 9(9).
        02   FILLER                PIC X(30).
        02   M-ADDRESS             PIC X(31).
        02   FILLER                PIC X(50).
    FD  PRINT-LIST
        :
        :
```

Figure 9-6

35. The FIND-MATCH paragraph (frame 32) needs only one change to work in a tape update program—the paragraph under the "trans# > master#" condition should be changed from GET-MASTER to COPY-MASTER, since that better describes what it does. The paragraph GET-MASTER is still useful however.

(a) Refer to Figure 9-6, and recode GET-MASTER for this tape update.

(b) Code the COPY-MASTER routine.

- - - - - - - - - - - - - - - - - - -

```
(a)  GET-MASTER.
         READ OLD-MASTER-STUDENT INTO MASTER-STU-RECORD
             AT END MOVE 'Y' TO MAS-EOF-SWITCH.

(b)  COPY-MASTER.
         WRITE MASTER-STU-RECORD.
         PERFORM GET-MASTER.
```

36. Consider the hierarchy in Figure 9-4 in the light of a tape update.

    (a) What changes would you need in the UPDATE-RECORD paragraph
    (see frame 33)? _____

    (b) Code any revisions needed.

- - - - - - - - - - - - - - - - - - -

(a) no changes needed; (b) no revisions needed

SUMMARY

You have seen how to write a structured COBOL program to update a sequential tape or disk file. The record-matching logic is the same for both, although there are small but significant differences in end-of-file processing and file usage. Since the tape file cannot be used for input and output within one program, tape update requires a bit more coding.

In this chapter we have considered only one type of file activity per program. We added, deleted, and updated in separate programs. In the next chapter, you will learn some techniques you can use to combine these activities in one program.

SELF-TEST

The Self-Test for this chapter is in the form of a complete Procedure Division for you to write. Since the chapter focussed on techniques, rather than new statements, a COBOL program is a practical way to test it.

In this exercise you will write a Procedure Division to add records to a disk file. Since you are adding records, you will have to create a new file. Feel free to refer to the hierarchy chart in Figure 9–2 as you write the program. Below, you will find the first three divisions of the program coded for you. Each record in the transaction file (NEWCUSTS) is to be added to the master file. If a duplicate is encountered, display 'DUPLICATE' and the entire transaction record before proceeding. Develop an appropriate end-of-file processing routine. Keep a count of the number of new customers added to the master file, and display that amount before ending the program.

```
IDENTIFICATION DIVISION.
PROGRAM-ID.
     NEW-CUSTOMERS.
ENVIRONMENT DIVISION.
INPUT-OUTPUT SECTION.
FILE-CONTROL.
     SELECT OLDMASTER ASSIGN TO DA-S-OLDONE.
     SELECT NEWCUSTS ASSIGN TO UR-S-CARDS.
     SELECT NEWMASTER ASSIGN TO DA-S-NEWONE.
DATA DIVISION.
FILE SECTION.
FD  OLDMASTER
     BLOCK CONTAINS 20 RECORDS
     LABEL RECORDS ARE STANDARD.
01   CUSTOMER-RECORD.
     02  CUST-NUMBER           PIC 9(6).
     02  CUST-DATA             PIC X(84).
FD  NEWCUSTS
     LABEL RECORDS ARE OMITTED.
01   NEW-CUSTOMER.
     02  NEW-NUMBER            PIC X(6).
     02  NEW-NAME              PIC X(25).
     02  NEW-ADDRESS           PIC X(34).
     02  NEW-PHONE             PIC X(10).
     02  FILLER                PIC X(5).
FD  NEWMASTER
     BLOCK CONTAINS 20 RECORDS
     LABEL RECORDS ARE STANDARD.
01   NEW-MAST-RECORD.
     02  NEW-MAST-NUMBER       PIC 9(6).
     02  NEW-MAST-REST         PIC X(84).
WORKING-STORAGE SECTION.
01   END-OF-FILE.
     02  EOF-MASTER            PIC X       VALUE 'N'.
     02  EOF-TRANS             PIC X       VALUE 'N'.
01   COUNT-ADDS                PIC 999     VALUE ZERO.
```

(continued on the next page)

```
01    MASTER-RECORD.
      02   MS-NUMBER              PIC 9(6).
      02   MS-NAME                PIC X(25).
      02   MS-ADDRESS             PIC X(34).
      02   MS-PHONE               PIC X(10).
      02   MS-CREDIT-HIST         PIC X(15)   VALUE SPACES.
```

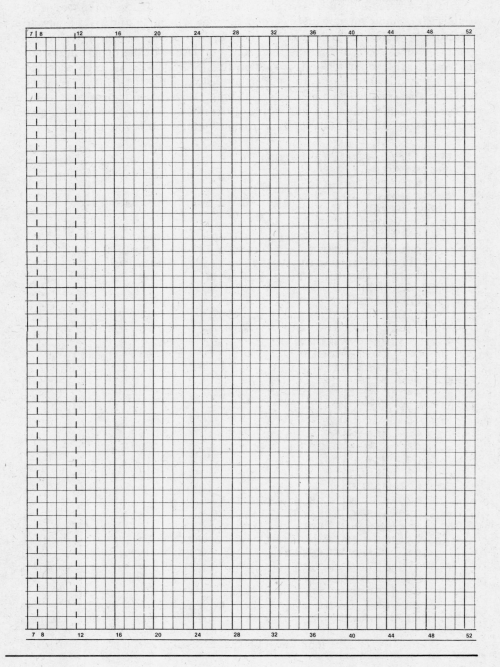

Answer Key

```
PROCEDURE DIVISION.
MAIN-LOGIC.
    OPEN INPUT OLDMASTER, NEWCUSTS
        OUTPUT NEWMASTER.
    PERFORM GET-MASTER.
    PERFORM GET-TRANSACTION.
    PERFORM PROCESS-RECORDS
        UNTIL EOF-MASTER = 'Y'
            OR EOF-TRANS = 'Y'.
    IF EOF-TRANS = 'Y'
        PERFORM COPY-MASTER
            UNTIL EOF-MASTER = 'Y'
    ELSE
        PERFORM ADD-CUSTOMER
            UNTIL EOF-TRANS = 'Y'.
    DISPLAY 'WE ADDED ' COUNT-ADDS ' RECORDS TO THE FILE'.
    CLOSE OLDMASTER, NEWCUSTS, NEWMASTER.
    STOP RUN.
PROCESS-RECORDS.
    IF NEW-NUMBER > CUST-NUMBER
        PERFORM COPY-MASTER
    ELSE
        IF NEW-NUMBER < CUST-NUMBER
            PERFORM ADD-CUSTOMER
        ELSE
            PERFORM ERROR-ON-ADD.
ADD-CUSTOMER.
    MOVE NEW-NUMBER TO MS-NUMBER.
    MOVE NEW-NAME TO MS-NAME.
    MOVE NEW-ADDRESS TO MS-ADDRESS.
    MOVE NEW-PHONE TO MS-PHONE.
    WRITE NEW-MAST-RECORD FROM MASTER-RECORD.
    ADD 1 TO COUNT-ADDS.
    PERFORM GET-TRANSACTION.
ERROR-ON-ADD.
    DISPLAY 'DUPLICATE' NEW-NUMBER.
    PERFORM COPY-MASTER.
    PERFORM GET-TRANSACTION.
COPY-MASTER.
    WRITE NEW-MAST-RECORD FROM CUSTOMER-RECORD.
    PERFORM GET-MASTER.
GET-MASTER.
    READ OLDMASTER
        AT END MOVE 'Y' TO EOF-MASTER.
GET-TRANSACTION.
    READ NEWCUSTS
        AT END MOVE 'Y' TO EOF-TRANS.
```

You may have coded your procedure differently. The major potential sources of error here are in the end-of-file processing and the record-matching routine. Make sure your end-of-file coding is arranged to write all records from the file that did not end first. Also be sure that an error was indicated by an "equal" condition in the record-matching routine. The new record transaction is added when NEW-NUMBER is less than CUST-NUMBER —or when CUST-NUMBER is greater than NEW-NUMBER.

We haven't included frame references here, since the details aren't tested that way. If you had a great deal of difficulty in writing the program, go back and study the figures in this chapter carefully. The logic of programming controls the coding.

CHAPTER TEN
More COBOL Programming Techniques

You have learned to handle sequential files on various devices, and to match records from two input files. All the programs you have seen so far have incorporated the most useful, and most used, COBOL statements. However, COBOL provides many additional statements. In this chapter you'll learn to use a selection of them to accomplish certain functions.

We'll focus on two general areas—data definition and flow of control. Appropriate data definition will let you use identical data names for different fields or different data-names for the same field. Both of these approaches become useful in complex applications.

So far, we've been using the standard sequence, selection, and repetition structures to control execution in our structured COBOL programs. In this chapter, we'll expand the repetition structure to include two more PERFORM options that make the programmer's life easier. And we'll look at the COBOL case structure—a control structure similar to selection that lets you perform one of any number of actions based on the value of a data-name.

When you complete this chapter, you will be able to:

- use qualified data-names and the CORRESPONDING option in Procedure Division statements;

- use REDEFINES in Data Division entries;

- use a PERFORM option to execute a paragraph a specific number of times;

- use a PERFORM option with a built-in counter; and

- code a case structure.

IDENTICAL DATA-NAMES

We said very early in this book that data-names must be unique within a program. We have carefully coded such names as IN-ADDRESS and OUT-ADDRESS to maintain unique data-names. There is another way to make seemingly identical data-names unique. In this section, you will learn to qualify data-names and specify certain operations to affect only items with identical names.

1. A record may contain several similar entries. For example, a personnel record might contain a birth date and a hire date. They might be subdivided like this:

```
01  PERSONNEL-RECORD.
    .
    .
    .
    02  DATE-OF-BIRTH
        03  D-MONTH     PIC 99.
        03  D-DAY       PIC 99.
        03  D-YEAR      PIC 99.
    02  DATE-OF-HIRE.
        03  D-MONTH     PIC 99.
        03  D-DAY       PIC 99.
        03  D-YEAR      PIC 99.
```

If a Procedure Division statement contained a reference to D-DAY, the computer wouldn't know which one you meant. So we "qualify" the name using a higher level name. Either D-DAY OF DATE-OF-BIRTH or D-DAY IN DATE-OF-BIRTH would be acceptable to the system.

Use the segment above as you write qualified data-names to reference the following:

(a) Year hired. _____

(b) Month of birthday. _____

Now write statements to accomplish the following:

(c) Establish July 15, 1980 as the hire date.

(d) Determine the approximate age (year only) at hire.

- - - - - - - - - - - - - - - - - - - -

(a) D-YEAR OF DATE-OF-HIRE
(b) D-MONTH OF DATE-OF-BIRTH
(c) MOVE 07 TO D-MONTH OF DATE-OF-HIRE.
    MOVE 15 TO D-DAY OF DATE-OF-HIRE.
    MOVE 80 TO D-YEAR OF DATE-OF-HIRE.
(d) SUBTRACT D-YEAR OF DATE-OF-BIRTH
        FROM D-YEAR OF DATE-OF-HIRE.

(NOTE: You could have used IN rather than OF in all of these.)

2. The qualification of data-names can occur on any level. You could use
    D-YEAR OF DATE-OF-HIRE OF PERSONNEL-RECORD, for example,
    and you could even add a file-name above that, if necessary, to make
    the data-name unique. Suppose a program used the PERSONNEL-
    RECORD of frame 1, along with a record called RETIREMENT that
    contains, among other things, this data:

```
01   RETIREMENT.
     02   FACTORS.
          03   D-YEAR      PIC 99.
          03   HEALTH      PIC X.
     :
     :
     02   DATE-OF-HIRE.
          03   D-YEAR      PIC 99.
          03   D-MONTH     PIC 99.
          03   D-DAY       PIC 99.
```

(a) Write a statement to determine the approximate age (year only) at
    retirement.

(b) Write statements to set DATE-OF-HIRE in RETIREMENT to the
    values in the PERSONNEL-RECORD.

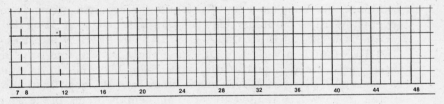

- - - - - - - - - - - - - - - - - -

(a) SUBTRACT D-YEAR IN DATE-OF-BIRTH
        FROM D-YEAR IN FACTORS.
(b) MOVE D-MONTH OF DATE-OF-HIRE OF PERSONNEL-RECORD
        TO D-MONTH OF DATE-OF-HIRE OF RETIREMENT.
    MOVE D-DAY OF DATE-OF-HIRE OF PERSONNEL-RECORD
        TO D-DAY OF DATE-OF-HIRE OF RETIREMENT.
    MOVE D-YEAR OF DATE-OF-HIRE OF PERSONNEL-RECORD
        TO D-YEAR OF DATE-OF-HIRE OF RETIREMENT.

3. Identical data-names can be used in MOVE statements with the
    CORRESPONDING option. For example, answer (b) above could have
    been

        MOVE CORRESPONDING DATE-OF-HIRE OF PERSONNEL-RECORD
            TO DATE-OF-HIRE OF RETIREMENT.

The group data-names are still qualified to make them unique, but three data items are moved. The data items are not in the same sequence in the two records but they are correctly moved with the CORRESPONDING option.

Write a statement to move all data items with the same names in CURRENT-DATA to HISTORICAL-DATA.

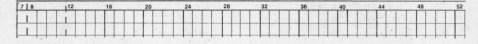

- - - - - - - - - - - - - - - - - -

```
MOVE CORRESPONDING CURRENT-DATA
     TO HISTORICAL-DATA.
```

4. Here is the format for the MOVE statement with the CORRESPONDING option:

$$\text{MOVE} \left\{ \begin{array}{l} \text{CORRESPONDING} \\ \text{CORR} \end{array} \right\} \text{ group-item-1 TO group-item-2.}$$

Notice that the abbreviation CORR is acceptable. Both the identifiers in a MOVE CORRESPONDING must be subdivided—they must contain elementary items (we call these subdivided items group items). As you have seen, they may be qualified names. The effect is to move all fields with matching names and qualification to the receiving group item. The level numbers of the items don't matter, but the qualification does. MOVE CORRESPONDING DATA-OF-HIRE OF PERSONNEL-RECORD TO RETIREMENT is a valid COBOL statement. But the data transferred would need matching qualification up to the data-names in the statement. If one needed three qualifiers and another two, the qualification would not match. Suppose you wanted all three elementary items in the sending field transferred with the above. How would they have to be defined in the 01 level RETIREMENT?

- - - - - - - - - - - - - - - - - -

```
01  RETIREMENT.
    02  D-MONTH    PIC 99.
    02  D-DAY      PIC 99.
    02  D-YEAR     PIC 99.
```

(The level 02 items could be in any order.)

5.

EMPLOYEE-RECORD		
NUMBER1	EMPLOYEE-NAME	ADDRESS1

WORKING-RECORD				
NUMBER1	FILLER	NAME	FILLER	ADDRESS1

Which variable values would be moved if you specified MOVE
CORRESPONDING EMPLOYEE-RECORD TO WORKING-RECORD?

- - - - - - - - - - - - - - - - - - -

NUMBER1 and ADDRESS1 (EMPLOYEE-NAME and NAME are not
affected)

The CORRESPONDING option and qualification may be used in programs
as appropriate. In some cases, they simplify programming and make for a
clearer, more understandable program. This section has shown you how to
use the same data-name to refer to different areas in storage. The next section will show you how to use different names to refer to the same area in
storage. We'll look at it on the record level first, then at the elementary
level.

REDEFINES

6. The records in each file we consider in this book are all the same length,
    such as 80 characters in a card file or 100 bytes in a tape file. But they
    need not all have the same description. For example, a student file might
    contain a record with personal data (name, address, number of years as
    student) for one student, followed by records of scholastic data for each
    year of education. A transaction file may contain information on records
    to be deleted, records to be added, and records to be updated. Since you
    need only an identifying number to delete a record, but more information
    to add one, these would necessarily contain different information.
        We said earlier that a level 01 data item must immediately follow an
    FD entry. In fact, all level 01 records following an FD entry (before the
    next FD) are descriptions for the records associated with that file. The
    DATA RECORDS clause we saw earlier can use IS or ARE and name one
    or more records (separated by a comma or a space) when it is used. In
    the File Section framework on the next page, the records PERSONAL-
    DATA and GRADE-DATA both define the record associated with
    STUDENT-FILE.

```
FILE SECTION.
FD   STUDENT-FILE
        .
        .
        .
01   PERSONAL-DATA.
        .
        .
        .
01   GRADE-DATA.
        .
        .
        .
FD   SEMESTER-UP
        .
        .
        .
01   UPDATE-RECORD.
        .
        .
        .
FD   PRINT-REPORT
        .
        .
        .
```

(a) Write a DATA RECORD clause for STUDENT-FILE.

(b) Write a DATA RECORD clause for SEMESTER-UP.

- - - - - - - - - - - - - - - - - - -

(a) DATA RECORDS ARE PERSONAL-DATA, GRADE-DATA
(b) DATA RECORD IS UPDATE-RECORD

7. Suppose the File Section included this coding:

```
FD   TRANSACTIONS
     LABEL RECORDS ARE OMITTED.
01   NEW-RECORD.
     02   TRANS-TYPE           PIC 9.
     02   TRANS-NAME           PIC X(30).
     02   TRANS-ADDRESS        PIC X(31).
     02   TRANS-NUMBER         PIC 9(8).
     02   TRANS-HISTORY        PIC X(10).
01   CHANGE-RECORD.
     02   FILLER               PIC X.
     02   NEW-NUMBER           PIC 9(8).
     02   NEW-ADDRESS          PIC X(31).
     02   FILLER               PIC X(40).
01   REMOVE-RECORD.
     02   FILLER               PIC X.
     02   REMOVE-NUMBER        PIC 9(8).
     02   FILLER               PIC X(71).
```

After a transaction record is read, one record of data is in the input area. You can refer to parts of it using any of the data-names above. Generally, you use a code within the input record to tell you which record is there. Here, the value of TRANS-TYPE will indicate which record describes the layout of the input record.

Suppose TRANS-TYPE = 1 means a new record is to be added, 2 means a record is to be changed, and 3 means a record is to be deleted from a master file. Examine the coding above as you answer these questions.

(a) If the value of TRANS-TYPE is 3, what name will refer to the number of the record to be deleted? _____

Which columns of the card will it be in? _____

(b) If the value of TRANS-TYPE is 2, which columns will contain the new address data? _____

(c) If the value of TRANS-TYPE is 1, which columns will contain the address? _____ Which columns will contain the record number? _____

(d) Which column in the input record will contain the TRANS-TYPE?

_____

- - - - - - - - - - - - - - - - - - - -

(a) REMOVE-NUMBER, columns 2-9; (b) columns 10-40; (c) columns 32-62, columns 63-70; (c) column 1, for any transaction type

8. In the File Section, we use separate level 01 record descriptions to redefine the same area. In the Working-Storage Section you can use REDEFINES to accomplish the same thing. For example, suppose you have defined an input record as PIC X(80). In the Working-Storage Section you can define the following.

```
01   UPDATE-NAME.
     02   UP-CODE                     PIC X.
     02   UP-NUMBER                   PIC 9(6).
     02   UP-NAME                     PIC X(24).
     02   FILLER                      PIC X(49).
01   UPDATE-ADDRESS  REDEFINES  UPDATE-NAME.
     02   FILLER                      PIC X.
     02   FILLER                      PIC X(6).
     02   UP-ADDRESS                  PIC X(31).
     02   FILLER                      PIC X(42).
```

When you access a record and move it to UPDATE-NAME, you can then check the UP-CODE, and update the name or address depending on

the result. The REDEFINES must immediately follow the item it redefines, with no intervening items—unless they, too, use REDEFINES.
And, in general, they must be the same length.

(a) How would you code PERSONAL-DATA and GRADE-DATA in the
Working-Storage Section to occupy the same space in storage?
(Code level 01 items only.)

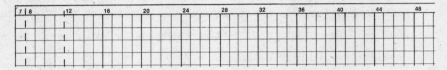

(b) What could appear between the two level 01 items?

- - - - - - - - - - - - - - - -

(a) 01   PERSONAL-DATA.
      .
      .
      .
    01   GRADE-DATA REDEFINES PERSONAL-DATA.
      .
      .
      .
              (or)
    01   GRADE-DATA.
      .
      .
      .
    01   PERSONAL-DATA REDEFINES GRADE-DATA.

(b) the items that make up the first; no other 01 items

9.   REDEFINES cannot be used at the 01 level in the File Section, as it can
      in Working-Storage. It can be used at other levels in both divisions,
      however.

```
02   UP-CODE                PIC X.
02   UP-NUMBER              PIC 9(6).
02   UPDATE-DATA-NAME.
     03   UP-NAME           PIC X(24).
     03   FILLER            PIC X(7).
02   UPDATE-DATA-ADDRESS    REDEFINES UPDATE-DATA-NAME.
     03   UP-ADDRESS        PIC X(31).
02   FILLER                 PIC X(42).
```

Now the area that includes the update data can be accessed using the
appropriate names. The redefined item (the one that includes
REDEFINES) must have the same level number as the item it redefines.
And the redefined item may not include a VALUE clause, though the first
item may. Which of the following show correct use of REDEFINES?

```
_____ (a)   02   A   REDEFINES B.
             02   B   PIC   XXX.


_____ (b)   02   B   PIC   XXX.
             02   C   REDEFINES B.
             03   D   PIC   X.
             03   E   PIC   99.


_____ (c)   02   F       PIC   X(10).
             02   G       PIC   X(2).
             02   H       REDEFINES F.


_____ (d)   02   I   PIC   XXX.
             02   J   PIC   999   VALUE ZERO
                                  REDEFINES I.


_____ (e)   02   K   PIC   999   VALUE ZERO.
             02   L   PIC   XXX   REDEFINES K.
```

- - - - - - - - - - - - - - - - - - -

b, e (In a, B must precede the item that redefines it. In c, item C
occurs between F and the item that redefines it. In d, the redefined item
contains a VALUE clause.)

10. Single items can be redefined as well as group items.

```
03   UP-PRICE                              PIC   X(5).
03   UP-PRICE-NUM REDEFINES UP-PRICE   PIC   S9(5).
```

Notice that here we changed the PICTURE of the data item. This is valid,
but you need to be careful. UP-PRICE-NUM can be used in arithmetic
statements, but UP-PRICE cannot, even though they represent the same
area of storage.

Code a level 02 item ITEM-NUMBER as eight characters. Then redefine it so it can be used in arithmetic.

- - - - - - - - - - - - - - - - - -

```
02   ITEM-NUMBER                                    PIC   X(8).
02   RE-ITEM-NUMBER REDEFINES ITEM-NUMBER   PIC   S9(8).
```


You've seen several uses of REDEFINES in COBOL programs. In Chapter
11, you'll learn some more powerful uses of the REDEFINES clause. Now
we're going to turn from the Data Division to the Procedure Division. The
rest of this chapter is devoted to various ways of controlling sequence of execution in a COBOL program.

PERFORM OPTIONS

11. You have seen how the PERFORM statement can be used to cause a paragraph to be executed once, or until a condition is true. You can also use PERFORM to execute a paragraph a specific number of times, using the format below.

PERFORM   paragraph $\begin{Bmatrix} \text{integer} \\ \text{data-name} \end{Bmatrix}$ TIMES

The statement PERFORM ADD-DAYS 7 TIMES would result in paragraph ADD-DAYS being executed 7 times with control then being returned to the statement following the PERFORM. Any data-name with an integer (whole number) value can be used as well. The value must be positive, or the paragraph won't be executed at all. Suppose the value of COUNTER is to determine the number of times ZAP-TOTALS is to be executed.

(a) How could COUNTER be defined: S99, 99, or 99V9? _____

(b) Code the PERFORM statement.

(c) What happens if COUNTER equals zero? _____

_____

- - - - - - - - - - - - - - - - - -

(a) S99 or 99
(b) PERFORM ZAP-TOTALS COUNTER TIMES.
(c) ZAP-TOTALS isn't executed; control will pass to the next statement after PERFORM.

12. Another format of the PERFORM statement is shown below. Notice this is a variation on PERFORM UNTIL. Here we have included the VARYING OPTION, which allows us to specify a data item to be varied each time the paragraph is performed.

PERFORM   paragraph

[VARYING data-name FROM $\begin{Bmatrix} \text{integer} \\ \text{data-name} \end{Bmatrix}$ BY $\begin{Bmatrix} \text{integer} \\ \text{data-name} \end{Bmatrix}$]

[UNTIL condition]

The VARYING option gives a data-name whose value is to be changed, a starting value (FROM), and an amount to change the value for each execution. Here is an example.

```
PERFORM     BUILD-CHART
       VARYING SAMPLE-DATA   FROM    1    BY    2
       UNTIL SAMPLE-DATA   >   100.
```

(a) What variable will be varied? _____

(b) What is the starting value? _____

(c) How many times will BUILD-CHART be executed? _____

- - - - - - - - - - - - - - - - - - -

(a) SAMPLE-DATA; (b) 1; (c) 50 times

13. When you need to increment a variable by a regular amount in the procedure that is to be performed, you can use a PERFORM statement with
the VARYING option. The VARYING option specifies a variable to be used
as a counter, what value it starts with, and how much it will vary in each
execution. An UNTIL segment specifies a condition for determining if the
paragraph should be executed. Examine the example below.

```
PERFORM LISTING
    VARYING COUNTER FROM A BY B
    UNTIL COUNTER GREATER THAN 60.
```

In this PERFORM statement:

(a) The variable that is varied is _____.

(b) It is varied in increments equal to the value of _____.

(c) The original value of the variable is equal to the value of _____.

(d) Control is returned to the statement following PERFORM when

_____.

- - - - - - - - - - - - - - - - - - -

(a) COUNTER; (b) B; (c) A; (d) COUNTER GREATER THAN 60

14. When a PERFORM statement with the VARYING option is executed, events
occur in a specific sequence.

format: PERFORM paragraph-name-1

VARYING data-name-1   FROM $\begin{Bmatrix} \text{literal-2} \\ \text{data-name-2} \end{Bmatrix}$

BY $\begin{Bmatrix} \text{literal-3} \\ \text{data-name-3} \end{Bmatrix}$ UNTIL condition.

- First, data-name-1 is set equal to data-name-2 (or literal-2).

- Second, the condition is tested; if true, the paragraph is not
executed.

- Third, if condition is false, the specified paragraphs are executed.

- Fourth, data-name-1 is incremented by data-name-3 (or literal-3).

- Fifth, the program recycles through the second, third, and fourth steps.

```
PERFORM LISTING
      VARYING COUNTER FROM BEGIN BY SPACING
      UNTIL COUNTER GREATER THAN 60.
```

For the example above, complete the steps below, using the actual data-names.

(a) First, COUNTER is set equal to _____.

(b) Second, _____.

(c) Third, paragraph LISTING is executed.

(d) Fourth, _____.

(e) Fifth, _____.

- - - - - - - - - - - - - - - - - - -

(a) BEGIN
(b) The condition COUNTER GREATER THAN 60 is tested.
(d) COUNTER is incremented by the value of SPACING.
(e) Recycle (b), (c), and (d).

15. Assume that when the PERFORM example of frame 14 is executed, COUNTER = 61, BEGIN = 1, and SPACING = 3.

(a) When the condition is tested the first time (second step in frame 14),

the value of COUNTER is _____.

(b) After COUNTER is incremented by SPACING the first time, its value

is _____.

- - - - - - - - - - - - - - - - - - -

(a) 1 (Data-name-1 is set equal to data-name-2 before the condition is tested.)
(b) 4 (1 + 3 = 4)

16. The data-name which follows the word FROM in the VARYING option is used only as the very first step in varying the value of data-name-1. The PERFORMed paragraph can make changes in data-name-2 without affecting the total number of times the paragraphs are executed. If it changes the values of data-name-1 (which follows VARYING) or data-name-3 (which follows BY), however, it could affect the number of executions. If the value of B in frame 16, for example, were set to 60 in LISTING, the condition would become true and LISTING would not be executed

again. Consider the PERFORM statement example of frame 14. A change in which of the following values during execution of LISTING could affect the number of times it is executed?

_____ (a) COUNTER

_____ (b) BEGIN

_____ (c) SPACING

- - - - - - - - - - - - - - - - - -

a, c

17. Write a statement to execute paragraph TIMELY, set NOW equal to THEN, then increment NOW by the value of NEVER until the value of NOW is less than the value of TOMORROW.

7	8		12	16	20	24	28	32	36	40	44	48	52

- - - - - - - - - - - - - - - - - - -

```
PERFORM TIMELY
     VARYING NOW FROM THEN BY NEVER
     UNTIL NOW LESS THAN TOMORROW.
```


18. The data-names or numeric literals that are used as data-name-2 (following FROM) and data-name-3 (following BY) need not be integers and they need not be positive. A programmer might, for example, wish to begin the value at -5 and increment it by intervals of .5. Write a statement specifying these values for varying X-RATE. The paragraph CINEMA should be executed until ATTENDANCE is more than 10,000.

- - - - - - - - - - - - - - - - - - -

```
PERFORM CINEMA
     VARYING X-RATE FROM -5 BY .5
     UNTIL ATTENDANCE GREATER THAN 10000.
```

(Remember that numeric literals can't include commas.)

19. The THRU option of PERFORM allows you to execute a sequence of paragraphs with one PERFORM.

PERFORM paragraph-1 [THRU paragraph-2]

In structured COBOL we use the THRU option only in a special circum-stance. You'll see here how it works. Then in the next section you'll learn to code and PERFORM a case structure, which requires a THRU option.

The THRU option of PERFORM allows you to execute a linear sequence of paragraphs. PERFORM APARA THRU BPARA results in transfer of control to APARA. Statements are executed normally until the last state-ment in BPARA is executed. Then control returns to the statement follow-ing the PERFORM...THRU. The range of the PERFORM may include other PERFORM statements, IFs, or any other kind of statement. But control must eventually reach the last statement in the specified last para-graph. Examine the segment framework below.

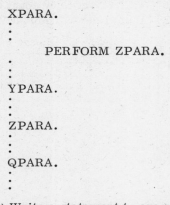

XPARA.
.
.

    PERFORM ZPARA.
.

YPARA.
.

ZPARA.
.

QPARA.
.
.

(a) Write a statement to execute the entire segment.

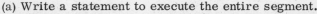

(b) How many paragraphs will be executed by your statement? _____

- - - - - - - - - - - - - - - - - - - -

(a) PERFORM XPARA THRU QPARA.
(b) 5 (XPARA, ZPARA, YPARA, ZPARA, QPARA)

20. When the THRU option is used in structured COBOL we use a special exit paragraph to serve as the final exit point. The EXIT statement is the only one in the final paragraph. It serves to terminate a range of paragraphs. Although its use isn't critical, EXIT makes it easier for you to make clear where the PERFORM THRU ends.

```
       XPARA.
         .
         .
             PERFORM ZPARA
       YPARA.
         .
         .
       ZPARA.
         .
         .
       QPARA.
         .
         .
       XPARA-EXIT.
             EXIT.
```

Write a statement to execute the segment shown above.

- - - - - - - - - - - - - - - - - - - -

       PERFORM XPARA THRU XPARA-EXIT.

CASE STRUCTURE

The three control structures (sequence, selection, and repetition) solve virtually all control functions in any programming solution. But some problems can be solved more efficiently in other ways. For example, we may need to make a selection that has more than two options. We can accomplish this with nested IFs, of course, but COBOL provides another way. We can code a case structure to transfer control to one of any number of paragraphs based on the value of a field, such as transaction type. This is one way of handling multiple file maintenance functions in one program. The case structure does nothing a nested IF can't do. But it does it in a more coherent, more understandable way. The case structure allows control to flow based on the value of a field. To use it, you need to know two forms of the GO TO statement.

21. The GO TO statement has the basic format below:

   GO TO paragraph-name.

The effect is to transfer control to the named paragraph—and leave it there. Unlike the PERFORM, GO TO does not return. It doesn't even keep track of where it came from. When GO TO is used extensively in programs, it becomes very difficult for us to understand what the program is doing, much less how it does it. In the case structure, we need to use GO TO to transfer control to the end of the case.

(a) Write a statement to transfer control to the exit paragraph in frame 20.

```
7 | 8    | 12    16    20    24    28    32    36    40    44    48
   |      |
   |      |
```

(b) What will happen when control reaches the exit paragraph of a segment invoked by PERFORM...THRU? _____

_____

- - - - - - - - - - - - - - - - - -

(a) GO TO XPARA-EXIT.
(b) Control will return to the statement following PERFORM...THRU.

22. We use another form of GO TO as the first statement in a case structure. The format shown below will transfer control to one of the named paragraphs, based on the value of a data-name.

```
GO TO   paragraph-1
        paragraph-2
        .
        .
        paragraph-n
        DEPENDING ON data-name.
```

With this format, the value of data-name determines which paragraph receives control. If data-name has value 1, paragraph-1 gets control. If data-name has value 6, paragraph-6 gets control. If data-name has value 0, or is greater than n, control falls through to the next statement after the GO TO...DEPENDING ON.

(a) Write a COBOL statement to transfer control to UPDATE-MASTER if TRANS-CODE is 1, ADD-RECORD if TRANS-CODE is 2, and DELETE-RECORD if it is 3.

```
   |    |
   |    |
   |    |
   |    |
   |    |
   |    |
```

(b) Where will control go if TRANS-CODE=0? _____

_____

(c) Where will control go if TRANS-CODE=17?

_____

- - - - - - - - - - - - - - - - -

(a) GO TO UPDATE-MASTER
       ADD-RECORD
       DELETE-RECORD
       DEPENDING ON TRANS-CODE.
(b) to the statement after GO TO
(c) to the statement after GO TO

23. Figure 10-1 shows a diagram of a case structure. The lettered boxes correspond to the parts of the structure. The statement that invokes the case would be PERFORM A-ENTER THRU A-EXIT. The first statement in A-ENTER would be the GO TO...DEPENDING ON. The last statement in each of B, C, D, and E would transfer control to the exit paragraph, A-EXIT.

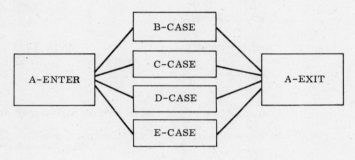

Figure 10-1

Refer to Figure 10-1 for paragraph names as you do the following:

(a) Write the first statement in A-ENTER (use CASE-CODE as data-name).

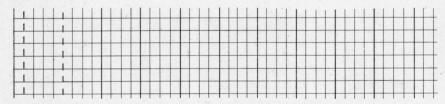

(b) Write the last statement in B-CASE.

(c) Write the A-EXIT paragraph.

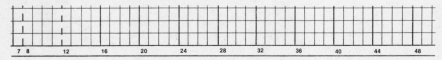

(a) GO TO B-CASE
         C-CASE
         D-CASE
         E-CASE
         DEPENDING ON CASE-CODE.
(b) GO TO A-EXIT.
(c) A-EXIT.
         EXIT.

24. The pseudocode for a typical case structure is shown below.

         CASE: transaction
                 CASE1
                     add customer
                 CASE2
                     delete customer
                 CASE3
                     handle charge
                 CASE4
                     handle credit
         ENDCASE

(a) How many paragraphs are represented in this case structure? _____ .

(b) What range of values do you expect for the transaction code?

_____

(c) Assume the operations can be done with a statement like PERFORM
    ADD-CUSTOMER. Write paragraph CASE3-HANDLE-CHARGE.

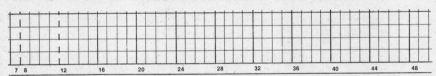

- - - - - - - - - - - - - - - - - - - -

(a) six (see frame 25)
(b) one to four
(c) CASE3-HANDLE-CHARGE.
        PERFORM HANDLE-CHARGE.
        GO TO CASE-EXIT.

25. On the next page is the complete case structure as coded in structured
    COBOL.

```
CASE-TRANSACTION.
     GO TO CASE1-ADD-CUSTOMER
          CASE2-DELETE-CUSTOMER
          CASE3-HANDLE-CHARGE
          CASE4-HANDLE-CREDIT
          DEPENDING ON TRANS-CODE.
     DISPLAY 'WRONG CODE', TRANS-NUM.
     GO TO CASE-EXIT.
CASE1-ADD-CUSTOMER.
     PERFORM ADD-CUSTOMER.
     GO TO CASE-EXIT.
CASE2-DELETE-CUSTOMER.
     PERFORM DELETE-CUSTOMER.
     GO TO CASE-EXIT.
CASE3-HANDLE-CHARGE.
     PERFORM HANDLE-CHARGE.
     GO TO CASE-EXIT.
CASE4-HANDLE-CREDIT.
     PERFORM HANDLE-CREDIT.
     GO TO CASE-EXIT.
CASE-EXIT.
     EXIT.
```

(a) Write the COBOL statement that would execute the case.

(b) What is the purpose of the statements immediately following GO TO... DEPENDING ON? _____

(c) One statement in the coding above is dispensable. Can you identify one that could be omitted with no effect? _____

- - - - - - - - - - - - - - - - - - -

(a) PERFORM CASE-TRANSACTION THRU CASE-EXIT.
(b) to deal with any transaction codes that aren't 1, 2, 3, or 4
(c) the last GO TO

26. Suppose you are going to update a master file. All the transactions represent changes to existing records, and a code (UPCODE) indicates what fields are to be changed. Here are the codes and what they mean.

(1) change name   (MOVE NEW-NAME TO MAST-NAME)
(2) change name
    and address   (MOVE NEW-ADDRESS TO MAST-ADDRESS)
(3) change address
(4) change address
    and phone   (MOVE NEW-PHONE TO MAST-PHONE)

(5) change name
     and phone
(6) change phone
(7) change all three

If a card has some other code, don't change anything. Just print the UP-NUMBER with the message "no change". Assume the structure will be invoked with PERFORM CHANGES THRU CHANGES-EXIT. Write the first paragraph of the case. (Create reasonable names.)

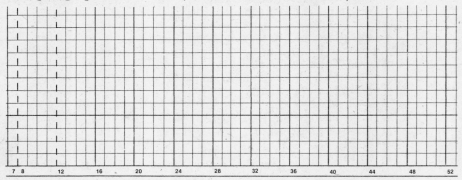

```
CHANGES.
    GO TO CASE1-NAME
        CASE2-NM-ADD
        CASE3-ADDRESS
        CASE4-ADD-PHN
        CASE5-NM-PHN
        CASE6-PHONE
        CASE7-ALL
        DEPENDING ON UP-CODE.
    DISPLAY UP-NUMBER 'NO CHANGE'.
    GO TO CHANGES-EXIT.
```

(You probably used different names. Be sure you listed seven paragraphs before the DEPENDING ON.)

27. Now write the paragraphs for UP-CODE values of 1 and 7 along with the last paragraph of the structure.

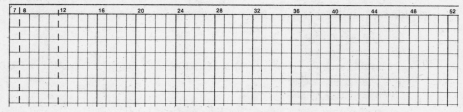

(form continued on next page)

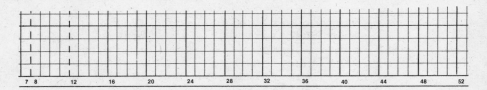

```
- - - - - - - - - - - - - - - - - - - -
     CASE1-NAME.
         MOVE NEW-NAME TO MAST-NAME.
         GO TO CHANGES-EXIT.
             .
             .
             .
     CASE7-ALL.
         MOVE NEW-NAME TO MAST-NAME.
         MOVE NEW-ADDRESS TO MAST-ADDRESS.
         MOVE NEW-PHONE TO MAST-PHONE.
         GO TO CHANGES-EXIT.              (could be omitted)
     CHANGES-EXIT.
         EXIT.
```

SUMMARY

You have now learned to code a COBOL case structure. Although this could be coded with nested IFs, the way shown here is much more understandable.

The only application of GO TO we will consider in this book is its use in a case structure. In general, the COBOL GO TO is avoided in structured programming because, even though it is easy to code, it is hard to follow. In the case structure, we always use GO TO to refer to a later point in the sequence. This keeps the logic simple. And the entire case module has a single entry point and exit. PERFORM and IFs can be used as needed within the case structure.

SELF-TEST

After you have written your answers to the Self-Test, check your answers in the Answer Key that follows. Be sure you understand any differences between your answers and ours before you begin the next chapter. Following each suggested answer is a frame reference in parentheses, in case you need to review.

In this Self-Test you will write several Structured COBOL program segments.

1. Suppose your master record is defined in Working-Storage as shown on the next page.

```
01   MASTER-RECORD.
     02   PART-NUMBER          PIC   9(6).
     02   PART-DESCRIPTION     PIC   X(20).
     02   PART-ON-HAND         PIC   9(4).
     02   PART-ON-ORDER        PIC   9(4).
     02   PART-UNIT-PRICE      PIC   99V99.
     02   PART-SELLING-PRICE   PIC   99V99.
     02   PART-MANUFACTURER    PIC   X(8).
```

When you add records to this file, the transaction record includes a new part number in positions 1 through 6, manufacturer in positions 7 through 14, a description in positions 15 through 34, equivalent parts in positions 35 through 50, and the unit price in positions 51 through 54. The last position on the card is a part code.

(a) Describe the transaction record so the appropriate data can be placed in master record using the CORRESPONDING option of the MOVE statement.

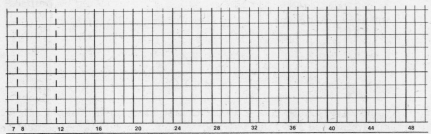

(b) Write the MOVE statement.

(c) How would you code a condition to test if the transaction record number is greater than the master record number?

2. Write a COBOL entry to describe an area (EXTRA-AREA) the same size as MASTER-RECORD to occupy the same area.

3. You want to cause a paragraph named CALCULATE to be executed exactly eight times. Write two different statements to do this, using the forms on the next page.

(a)

(b)

4. Suppose you are processing changes to a customer account master file.
    The changes are input on cards. There are several types of cards, de-
    pending on the field in the master record to be changed.

    A card is read and the matching master record is found in another
    routine in the program. Then control is passed to this routine. In this
    routine, the card type is examined and the appropriate change is made.
    The card types are:

        1 - Change to customer's name
        2 - Change to customer's address
        3 - Change to service description
        4 - Change to monthly rate
        5 - Change to account manager

    This code is in field CHANGE-TYPE, described as PICTURE 9. No
    other card type can enter this routine, as the card type is validated else-
    where in the program.

    Here is a structure chart for the case structure.

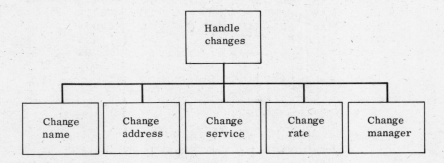

(a) Using a PERFORM to handle the actual processing for each type, code
    a case structure for this problem. (Include at least the first two and
    last two paragraphs.)

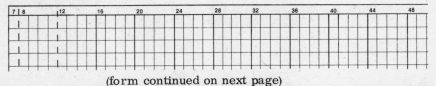

(form continued on next page)

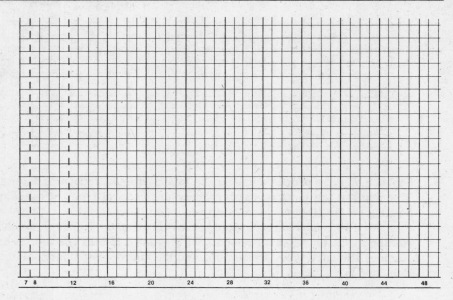

(b) Code a statement to invoke the case.

Answer Key

1. (a)
```
01  ADD-RECORD.
    02   PART-NUMBER         PIC   9(6).
    02   PART-MANUFACTURER   PIC   X(8).
    02   PART-DESCRIPTION    PIC   X(20).
    02   FILLER              PIC   X(16).
    02   PART-UNIT-PRICE     PIC   99V99.
    02   FILLER              PIC   X(25).
    02   PART-CODE           PIC   X.           (5)
```

(b)
```
MOVE CORRESPONDING ADD-RECORD
    TO MASTER-RECORD.                    (3)
```

(c)
```
...PART-NUMBER OF ADD-RECORD >
    PART-NUMBER OF MASTER-RECORD...      (4)
```

2.
```
01  EXTRA-AREA  REDEFINES  MASTER-RECORD
              PIC  X(50).                 (9)
```

3. (a) `PERFORM CALCULATIONS 8 TIMES.`   (11)
   (b)
```
PERFORM CALCULATIONS
    VARYING TIME-COUNT FROM 1 BY 1
    UNTIL TIME-COUNT > 8.                (17)
```

4. (a)
```
        HANDLE-CHANGES.
             GO TO CASE-NAME
                   CASE-ADDRESS
                   CASE-SERVICE
                   CASE-RATE
                   CASE-MANAGER
                   DEPENDING ON CHANGE-TYPE.
             GO TO CHANGE-EXIT.
        CASE-NAME.
            PERFORM CHANGE-NAME.
            GO TO CHANGE-EXIT.
        CASE-ADDRESS.
            PERFORM CHANGE-ADDRESS.
            GO TO CHANGE-EXIT.
                .
                .
        CASE-MANAGER.
            PERFORM CHANGE-MANAGER.
            GO TO CHANGE-EXIT.
        CHANGE-EXIT.
            EXIT.                                    (25)
```

(b)
```
   PERFORM HANDLE-CHANGES THRU CHANGE-EXIT.       (24)
```

CHAPTER ELEVEN
Tables

Many COBOL applications require the use of tables, which are simply repetitions of data in the same format. We can describe repeated occurrences of data items having the same format with a single data-name. We can then use subscripts or indexes to refer to a specific occurrence of the data-name. For example, if an input file includes values for 365 different days, we may describe a table to hold 365 occurrences of usage figures. Then ELECTRICITY (1) would refer to the first value, and so on. The data-name and its subscript refer to a single occurrence of the table value. Tables can greatly simplify coding of data-names, and allow for very efficient ways to process data.

In this chapter you will learn to describe tables in the Data Division, to assign values to these tables, and to use them in the Procedure Division to solve problems.

When you have completed this chapter, you will be able to:

- define tables in the Data Division;

- initialize a one- or two-dimensional table in the Procedure Division;

- access elements in a one- or two-dimensional table using subscripts; and

- use indexes in SET and SEARCH commands.

TABLE DESCRIPTION ENTRY: SINGLE OCCURS

1. A table is a collection of related data items with identical picture descriptions. For example, a table might include a list of social security numbers, a list of scores on successive exams, or a set of wholesale prices. Which of the following could be a table?

   _____ (a) a name, an address, and a maximum credit limit

   _____ (b) a list of state abbreviations, all described as XX

   _____ (c) any collection of items, as long as they all have the same pictures

- - - - - - - - - - - - - - - - - - - -

b, c

2. Each item in a table can be referred to by a number (called a subscript) that identifies its position in the table. For example, you may have a table of seven items that includes the names of the days of the week where WK-DAY (1) has the value SUNDAY.

    (a) What is the value of WK-DAY (3)? _____

    (b) What term refers to the number in parentheses? _____

- - - - - - - - - - - - - - - - - - -

(a) TUESDAY; (b) subscript

3. An input card may contain a variable called IN-DAY. The variable itself may be used as a subscript to access a table entry. If the value of IN-DAY is 6, then the value of WK-DAY is FRIDAY. Suppose the value of IN-DAY is 4. Which of the statements below would put the corresponding value to WK-DAY on the system printer?

    _____ (a) DISPLAY IN-DAY.

    _____ (b) DISPLAY IN-DAY (WK-DAY).

    _____ (c) DISPLAY WK-DAY (IN-DAY).

    _____ (d) DISPLAY WK-DAY.

- - - - - - - - - - - - - - - - - - -

c

4. A table is defined in the Data Division, using a new entry, the OCCURS clause. As you can see in the example below, the OCCURS clause specifies the number of elements in the table.

    ```
    01  WEEK-DAYS.
        02  WK-DAY OCCURS 7 TIMES PIC X(9).
    ```

    This entry sets up a table of seven items, each nine characters long. A total of 9 times 7, or 63, bytes (each character occupies 1 byte) will be needed to store the table. Several rules about OCCURS apply to this definition:

    - OCCURS does not appear at the 01 level but at a lower level.

    - The PICTURE appears at the lowest level.

    - The subscript is used with the OCCURS level—you could use WK-DAY (1), but not WEEK-DAYS (1).

(a) Suppose you wanted to describe a table of the names of the months. Using the example as a model, write a Data Division description of MONTH-LIST.

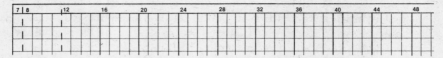

(b) Suppose an input record includes these data items:

```
02   PURCHASE-DAY.
     03  PMONTH    PIC 99.
     03  PDAY      PIC 9.
```

What expression could you use to access elements of the tables in this frame to obtain:

The name of the day referred to? _____

The name of the month referred to? _____

- - - - - - - - - - - - - - - - - - - -

(a)
```
01   MONTH-LIST.
     02   MONTH-NAME OCCURS 12 TIMES PIC X(9).
```

(b)
```
WK-DAY (PDAY)
MONTH-NAME (PMONTH)
```

5. Let's consider the MONTH-LIST table from frame 4 again. How can we set up this table, once storage is reserved for it in the Data Division? One way is by using an input file. Suppose each month-name is punched in the first nine positions of a separate card.

(a) How many cards would be in that input file? _____

(b) Write a record description for the input records.

- - - - - - - - - - - - - - - - - - -

(a) 12

(b)
```
01   IN-RECORD.
     02   IN-MONTH    PIC X(9).
     02   FILLER      PIC X(71).
```

6. Examine the sets of statements on the next page. Which, if any, will assign the input values to the table entries?

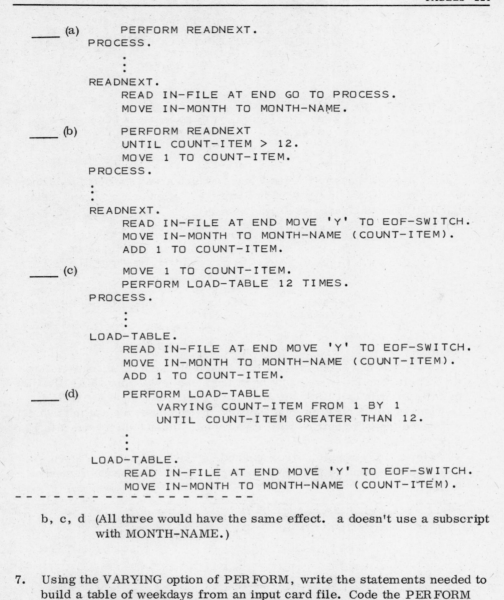

```
____ (a)        PERFORM READNEXT.
           PROCESS.
               .
               .
               .
           READNEXT.
               READ IN-FILE AT END GO TO PROCESS.
               MOVE IN-MONTH TO MONTH-NAME.

____ (b)        PERFORM READNEXT
                UNTIL COUNT-ITEM > 12.
                MOVE 1 TO COUNT-ITEM.
           PROCESS.
               .
               .
               .
           READNEXT.
               READ IN-FILE AT END MOVE 'Y' TO EOF-SWITCH.
               MOVE IN-MONTH TO MONTH-NAME (COUNT-ITEM).
               ADD 1 TO COUNT-ITEM.

____ (c)        MOVE 1 TO COUNT-ITEM.
                PERFORM LOAD-TABLE 12 TIMES.
           PROCESS.
               .
               .
               .
           LOAD-TABLE.
               READ IN-FILE AT END MOVE 'Y' TO EOF-SWITCH.
               MOVE IN-MONTH TO MONTH-NAME (COUNT-ITEM).
               ADD 1 TO COUNT-ITEM.

____ (d)        PERFORM LOAD-TABLE
                    VARYING COUNT-ITEM FROM 1 BY 1
                    UNTIL COUNT-ITEM GREATER THAN 12.
               .
               .
               .
           LOAD-TABLE.
               READ IN-FILE AT END MOVE 'Y' TO EOF-SWITCH.
               MOVE IN-MONTH TO MONTH-NAME (COUNT-ITEM).
```

- -

b, c, d (All three would have the same effect. a doesn't use a subscript
with MONTH-NAME.)

7. Using the VARYING option of PERFORM, write the statements needed to
build a table of weekdays from an input card file. Code the PERFORM
and the paragraph it performs. (Use IN-FILE, IN-DAY, and COUNTER
as needed.)

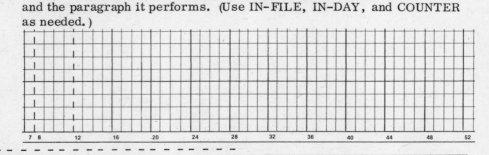

- -

```
      PERFORM LIST-DAYS
          VARYING COUNTER FROM 1 BY 1
          UNTIL COUNTER GREATER THAN 7.
PROCESS.
   .
   .
   .
LIST-DAYS.
     READ IN-FILE AT END MOVE 'Y' TO EOF-SWITCH.
     MOVE IN-DAY TO WK-DAY (COUNTER).
```

8. Tables such as those in frames 3 and 4, which aren't expected to change,
    can be given values in the Working-Storage Section of a program, using
    the REDEFINES clause, as shown below.

```
01   MONTHS.
     02   MONTH-1              PIC X(9) VALUE 'JANUARY  '.
     02   MONTH-2              PIC X(9) VALUE 'FEBRUARY '.
     .
     .
     .
     02   MONTH-12             PIC X(9) VALUE 'DECEMBER '.
01   MONTH-LIST REDEFINES MONTHS.
     02   MONTH-NAMES OCCURS 12 TIMES
                     PIC X(9).
```

As you learned earlier, the REDEFINES clause must directly follow
the item it redefines, and must be at the same level. Since VALUE can't
be included with OCCURS, the above is a useful technique for coding a
constant table. A program that includes the coding above can immediately
reference the table entries with a subscript, either a digit from 1 to 12 or
a data-name.

Refer to the example above, and code a Working-Storage record to
give weekday name values to seven items. Then redefine the record as a
table.

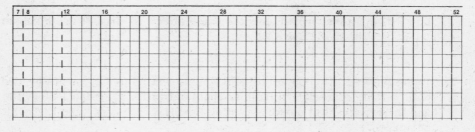

- - - - - - - - - - - - - - - -

```
01   DAYS-OF-WEEK.
     02   DAY-1               PIC X(9) VALUE 'SUNDAY   '.
     .
     .
     02   DAY-7               PIC X(9) VALUE 'SATURDAY '.
01   WEEK-DAYS REDEFINES DAYS-OF-WEEK.
     02   WK-DAY OCCURS 7 TIMES
                     PIC X(9).
```

9. The entries in a table must all be the same size and format. For example, an input record may include amounts purchased in 7 different years, from 1975 through 1981. Each entry will have seven level 02 items SUM-PURCH to refer to the entire table, and R-SUM to refer to each item.

(a) Write the description for the table in the answer to frame 8:

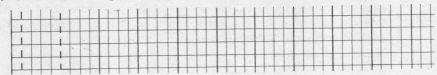

(b) How could you refer to the purchase sum of 1978? _____

- - - - - - - - - - - - - - - - - - -

(a)
```
02   SUM-PURCH.
     03   YR-SUM OCCURS 7 TIMES
                    PIC 9(5)V99.
```

(b) YR-SUM (4)

10. Subscripted data-names can be used in most COBOL statements. Suppose any customer who purchased more than twice as much in 1981 as in 1975, is to be issued a new "gold-plated" credit card. Paragraph NEW-CREDIT-CARD is to be executed, then control is to be returned to the normal sequence. Write a statement to accomplish this.

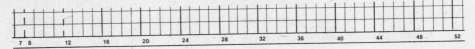

- - - - - - - - - - - - - - - - - - -

```
IF YR-SUM (7) GREATER THAN 2 * YR-SUM (1)
    PERFORM NEW-CREDIT-CARD.
```

11. In the record-description entry below, a table is included in the input data as CABLE. Notice that 80 positions are accounted for.

```
FILE SECTION.
FD  IN-FILE
    LABEL RECORDS ARE OMITTED.
01  IN-RECORD.
    02 CLUE                      PIC X.
    02 C-NUMBER                  PIC 9(8).
    02 C-NAME                    PIC X(21).
    02 C-ADDRESS                 PIC X(30).
    02 CABLE OCCURS 5 TIMES      PIC X(4).
```

When an input card is read, values are assigned to the input record, including the 5 table elements. Assume card columns 61 through 80 contain ABCDEFGHIJKLMNOPQRST. CABLE (1) contains ABCD. What is the value of:

(a) CABLE (3) _____

(b) CABLE (5) _____

(c) Suppose CLUE in IN-RECORD contains a number from 1 to 5. Whatever the value of CLUE, the corresponding occurrence of CABLE is to be written upon the console typewriter. Write the statement necessary to accomplish this.

- - - - - - - - - - - - - - - - - - - -

(a) IJKL
(b) QRST
(c) DISPLAY CABLE (CLUE) UPON CONSOLE.

12. A table may contain many elements. Suppose, for example, you have this table.

```
01   SCHOOL-ENROLLMENT.
     02   ELEMENTARY          PIC 9(4)
                              OCCURS 98 TIMES.
```

This table is to contain an enrollment for each school in the system. If the elementary schools are coded 1 to 98, this will be a useful table. If school names are used rather than codes, the following would be a more effective table.

```
01   SCHOOL-ENROLLMENT.
     02   ELEMENTARY     OCCURS 98 TIMES.
          03   SCHOOL-NAME     PIC X(20).
          03   SCHOOL-POP      PIC 9(4).
```

Suppose an input file (SCHOOL-MASTER) contains all sorts of school information, including ELEM-NAME and ENROLLED. The pseudocode segment is shown below. A data-name EL has been defined with VALUE ZERO for use as the variable subscript.

```
     Get input record
     PERFORM UNTIL no more records
          load table
     ENDPERFORM
Load Table
     increment subscript
     move data to table element
     get input record
```

Create the SCHOOL-ENROLLMENT table from the SCHOOL-MASTER file, following the pseudocode.

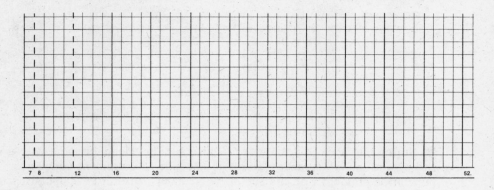

```
        READ SCHOOL-MASTER
            AT END MOVE 'Y' TO SCHOOL-EOF.
        PERFORM LOAD-TABLE
            UNTIL SCHOOL-EOF = 'Y'.
            .
            .
            .
    LOAD-TABLE.
        ADD 1 TO EL.
        MOVE ELEM-NAME TO SCHOOL-NAME (EL).
        MOVE ENROLLED TO SCHOOL-POP (EL).
        READ SCHOOL-MASTER
            AT END MOVE 'Y' TO SCHOOL-EOF.
```

13. If exactly 98 records were in the input file, the table would now be
    created. Suppose the input file contained more than 98 records, but you
    only want the first 98 represented in your table. How would you modify
    the coding in the preceding frame?

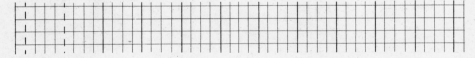

```
    PERFORM LOAD-TABLE 98 TIMES.
        (or)
    PERFORM LOAD-TABLE
        VARYING EL FROM 1 BY 1
        UNTIL EL > 98.
```

   (In the second case, you would omit ADD 1 TO EL as well.)

14. Now that the table is created (or built or loaded), we are ready to use it.
    Suppose we need to list the names of all schools that have fewer than 200
    students enrolled. The coding on the next page will accomplish this.

```
PERFORM FIND-LOW
    VARYING EL FROM 1 BY 1
    UNTIL EL > 98.
:
:
FIND-LOW.
    IF SCHOOL-POP (EL) < 200
        DISPLAY ELEM-NAME (EL)
    ELSE
        NEXT SENTENCE.
```

Notice that PERFORM VARYING changes the subscript, and varies it throughout the table range—from 1 to 98. The IF statement compares the population element with the cut-off point (200). When a low population is located, the school-name of the same subscript is printed. The searching paragraph then continues incrementing the subscript. This routine would print from 0 to 98 school-names, depending on how many had fewer than 200 students enrolled.

Now you want to count and list the schools that have more than 500 enrolled. Modify the coding to accomplish this. Display the count as OVER-SCHOOL.

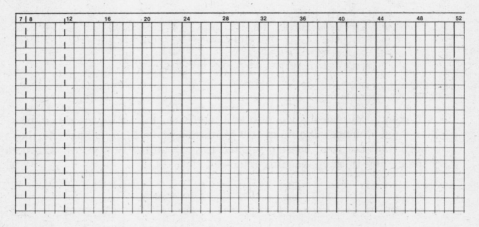

- - - - - - - - - - - - - - - - - -

```
    MOVE ZERO TO OVER-SCHOOL.
    PERFORM FIND-OVER
        VARYING EL FROM 1 BY 1
        UNTIL EL > 98.
    DISPLAY OVER-SCHOOL 'SCHOOLS'.
:
:
FIND-OVER.
    IF SCHOOL-POP (EL) > 500
        PERFORM LIST-IT
    ELSE
        NEXT SENTENCE.
:
:
LIST-IT.
    ADD 1 TO OVER-SCHOOL.
    DISPLAY ELEM-NAME (EL).
```

15. Now modify the coding above to find the total population in those schools which have more than 500 children. Display the total population along with the number of schools involved.

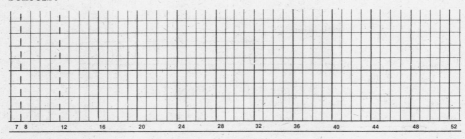

```
        MOVE ZERO TO OVER-SCHOOL, TOTAL-POP.
        PERFORM FIND-OVER
            VARYING EL FROM 1 BY 1
            UNTIL EL > 98.
        DISPLAY OVER-SCHOOL, TOTAL-POP.
    .
    .
    .
FIND-OVER.
    no changes
LIST-IT.
    ADD 1 TO OVER-SCHOOL.
    ADD SCHOOL-POP (EL) TO TOTAL-POP.
    DISPLAY ELEM-NAME (EL).
```

16. Write a short routine to find and display the total population in all 98 schools.

```
MOVE ZERO TO TOTAL-POP.
PERFORM ADD-THEM
     VARYING EL FROM 1 BY 1
     UNTIL EL > 98.
DISPLAY TOTAL-POP.
     ⋮
ADD-THEM.
     ADD SCHOOL-POP (EL) TO TOTAL-POP.
```

MULTI-DIMENSIONAL TABLES

In the preceding frames, you have been processing a one-dimensional table, using the usual control structures. COBOL also allows two- and three-dimensional tables. In this section, we'll look at how to define and process two-dimensional tables using the same techniques.

17. A one-dimensional table might represent either a list of student names or a set of scores for any one student. A two-dimensional table can include a set of scores for each of the students. The table in Figure 11-1 would contain how many table elements?

Figure 11-1. Scores Table

---

72 (students * scores, or the number of elements in one dimension times the number of elements in the other)

18. As you know, the OCCURS clause may be used to denote repeated occurrences of similar items. To define a two-dimensional table, the OCCURS clause is used twice as shown below. The PICTURE clause is used only after the last OCCURS.

```
01   SALES-TABLE.
     02   SALESMAN OCCURS 14 TIMES.
          03   SALES OCCURS 12 TIMES
                    PIC 9(4)V99.
```

Write the entries necessary to describe TEST-TABLE as shown in Figure 11-1.

```
01   TEST-TABLE.
     02   STUDENT OCCURS 9 TIMES.
          03 SCORE OCCURS 8 TIMES PIC 999.
```

19. Now look at this example again:

```
01   SALES-TABLE.
     02   SALESMAN OCCURS 14 TIMES.
          03 SALES OCCURS 12 TIMES
               PIC 9(4)V99.
```

In order to refer to one entry in a two-dimensional table, you need two subscripts, written in the form (1, 2). The first subscript refers to the variable described by the first OCCURS and must be followed by a comma and a space. The second subscript refers to the variable described by the second OCCURS. Both subscripts follow the name of the last variable. Which of the following are correct?

_____ (a) SALESMAN (2)   _____ (c) SALES (14, 12)

_____ (b) SALES (2)   _____ (d) SALES (1, 17)

----

c   (In d, the second subscript is larger than 12.)

All COBOL compilers accept this format. Some allow you to omit the space.

20. Refer to Figure 11-1. SCORE (1, 8) refers to Allen's score on the eighth test. Write the entries to refer to the items on the following page.

(a) OHanlon's seventh score _____

(b) Loveland's first score _____

(c) Garibaldi's fourth score _____

- - - - - - - - - - - - - - - - - - - -

(a) SCORE (8, 7)
(b) SCORE (7, 1)
(c) SCORE (3, 4)

21. Suppose you are interested in finding out which students, if any, received scores of 100 on a given test. The input will be a test number—the second subscript. Your task will be to find any scores of 100, and identify (DISPLAY) the first subscript. This table look-up problem works much like a one-dimensional table—you keep one subscript (the given test number) constant and vary the other to check all nine students. Use datanames from frame 18 with SUB-STU and SUB-TEST, as subscripts, and write the commands needed to find and DISPLAY the value of SUB-STU when SUB-TEST is fixed to refer to one test and the value of the table entry is 100.

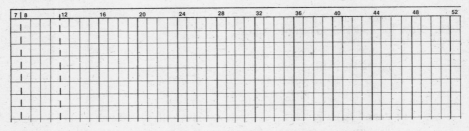

- - - - - - - - - - - - - - - - - - - -

```
        MOVE 1 TO SUB-STU.
        PERFORM CHECK-SCORE 9 TIMES.
            :
            :
    CHECK-SCORE.
        IF SCORE (SUB-STU, SUB-TEST) = 100
            DISPLAY SUB-STU.
        ADD 1 TO SUB-STU.
```

22. Table look-up in a two-dimensional table often requires the use of nested IFs or nested PERFORMs. Suppose you were trying to identify any tests for which students received a 100. We can add another level of PERFORM around the one above.

(a) What subscript will change in the outer loop? _____

(b) How many times will the inner loop (the coding above) be executed?

_____

- - - - - - - - - - - - - - - - - - - -

(a) second (SUB-TEST)

(b) 72 (9 times for each of the tests)

23. The coding below demonstrates the use of nested PERFORMs to locate elements in a two-dimensional table. Notice that the first segment includes PERFORM VARY-TEST, while VARY-TEST includes PERFORM CHECK-SCORE.

```
        MOVE 1 TO SUB-TEST.
        PERFORM VARY-TEST 8 TIMES.
          .
          .
    VARY-TEST.
        MOVE 1 TO SUB-STU.
        PERFORM CHECK-SCORE 9 TIMES.
        ADD 1 TO SUB-TEST.
    CHECK-SCORE.
        IF SCORE (SUB-STU, SUB-TEST) = 100
            DISPLAY SUB-STU.
        ADD 1 TO SUB-STU.
```

(a) What will be the value of the subscripts the 19th time CHECK-SCORE is entered? _____

(b) Where could you insert DISPLAY 'TEST NUMBER', SUBTEST to cause the test number to be printed before its associated student numbers? _____

- - - - - - - - - - - - - - - - - - -

(a) (3, 1)

(b) at the beginning of VARY-TEST

TEST-TABLE, as diagrammed in Figure 11-1, might be used in several ways. You might want to get a student's final average, or find the average score on any test. Or, you might be interested in the overall average for all students. In the next sequence of frames you will see how to process the data from a two-dimensional table.

24. As you've seen, you can access all table elements from one row (across) or one column (down) in a two-dimensional table, by holding constant the subscript of the variable for the specific row or column. Then you vary the subscript that refers to the separate elements in that specific row or column. For example, to find the average score on the fourth test, the second subscript must first be set at 4. Then the first subscript is varied from 1 through 9 as the scores of the nine students are added together. Thus, the items added are SCORE (1, 4), SCORE (2, 4), SCORE (3, 4), through SCORE (9, 4). Finally, of course, the sum would be divided by nine. In averaging student Fernandez' scores, the steps would be:

(a) set the _____ subscript to _____.
             (first/second)

(b) vary the _____ subscript from 1 through _____.
             (first/second)

(c) add the elements—the third element is _____.

(d) divide the sum of the elements by _____.

- - - - - - - - - - - - - - - - - - - -

(a) first, 2; (b) second, 8; (c) SCORE (2, 3); (d) eight

25. Assume the student/score table is entered into the computer as described. Use the variable KK as the variable subscript, and write the COBOL statements to find Kirby's average. Assume the data-names you will need are SUBTOTAL and FINAL-T.

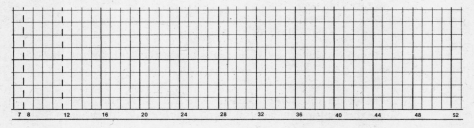

- - - - - - - - - - - - - - - - - - -

```
      MOVE 1 TO KK.
      PERFORM ADD-PARA 8 TIMES.
      DIVIDE SUBTOTAL BY 8 GIVING
          FINAL-T.
        .
        .
        .
  ADD-PARA.
      ADD SCORE (6, KK) TO SUBTOTAL.
      ADD 1 TO KK.
```

Other answers for frame 25 may also be correct. For example, you may have written:

```
      PERFORM ADD-PARA VARYING KK FROM 1 BY 1
          UNTIL KK GREATER THAN 8.
      DIVIDE 8 INTO SUBTOTAL GIVING FINAL-T.
        .
        .
        .
  ADD-PARA.
      ADD SCORE (6, KK) TO SUBTOTAL.
```

INDEXING

Tables can be created in more than two dimensions. These are not commonly used, but the techniques are similar to processing two-dimensional tables. To define a three-dimensional table, you would need three levels of OCCURS; as before, you use a PICTURE only with the lowest level. To search or load a three-level table, you need three levels of IF or PERFORM.

Table handling is one of the more difficult, yet useful features of any programming language. Several versions of COBOL provide additional statements and features to make it easier for the programmer to use. A variable, called an INDEX, can be defined with the OCCURS variable. This INDEX can be given a value in a SET statement. The SEARCH statement (instead of one IF level) will increment the INDEX, and test for a condition in a table-processing operation. Like IFs and PERFORMs, SEARCH statements can be nested to process multi-dimensional tables. The next section will introduce the indexing features.

26. In COBOL, we can use indexing instead of subscripting to refer to table elements. The index is fairly similar to a data-name subscript in appearance, but it's quite different to the computer. When you use an index, you can use a special statement (SEARCH), which simplifies the type of processing we have been doing and allows us to do another type as well. The INDEX variable is defined in the OCCURS clause, as shown below.

```
01   CODE-TABLE.
     02   CODE-NUMBERS    PIC 999
                          OCCURS 20 TIMES
                          INDEXED BY X-CODE.
```

This defines CODE-TABLE with an index, X-CODE. The table elements can still be referenced with subscripts or digits, but you will see than the index variable is easy to use. The index, by the way, is defined by its appearance with OCCURS. You do not use a PIC clause anywhere to describe X-CODE.

Define SCHOOL-ENROLLMENT as a table with 98 elements called ELEMENTARY. Use X-SCHOOL as the index: use SCHOOL-NAME PIC X(20) and SCHOOL-POP PIC 9(4) as the items in ELEMENTARY.

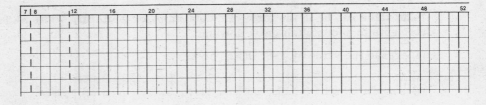

```
01   SCHOOL-ENROLLMENT.
     02   ELEMENTARY              OCCURS 98 TIMES
                                  INDEXED BY X-SCHOOL.
          03   SCHOOL-NAME        PIC  X(20).
          03   SCHOOL-POP         PIC  9(4).
```

27. An index cannot be specified in a MOVE or arithmetic statement; it cannot be DISPLAYed. A special statement is used to assign a value to an index, or to equate an index value with a standard data-name. This is the format:

    SET name1 TO name2

    "Name1" can be an index or a data-name. "Name2" can be an index, a data-name, or a literal. But at least one of the names must be an index. Index names must always have values between 1 and the table size; you can't set an index to zero. The effect of SET is equivalent to assigning the value of name2 to name1. Notice this is the reverse of a MOVE statement.

    Suppose we prefix our indexes with X- (this is a good practice that helps you keep track of indexes in your coding). Which of the following are valid SET statements?

    _____ (a) SET X-SCHOOL TO IN-VALUE.

    _____ (b) SET 'OUT-VALUE' TO X-SCHOOL.

    _____ (c) SET 7 TO X-SCHOOL.

    _____ (d) SET OUT-VALUE TO IN-VALUE.

    _____ (e) SET X-SCHOOL TO 1.

- - - - - - - - - - - - - - - - - - -

    a, b, e (In b, name1 cannot be a literal. In d, neither name is an index.)

28. The SET statement can also be used to increase or decrease the value of an index.

    SET index-name UP BY   value
    SET index-name DOWN BY value

    The value can be in the form of a data-name or a literal. Write SET statements to accomplish the following:

    (a) Increase the value of X-SCHOOL by 1.

    (b) Assign the value of N-CODE to X-SCHOOL.

(c) Assign the value of X-SCHOOL to OUT-CODE.

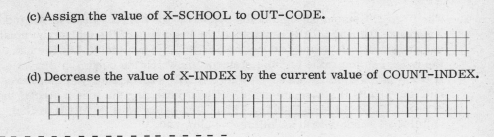

(d) Decrease the value of X-INDEX by the current value of COUNT-INDEX.

- - - - - - - - - - - - - - - - - - -

(a) SET X-SCHOOL UP BY 1.
(b) SET X-SCHOOL TO N-CODE.
(c) SET OUT-CODE TO X-SCHOOL.
(d) SET X-INDEX DOWN BY COUNT-INDEX.

29. The SEARCH statement can be used with an indexed table to locate specific table elements. SEARCH initiates a sequential search, just like the ones you've seen with PERFORM VARYING. Here is a basic SEARCH format:

```
SEARCH  table-name
      [AT END  statement]
      WHEN  condition
              statement
```

The effect is that the named table (at the OCCURS level) is searched from the current value of the index. If the condition is met for any element, the statement following WHEN is executed. If the end of the table is reached, the AT END clause is executed.

Suppose a table is defined as shown below.

```
01   CODE-TABLE.
     02    CODE-NUMBERS    PIC 999
                           OCCURS 20 TIMES
                           INDEXED BY X-CODE.
```

Follow the format above and write a SEARCH statement to PERFORM CODE-FOUND if CODE-NUMBER (X-CODE) is equal to IN-CODE. If the condition never becomes true, PERFORM CODE-NOT-FOUND.

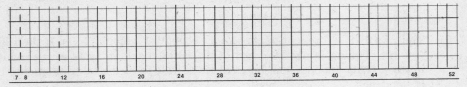

- - - - - - - - - - - - - - - - - -

```
SEARCH CODE-NUMBER
      AT END PERFORM CODE-NOT-FOUND
      WHEN CODE-NUMBER (X-CODE) = IN-CODE
          PERFORM CODE-FOUND.
```

30. The SEARCH statement begins the search at the current value of the index. To ensure that the SEARCH starts at the beginning of the table, you must set the index to 1 before issuing the SEARCH. When the SEARCH ends, the index has the value of table element for which the condition was true. If you want to continue a search where it was interrupted, you must execute the SEARCH statement again, without resetting the index. Recall the SCHOOL-ENROLLMENT table. The coding below uses SEARCH to find and list all schools with enrollments below 200.

```
        :
        :
        SET X-SCHOOL TO 1.
        PERFORM FIND-THEM
            UNTIL END-OF-TABLE = 'Y'.
        :
        :
    FIND-THEM.
        SEARCH ELEMENTARY
            AT END MOVE 'Y' TO END-OF-TABLE
            WHEN SCHOOL-POP (X-SCHOOL) < 200
                PERFORM LIST-IT.
```

The search is repeated until the end of the table is reached. Every time a school with population less than 200 is found it is listed, but the PERFORM UNTIL control doesn't terminate until Y is moved to END-OF-TABLE.

Write a SEARCH statement to find and print the population-name and population of the school whose name matches IN-SCHOOL. If it isn't in the table, print IN-SCHOOL.

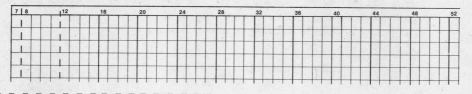

```
SEARCH ELEMENTARY
    AT END DISPLAY IN-SCHOOL, 'NOT LISTED'
    WHEN ELEM-NAME (X-SCHOOL) = IN-SCHOOL
        DISPLAY ELEM-NAME (X-SCHOOL), SCHOOL-POP (X-SCHOOL).
```

31. The SEARCH statement performs a sequential search. Even if the item you are seeking is near the end of the table, each entry is still examined in turn. This process can be used if the values of the table elements are in sequence, or if they aren't.

If the table entries are in sequence, a more efficient type of search, called a binary search, can be performed. A binary search requires a key field in each table entry. It searches by first checking the key field value at the midpoint of the table. If the value it is searching for is higher, it then checks the key field value at the midpoint of the top half of the table. It continues bisecting the remaining portion of the table until the desired key is located. Binary searching can cut access time drastically for many tables. Which of the tables described below could have a binary search?

_____ (a) A tax table arranged by income levels

_____ (b) A table in which names are alphabetized

_____ (c) A list of employees' names and addresses, entered as they are hired.

- - - - - - - - - - - - - - - - - - - -

a, b (c may have some logical sequence, but data isn't specified as a key.)

32. The description of a table that will be processed with a binary search requires a KEY entry in addition to an index.

```
01   CODE-TABLE.
     02   CODE-NUMBER      PIC 999
                           OCCURS 20 TIMES
                           INDEXED BY X-CODE
                           ASCENDING KEY IS CODE-NUMBER.
```

The KEY can be ASCENDING or DESCENDING; in most applications, though, the table is in ascending sequence. Modify the SCHOOL-ENROLLMENT description (see Figure 11-1) to allow a binary search. Assume the names are in alphabetical order.

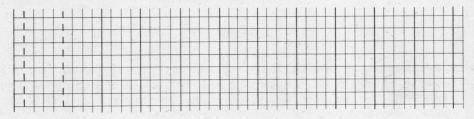

- - - - - - - - - - - - - - - - - - - -

```
01   SCHOOL-ENROLLMENT.
     02   ELEMENTARY          OCCURS 98 TIMES
                              INDEXED BY X-SCHOOL
                              ASCENDING KEY IS SCHOOL-NAME.
          03   SCHOOL-NAME    PIC  X(20).
          03   SCHOOL-POP     PIC  9(4).
```

33. A binary search is initiated by a SEARCH ALL statement, coded as in the format on the next page.

```
SEARCH ALL  table-name
     [AT END  statement]
     WHEN  condition
          statement.
```

As with the sequential SEARCH, the AT END clause is necessary if there is any chance the condition won't be met. Most programmers include it. In SEARCH ALL, the KEY variable must be included in the condition. Suppose the CODE-TABLE is searched for a code equal to IN-CODE.

```
SEARCH ALL CODE-NUMBER
     AT END MOVE 'Y' TO CODE-END
     WHEN CODE-NUMBER (X-CODE) = IN-CODE
          PERFORM MATCH-UP.
```

Code a statement to perform a binary search of the school enrollment table you defined in frame 32 to display the population of the school entered as "IN-SCHOOL".

```
SEARCH ALL ELEMENTARY
     AT END MOVE 'Y' TO SCHOOLS-OUT
     WHEN SCHOOL-NAME (X-SCHOOL) = IN-SCHOOL
          DISPLAY SCHOOL-POP (X-SCHOOL).
```

SUMMARY

In this chapter you have learned to describe one- and two-dimensional tables. You have learned to code values for a table in Working-Storage, as well as to load a table from an input file. You have seen how the familiar PERFORM and IF statements are used to process tables.

You have seen how indexing allows you to use SEARCH statements to perform a binary or sequential search of a one-dimensional table. The SEARCH greatly simplifies table processing. Like IF and PERFORM, SEARCH statements can be nested to handle two-dimensional tables. You will find more options of SEARCH and uses of indexing in the COBOL reference manual for your computer system.

SELF-TEST

After you have written your answers to the Self-Test, check your answers in the Answer Key that follows. Be sure you understand any differences between your answers and ours before you begin the next chapter. Following each suggested answer is a frame reference in parentheses, in case you need to review.

In this Self-Test you will write several related segments for a table-handling program.

1. Your program will use a table with 100 elements. Each element includes the item number (seven characters) and a one-digit sale code.

    (a) Describe the table.

    (b) Now assume the table will be in item-number sequence. Describe the table with a key and an index (X-ITEM).

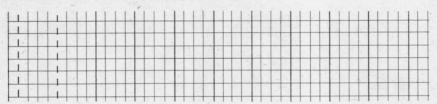

2. Your table will be created from a card file, which contains IN-NUMBER and IN-CODE. The main logic contains these statements:

```
PERFORM GET-TABLE-RECORD.
PERFORM LOAD-TABLE
     VARYING X-ITEM FROM 1 BY 1
     UNTIL X-ITEM > 100.
```

    Write the LOAD-TABLE paragraph to build the table you described in 1(b).

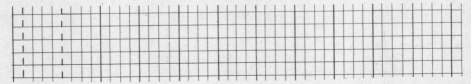

3. Another input file contains information on items ordered by customers. Each item ordered (ORDER-NUMBER) must be checked against the table. If the item number is in the table, ORDER-DISCOUNT is set to the item code for that table entry. If the item isn't in the file, ORDER-DISCOUNT is set to zero.

    Write statement(s) to do a sequential search of the file and set ORDER-DISCOUNT to the appropriate value.

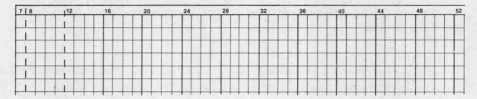

4. Suppose the program specifications have changed. Now if the item is in the table, you need to store the value of the index in ITEM-POSITION in addition to storing the code in ORDER-DISCOUNT. Write a statement to do this with a binary search.

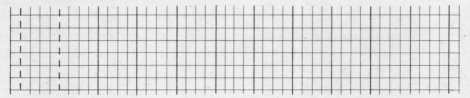

Answer Key

(You may have used different names in your coding.)

1. (a)
```
01  SALE-TABLE.
    02  SALE-ITEM OCCURS 100 TIMES.
        03  ITEM-NUMBER      PIC X(7).
        03  ITEM-SALE-CODE   PIC 9.          (9)
```

(b)
```
01  SALE-TABLE.
    02  SALE-ITEM OCCURS 100 TIMES
                INDEXED BY X-ITEM
                ASCENDING KEY IS ITEM-NUMBER.
        03  ITEM-NUMBER      PIC X(7).
        03  ITEM-SALE-CODE   PIC 9.      (26, 32)
```

2.
```
LOAD-TABLE.
    MOVE IN-NUMBER TO ITEM-NUMBER (X-ITEM).
    MOVE IN-CODE TO ITEM-SALE-CODE (X-ITEM).
    PERFORM GET-TABLE-RECORD.                (6)
```

3. SET X-ITEM TO 1.
    SEARCH SALE-ITEM
        AT END MOVE ZERO TO ORDER-DISCOUNT
        WHEN ORDER-NUMBER = ITEM-NUMBER (X-ITEM)
            MOVE ITEM-SALE-CODE (X-ITEM) TO ORDER-DISCOUNT.

    (You could have used PERFORM and varied X-ITEM.)   (28, 29)

4. SEARCH ALL SALE-ITEM
        AT END MOVE ZERO TO ORDER-DISCOUNT
        WHEN ORDER-NUMBER = ITEM-NUMBER (X-ITEM)
            MOVE ITEM-SALE-CODE (X-ITEM) TO ORDER-DISCOUNT
            SET ITEM-POSITION TO X-ITEM.   (33)

CHAPTER TWELVE
Random Access Files

So far in this book, we have discussed files on card, printer, magnetic tape, and disk. All these files are sequentially organized; they are created in a specific sequence and accessed only in that sequence.

In this chapter we will talk about some other ways files may be organized —all of which permit random access as well as access in the sequence the file was created. These files (which may be relative, direct, or indexed files) must all be stored on mass-storage devices, most commonly the disk. As in sequential disk files, records can be updated in place.

Random access allows accessing of any record, when its key value is known. It isn't necessary to read the preceding records in the file. If only 20 scattered records are needed from a file of 300 or 3000 records, random access is the only way to go. For example, all the records in a file of department store customers do not have transactions everyday—or even every month. And only a small percentage of college students change their names or majors every week.

In this chapter, we will first survey various types of files that permit random access. We shall see the advantages of each and compare the key requirements. Then we will examine one type, the Indexed Sequential Access Method (ISAM) file in detail. You'll learn to create, access, and update an ISAM file. You'll also learn the requirements for processing Virtual Storage Access Method (VSAM) files.

When you complete your study of this chapter, you will be able to:

- identify the type of key required for random access files;

- differentiate between relative and direct files;

- code a program to create an ISAM file;

- code statements to sequentially access and update records in an ISAM file;

- code statements to randomly access and update records in an ISAM file; and

- identify differences between statements needed for ISAM and VSAM files.

In all random access files, each record must be uniquely identified by some value within it or by its location. The system (or the access method) must have some way to make the connection between the key and the record. In this section, we'll see how this is done in the common types of random access files, and survey the particular strengths of each type.

TYPES OF RANDOM ACCESS FILES

1. Three general types of random access files are called relative, direct, and indexed. Records in a relative file are accessed according to when they are placed in the file. The relative position in the file becomes the key. The 48th record placed in the file is ever-afterward record number 48. Records in a direct file, on the other hand, have two-part keys. The first part gives the track number—this is assigned when the file is created. The system goes directly to that track and searches for the record identifier that makes up the second part of the key. In the third type, indexed files, the key is simply a record identifier, as you've used before, and every record has a unique one. The system maintains indexes, in which it looks up key locations as needed.

    (a) Which type of random access file requires you to give the location of a record for random access? _____

    (b) Which type of random access file requires you to know the sequence the file was created in? _____

    (c) Which type of random access file requires you to specify only the record identifier? _____

    (d) In which type of random access file can the desired record be accessed most directly? _____

- - - - - - - - - - - - - - - - - - - -

    (a) direct (You need the track number as part of key.)
    (b) relative
    (c) indexed
    (d) relative (No index or track is consulted.)

2. The key of a relative file is similar to a subscript of a table. Records can be accessed randomly, as the system goes directly to the area where the record is stored. Since the sequence numbers are all used, however, records cannot be inserted into a relative file. They can only be added to the end. Records can be accessed sequentially, but it isn't very useful in a relative file. The records are arranged by a time rather than by anything unique to the contents. To use random access, you must

figure out the positional key. Once the relative position of a record is known, random access of records in relative files is very efficient.

(a) Which would be easiest in a relative file—adding records, updating records, or deleting records? _____

(b) What does the key for a relative file consist of?

_____

- - - - - - - - - - - - - - - - - - - -

(a) updating records;   (b) the sequence number it was created with

3. Direct files are also efficient for random access, since the track address is part of the key. The system goes directly to the track, then searches the track for the particular record. Like relative files, direct files must be complete when they are created—records can't be inserted later, just added to the end. The track part of the key is derived mathematically when the file is created. For example, the record identifier might be divided by the number of tracks available, and the remainder used as the track indicator. The same formula would be used when the record is accessed randomly. Sequential access of records from a direct file is not very useful, since the assignment of records to tracks does not depend on the record itself.

(a) What are the two parts of a direct file key?

_____

(b) With direct files, how does the system go from the key to the desired record? _____

_____

(c) Why can't you add records into a direct file?

_____

- - - - - - - - - - - - - - - - - - - -

(a) Track identifier and record identifier.
(b) It goes directly to the track indicated, then searches for the record.
(c) The file must be complete when created.

4. There are two types of indexed files, commonly known as ISAM and VSAM. ISAM files use the Indexed Sequential Access Method, and they can be used on computer systems ranging from microcomputers to the IBM 370. VSAM files use the Virtual Storage Access Method, and are used primarily with very large, virtual storage systems. VSAM is part of the current ANS COBOL standard. Both types of indexed file use unique record identifiers embedded in records as keys, just as we used earlier

in sequential files. ISAM and VSAM are both created sequentially, but they can be accessed either sequentially or randomly. Sequential access of records in an indexed file is slower than sequential access of a sequential disk file. And random access of an indexed file is slower than random access of a relative or direct file. However, the ease of key specification and of adding records combine to make indexed files the most widely used type of random access files available today.

(a) Which are more efficient for random access, relative or indexed files?

   _____

(b) What is included in an indexed file key? _____

(c) How can indexed files be accessed? _____

(d) Name the two types of indexed files. _____

(e) To which type(s) of random access files can records be added?

   _____

- - - - - - - - - - - - - - - - - - -

(a) relative; (b) a record identifier; (c) sequentially or randomly;
(d) ISAM and VSAM; (e) indexed (ISAM and VSAM)

When random access files are created, the system allocates space, builds tables or indexes, and stores the records. Control of that process is beyond the scope of this book. The COBOL manual for an installation can give you the organizational details. We will show you only how to use the files.

We will discuss ISAM file programming in some detail, since most COBOL compilers permit this type of indexed file. We will also cover the major differences between ISAM and VSAM processing. We won't cover the organization of ISAM and VSAM files. Beginning programmers seldom need this information. The COBOL reference manuals for any computer system will include organizational details about the indexed files supported.

ISAM FILES

5.   ISAM files have embedded keys—from 1 to 255 bytes long. When an ISAM file is created, the records must be arranged so that these keys are in ascending sequential order. The first byte of the record must not contain the key; that byte must be reserved for a special delete code called a flag. We'll look at the delete feature in the next frame. The unique identifier within the record becomes known to the COBOL compiler as the RECORD KEY.

   (a) Which record description on the next page could describe records in an ISAM File?

```
_____  01  REC-DATA.
            02  REC-NUMBER      PIC  9(7).
            02  REC-INFO        PIC  X(83).
            02  REC-DELETE      PIC  X.


_____  01  REC-DATA.
            02  REC-INFO        PIC  X(83).
            02  REC-NUMBER      PIC  9(7).
            02  REC-MORE        PIC  X(10).


_____  01  REC-DATA.
            02  REC-DELETE      PIC  X.
            02  REC-INFO        PIC  X(83).
            02  REC-NUMBER      PIC  9(7).
            02  REC-MORE        PIC  X(10).
```

(b) In what sequence would the keys below be arranged for creating an
ISAM file?

    17   28   12   16   42

_____

(c) In question (a) above, what would be the name of the RECORD KEY?

_____

- - - - - - - - - - - - - - - - - - -

(a) the third (others have no delete flag position); (b) ascending (12, 16,
17, 28, 42); (c) REC-NUMBER

6. The first position in an ISAM file record is reserved for a "delete flag."
When the record is to be deleted, a special value, called HIGH-VALUES,
is placed in the delete-field. This value is the highest possible hexadeci-
mal value (FF)—even higher than 9! The system recognizes this signal
and doesn't read the record under certain conditions. When records are
first placed in an ISAM file, this delete flag must be initialized to something besides HIGH-VALUES. Most programmers use LOW-VALUES.
(HIGH-VALUES and LOW-VALUES are figurative constants.)

    When we want to delete a record from an ISAM file we actually update
the record by moving HIGH-VALUES to the delete-flag field. Sequential
access will ignore the record, although it can still be accessed randomly,
as you'll see. The record can be eliminated from the file when it is reorganized.

(a) Where in an ISAM record is the delete-flag location?

_____

(b) What is the effect of having HIGH-VALUES in the delete-flag field?

_____

(c) What value is generally used to initialize the delete-flag position?

_____

(d) Can records be accessed from an ISAM file after they are deleted?

_____

- - - - - - - - - - - - - - - - - - - -

(a) first character; (b) marks it as deleted—it will be ignored on sequential access; (c) figurative constant LOW-VALUES; (d) yes—randomly

7. A COBOL program to create an ISAM file has certain requirements beyond those for sequential files. In the Environment Division, the ASSIGN clause specifies the installation standard. In the form we've been using, that means DA-I-ddname. The "I" stands for indexed. A RECORD KEY clause must be included as well, and an ACCESS clause may be included. Here is an example:

```
SELECT ISFILE
    ASSIGN TO DA-I-CUSTS
    ACCESS IS SEQUENTIAL
    RECORD KEY IS CUST-NUMBER.
```

SEQUENTIAL is the default access method, so the ACCESS clause can be omitted. The RECORD KEY clause names the field in each record by which they are sequenced.

Suppose you are going to create an ISAM file named STUDENTS, with system name DA-I-STU1980. The records are organized by SOCIAL-SECURITY number. Write an Environment Division entry for this file.

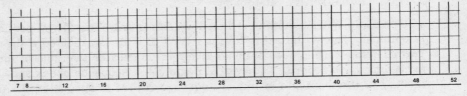

- - - - - - - - - - - - - - - - - - -

```
SELECT STUDENTS
    ASSIGN TO DA-I-STU1980
    ACCESS IS SEQUENTIAL
    RECORD KEY IS SOCIAL-SECURITY.
```

8. An ISAM file generally has standard labels. Blocking is permitted, and it results in faster sequential access. Blocking doesn't help with random access, though, since it is unlikely two randomly accessed records would be in the same block.

The FD entry for creation of an ISAM file is no different from that for a sequential disk file. When it is created, an ISAM file is opened as OUTPUT—again no different from sequential disk.

(a) Suppose the records in STUDENTS are blocked by four. The record is described as STU-RECORD. Write an FD entry to be used when creating the ISAM file.

(b) Write a statement to open the file for ISAM creation.

```
(a)  FD  STUDENTS
         BLOCK CONTAINS 4 RECORDS
         DATA RECORD IS STU-RECORD
         LABEL RECORDS ARE STANDARD.
(b)  OPEN OUTPUT STUDENTS.
```

9. The output statement (WRITE) for creating an ISAM file includes a new clause—INVALID KEY.

> WRITE record-name [FROM identifier]
>   INVALID KEY statement

The basic WRITE statement functions as always. The FROM portion is optional. The statement following INVALID KEY is executed if the record being written does not have a key value greater than that of the preceding valid record. The system performs a sequence check and alerts you if a duplicate or out-of-sequence record is encountered. An appropriate INVALID KEY action might be to print a message and get the next input record. When the INVALID KEY clause is activated, no record is written. The action after INVALID KEY generally makes a record of data not written to the ISAM file.

Suppose records to be put in the ISAM file STUDENTS have the keys below.

1. 191392073
2. 376401945
3. 298123012
4. 376401945
5. 378401822

(a) Which ones will activate the INVALID KEY clause? _____

(b) Write a statement to put a record in the ISAM file, and execute OUT-OF-SEQUENCE if any are invalid.

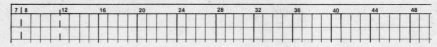

- - - - - - - - - - - - - - - - - - -

(a) numbers 3 and 4

(b) ```
WRITE STU-RECORD
     INVALID KEY PERFORM OUT-OF-SEQUENCE.
```

10. Figure 12-1 below shows the first three divisions of a program to create an ISAM file. Notice that the ISAM record has the first byte set aside for the delete flag. The SOCIAL-SECURITY field is the RECORD KEY. We will build the ISAM record in Working-Storage, so we can use a VALUE clause to initialize the delete-flag field.

```
IDENTIFICATION DIVISION.
PROGRAM-ID.
     LOADISAM.
ENVIRONMENT DIVISION.
INPUT-OUTPUT SECTION.
FILE-CONTROL.
     SELECT SEQSTUDENT
          ASSIGN TO DA-S-INDISK.
     SELECT STUDENTS
          ASSIGN TO DA-I-INDEXDSK
          ACCESS IS SEQUENTIAL
          RECORD KEY IS SOCIAL-SECURITY.
DATA DIVISION.
FILE SECTION.
FD   SEQSTUDENT
     LABEL RECORDS ARE STANDARD.
01   SEQ-RECORD.
     02   SEQ-SSNO            PIC X(9).
     02   FILLER             PIC X(51).
FD   STUDENTS
     LABEL RECORDS ARE STANDARD.
01   ISAM-RECORD.
     02   STU-DELETE          PIC X.
     02   SOCIAL-SECURITY     PIC X(9).
     02   FILLER             PIC X(51).
     02   FILLER             PIC X(19).
WORKING-STORAGE SECTION.
01   SEQ-EOF-SWITCH          PIC X        VALUE 'N'.
01   WS-RECORD.
     02   WS-DELETE           PIC X        VALUE LOW-VALUES.
     02   WS-BODY.
          03   WS-SSNO         PIC X(9).
          03   FILLER          PIC X(51).
     02   FILLER             PIC X(19)    VALUE SPACES.
```

Figure 12-1
```

The pseudocode below represents the Procedure Division of a program to create an ISAM file. Notice that we'll simply display out of sequence records.

Main-logic.
      Get input record
      PERFORM UNTIL no more records
            build ISAM file
      ENDPERFORM
      Terminate program

Build ISAM file
      Construct record
      Put record in ISAM file
      IF   record in sequence
            put in ISAM file
      ELSE
            display out of sequence record.
      ENDIF
      Get input record

Write a structured COBOL Procedure Division to create the file.

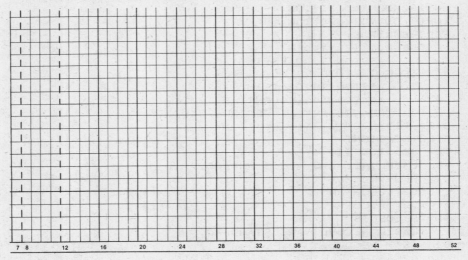

```
PROCEDURE DIVISION.
MAIN-LOGIC.
    OPEN INPUT SEQSTUDENT
        OUTPUT STUDENTS.
    PERFORM GET-INPUT.
    PERFORM BUILD-ISAM-FILE
        UNTIL SEQ-EOF-SWITCH = 'Y'.
    CLOSE SEQSTUDENT, STUDENTS.
    STOP RUN.
```

(continued on the next page)

```
BUILD-ISAM-FILE.
    MOVE WS-RECORD TO ISAM-RECORD.
    WRITE ISAM-RECORD
        INVALID KEY DISPLAY WS-BODY.
    PERFORM GET-INPUT.
GET-INPUT.
    READ SEQSTUDENT INTO WS-BODY
        AT END MOVE 'Y' TO SEQ-EOF-SWITCH.
```

11. After an ISAM file is created, you can open it as INPUT (for read only) or as I-O (for update). You can retrieve records with a READ statement. When access is sequential, you use an AT END clause, as with sequentially organized files. The sequential access procedure is identical to that for a sequential file. During sequential access, any records already containing a delete flag (hex FF) in the first byte are not retrieved.

   (a) Suppose you are sequentially accessing records in an ISAM file that contains 3000 records? How many records will you read if your

   transaction file contains 600 records? _____

   (b) What will be involved in end-of-file processing if the transaction file

   ends first? _____

- - - - - - - - - - - - - - - - - - -

   (a) 3000 (approximately); (b) close files—no more processing must be done

12. Sequential update of an ISAM file is also similar to the updating of sequential files. You open the file as I-O. You use AT END with READ. But when you replace the ISAM record in the file, you use the INVALID KEY option in the WRITE statement just as when the file was created. But now the INVALID KEY statement is activated only if no record was read with the key of the record you are trying to write. If one was read, the WRITE puts the changed version in the same location in ISAM file. Records cannot be added to the ISAM file sequentially (only randomly). Records can be marked for deletion, however, as part of an update procedure. To delete a record, you set the first byte to HIGH-VALUES.

   (a) In sequential update of ISAM files, which I/O statement uses

   INVALID KEY? _____

   (b) Under what conditions is the INVALID KEY option activated?

   _____

   (c) Write a statement to mark STU-RECORD for deletion.

```
| | | | | | | | | | | | | | | | | | | | | | | | | | | | | | | | | | | | | | | | | | | | |
  7 8    12    16    20    24    28    32    36    40    44    48
```

- - - - - - - - - - - - - - - - - - -

(a) WRITE

(b) no record was read with that key

(c) MOVE HIGH-VALUES TO STU-DELETE.

RANDOM ACCESS OF ISAM RECORDS

13. Before the system can access a record randomly, you have to tell it which record you want. The system will take the source key you provide and find the record with a matching RECORD KEY. Recall that the RECORD KEY must be embedded in the ISAM record. The source key must be located in Working-Storage. Some compilers call the source key a NOMINAL KEY, others call it a SYMBOLIC KEY; they are used identically. We'll use NOMINAL KEY because it's more widespread.

   The NOMINAL KEY clause is coded in addition to the RECORD KEY clause in the Environment Division. The key of the record you want to access must be placed in this source-key variable before you attempt to read the record.

   (a) Write RECORD KEY and NOMINAL KEY clauses for an ISAM file. The ISAM record contains PART-NUMBER, and the Working-Storage Section contains ITEM-CODE.

   (b) A transaction record contains an item called IN-ITEM. Write a statement that will put the transaction record value in the NOMINAL KEY field.

- -

   (a) RECORD KEY IS PART-NUMBER
   NOMINAL KEY IS ITEM-CODE
   (SYMBOLIC KEY IS ITEM-CODE would be used for some computer systems.)

   (b) MOVE IN-ITEM TO ITEM-CODE.

14. When records are accessed randomly from an ISAM file, we won't reach the end of the file but will go directly to each record. Therefore, we won't use the AT END clause in the READ statement. Instead, we use the INVALID KEY clause in each READ for random access. The INVALID KEY option is written the same in both READ and WRITE. When used with READ, however, it is activated when no RECORD KEY in the ISAM file matches the current value of the NOMINAL KEY (or SYMBOLIC KEY).

The pseudocode below reflects a program segment that randomly accesses records from ISAMFILE and displays each requested ISAM-RECORD. If a record isn't in the file, the transaction number (IN-ITEM) is displayed with the message NOT IN FILE. The ISAM file is the one you wrote entries for in frame 13.

```
Main-logic
     Get record
     PERFORM UNTIL  no more transactions
          Get-info
     ENDPERFORM
     Print ending message
Get-info
     set key
     get ISAM record
     IF    not in file
          display message
     ELSE
          display ISAM record
     ENDIF
     get transaction record
```

Here is some of the COBOL coding for the main-logic paragraph.

```
PERFORM GET-TRANS.
PERFORM GET-INFO
     UNTIL TRANS-EOF = 'Y'.
DISPLAY 'ALL TRANS LISTED'.
```

Write a structured COBOL GET-INFO paragraph.

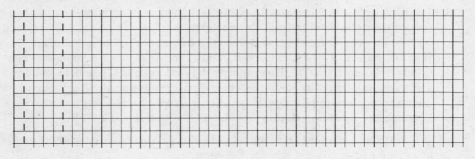

- - - - - - - - - - - - - - - - - - - -

```
GET-INFO.
    MOVE IN-ITEM TO ITEM-CODE.
    READ ISAMFILE
        INVALID KEY MOVE 'Y' TO NOT-IN-FILE.
    IF NOT-IN-FILE = 'Y'
        DISPLAY IN-ITEM, 'NOT IN FILE'
        MOVE 'N' TO NOT-IN-FILE
    ELSE
        DISPLAY ISAM-RECORD.
    PERFORM GET-TRANS.
```

15. ISAM files can be processed randomly for record retrieval as you saw in frame 14. They can also be processed randomly for adding records and for updating records, which includes deletion. Updating records involves setting the source key, reading the record, making changes, and rewriting the record. The REWRITE statement is very similar to the WRITE—you may use the FROM option, and you must use INVALID KEY option. The record will be rewritten over the record whose record key matches the source key. You must be careful not to change that value. The INVALID KEY option on REWRITE is activated if the record does not exist in the file. But if the INVALID KEY clause on the READ wasn't activated, this won't be a problem.

Suppose the ELSE clause in frame 14 were written as ELSE PERFORM UPDATE-ISAM. Write the update paragraph to change IS-ADDRESS to IN-ADDRESS and put the updated record back into the ISAM file.

- - - - - - - - - - - - - - - - - -

```
UPDATE-ISAM.
    MOVE IN-ADDRESS TO IS-ADDRESS.
    REWRITE ISAM-RECORD
        INVALID KEY DISPLAY 'PROBLEM ON REWRITE', IN-ITEM.
```

16. Deleting records from an ISAM file is actually an update—you set the delete flag (the first byte of the record) to HIGH-VALUES. As we said earlier, records marked as deleted aren't accessed sequentially. They may be still in the file, however, and if so, they can be accessed randomly! When an ISAM file contains deleted records, random access will get them any time the keys match. A good programming technique is to check the delete byte value after each record is randomly accessed. Suppose the first position in ISAM-RECORD is IS-DELETE.

(a) Write a statement to mark the ISAM-RECORD indicated by the current value of the source key for deletion.

(b) Suppose your random update routine includes GET-ISAM as a separate paragraph. Write GET-ISAM including a check to see if the record is deleted as well as a check to know if the record is found. PERFORM DELETE-MARK, or NOT-FOUND, as appropriate. Use the form on the following page.

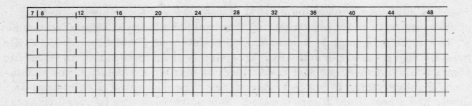

```
(a)  MOVE HIGH-VALUES TO IS-DELETE.
(b)  GET-ISAM.
         READ ISAMFILE
             INVALID KEY PERFORM NOT-FOUND.
         IF IS-DELETE = HIGH-VALUES
             PERFORM DELETE-MARK.
```

17. When we want to add records to an ISAM file, we use the WRITE state-
    ment with the INVALID KEY option, after setting the source-key value
    to the key of the new record. The INVALID KEY option is activated if
    that key already exists in the file. Suppose you have constructed WS-
    ISAM-RECORD to be added to ISAMFILE. You have already put IN-ITEM
    into ITEM-CODE, which is the NOMINAL KEY. Write a statement to add
    the record as ISAM-RECORD. If there already is a record with that key,
    execute paragraph DUPLICATE-KEY.

```
WRITE ISAM-RECORD FROM WS-ISAM-RECORD
     INVALID KEY PERFORM DUPLICATE-KEY.
```

18. You have seen that the INVALID KEY clause is activated under different
    conditions in different statements. Match the statements indicated below
    with the condition that activates the INVALID KEY clause.

    _____ (a) WRITE (create ISAM file)   1. record not in file
                                             2. record is in file
    _____ (b) WRITE (add record)   3. record out of key sequence

    _____ (c) REWRITE (update)

    _____ (d) REWRITE (delete)

    _____ (e) READ (read only)

    _____ (f) READ (update)

    (a) 3; (b) 2; (c) 1; (d) 1; (e) 1; (f) 1

You have seen the common ISAM statements and techniques. There is, of course, more to ISAM programming than you have learned here. You can now write simple programs to create and/or maintain an ISAM file. An ISAM file must be reorganized periodically. This simply involves reading an ISAM file sequentially onto a sequential disk. Records marked for deletion are eliminated, and everything is put in key sequence. The sequential disk is used as input, and a new ISAM file is created. Now no records are in overflow areas, and both sequential and random access are more efficient. Also the sequential disk provides a backup copy of the file, which can be used if necessary. Most computer installations provide standard programs for ISAM file reorganization.

COBOL CODING: ISAM/VSAM

Now let's look briefly at the COBOL coding differences between ISAM and VSAM files.

Environment Division for VSAM

19. In the File Control paragraph, ISAM files require SELECT and ASSIGN clauses. The ACCESS clause must specify RANDOM for random access, and may be used for the default, SEQUENTIAL. The RECORD KEY clause is always required. The NOMINAL KEY (or SYMBOLIC KEY) clause is needed for random access. VSAM files also require SELECT, ASSIGN, and RECORD KEY. A new clause, ORGANIZATION INDEXED, is required in the SELECT entry as well. VSAM has three ACCESS options: RANDOM, SEQUENTIAL and DYNAMIC—dynamic access uses both sequential and random in the same program. VSAM files can also specify two optional clauses—PASSWORD and STATUS. The password is used with protected files. STATUS is a two-character data item that holds a code indicating whether or not an I/O statement finished successfully—whether a record was read or written. The error status codes and their use are beyond the scope of this book.

   Identify whether each clause below is used with ISAM files, VSAM files, or both.

   _____ (a) SELECT   _____ (f) NOMINAL KEY

   _____ (b) ASSIGN   _____ (g) PASSWORD

   _____ (c) ACCESS   _____ (h) STATUS

   _____ (d) ORGANIZATION   _____ (i) SYMBOLIC KEY

   _____ (e) RECORD KEY

- - - - - - - - - - - - - - - - - - - -

   Both: a, b, c, e; ISAM: f, i; VSAM: d, g, h

Data Division for VSAM

20. Records in an ISAM file may be blocked; the FD entry may include the BLOCK CONTAINS clause. While VSAM records may be blocked, the system takes care of the blocking, so VSAM FD entries may not include the BLOCK CONTAINS clause. The ISAM record has a delete code in the first position. VSAM records do not include a delete code—the records are deleted directly rather than marked for deletion. As in ISAM records, the VSAM RECORD KEY must be embedded in the record.

Identify whether each of the following would apply to ISAM, VSAM, or neither type of file.

_____ (a) BLOCK CONTAINS 4 RECORDS

_____ (b) delete flag in first byte

_____ (c) no BLOCK CONTAINS clause

- -

(a) ISAM; (b) ISAM; (c) VSAM

21. Sequential access of records from a VSAM file is very similar to that from an ISAM file. The Procedure Division coding for creating the files is identical. Sequential update for both files involves using a READ with the AT END clause. Where ISAM uses a WRITE statement, however, VSAM uses REWRITE. Both use the INVALID KEY clause, which is activated if a previous READ wasn't successfully executed. Random access and adding records to ISAM files require that you set the NOMINAL or SYMBOLIC KEY to the value of the RECORD KEY you wish to access or add. In VSAM files, you set the RECORD KEY itself before issuing a READ or adding a record. Identify which statement would be used to perform each operation below for a VSAM file:

(a) Create a VSAM file. _____

(b) Put an updated record back into the VSAM file (sequentially).

_____

(c) Put an updated record back into the VSAM file (randomly).

_____

(d) Indicate the record to be added to the VSAM file.

_____

- -

(a) WRITE with INVALID KEY.
(b) REWRITE with INVALID KEY.
(c) REWRITE with INVALID KEY.
(d) MOVE value to RECORD KEY.

In some computer systems, VSAM files, and occasionally even ISAM, may require error status checking after I/O operations. A special indicator is automatically set with values after each input or output operation. The value may indicate a successful operation or the type of error that occurred. Before you actually run a program to create or use any random access file, be sure you scan the reference manual for your system to see if status checking is required. You will also be able to determine whether your COBOL compiler uses a NOMINAL or a SYMBOLIC key for ISAM files.

SUMMARY

In this chapter we have presented an overview of the features and advantages of the three general types of random access files: direct, relative, and indexed. We discussed coding for one type of indexed file (ISAM) in detail, then saw how coding for VSAM files is similar. In the Summary Exercise, you will write segments of a program that uses random access to update an ISAM file.

Summary Exercise

22. Write the first COBOL division for a program named SUMMARY. Include at least one optional paragraph.

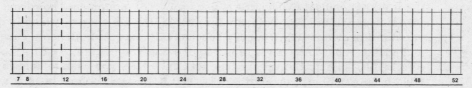

```
IDENTIFICATION DIVISION.
PROGRAM-ID.
    SUMMARY.
AUTHOR.
    RUTH ASHLEY.
```

(You may have used another optional paragraph.)

23. Your program will use the three files and data described in the Data Division in Figure 12-2 on the next page. Part of the Environment Division of the COBOL program follows this figure.

```
DATA DIVISION.
FILE SECTION.
FD  UPDATE-INFO
    LABEL RECORDS ARE OMITTED.
01  UPDATE-RECORD.
    02  TRANSACTION-CODE            PIC 9.
    02  CARD-NUMBER                 PIC 9(6).
    02  NEW-NAME                    PIC X(22).
    02  NEW-ADDRESS                 PIC X(30).
    02  NEW-YEAR                    PIC XX.
    02  NEW-MAX-CREDIT              PIC 9(4)V99.
    02  FILLER                      PIC X(4).
    02  UPDATE-ACTION               PIC 9(4)V99.
    02  FILLER                      PIC X(3).
FD  ERROR-FILE
    LABEL RECORDS ARE OMITTED.
01  ERROR-LIST                      PIC X(133).
FD  INDEXED-FILE
    BLOCK CONTAINS 5 RECORDS
    LABEL RECORDS ARE STANDARD.
01  ISAM-RECORD.
    02  DELETE-FLAG                 PIC 9.
    02  PERSONAL.
        03  ISAM-NAME               PIC X(22).
        03  ISAM-NUMBER             PIC 9(6).
        03  ISAM-ADDRESS            PIC X(30).
    02  HISTORY.
        03  ISAM-YR-OPEN            PIC XX.
        03  ISAM-MAXIM              PIC 9(4)V99.
        03  ISAM-MAX-BILL           PIC 9(4)V99.
        03  ISAM-BALANCE-DUE        PIC 9(4)V99.
        03  ISAM-PAYCODE            PIC 9.
WORKING-STORAGE SECTION.
01  INFO-EOF                        PIC X    VALUE 'N'.
01  NOM-KEY                         PIC 9(6).
01  AMOUNT                          PIC 9(4)V99.
01  LISTING.
    02  CARRIAGE                    PIC X.
    02  PROBLEM                     PIC X(80).
    02  E-MESSAGE                   PIC X(52).
```

Figure 12-2

```
ENVIRONMENT DIVISION.
INPUT-OUTPUT SECTION.
FILE-CONTROL.
    SELECT UPDATE-INFO      ASSIGN TO UR-S-CARD1.
    SELECT ERROR-FILE       ASSIGN TO UR-S-PRINT2.
```

Using the information in Figure 12-2 and the partial program above, code the Environment Division entry needed for the ISAM file. We'll be updating it randomly. (A form for your use follows on the next page.)

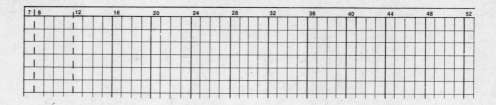

```
    SELECT INDEXED-FILE
        ASSIGN TO DA-I-MASTER3
        RECORD KEY IS ISAM-NUMBER
        NOMINAL KEY IS NOM-KEY
        ACCESS IS RANDOM.
```

(You may have used a different system name, but you should have used these key fields.)

24. This program will be a random update of an ISAM file. The transaction-code in the update record has a value of 1 through 3—where 1 indicates a record to be added to the file, 2 a charge to be added to the balance, and 3 a credit to be subtracted from the balance. A case structure is used to handle the transactions.

A detailed pseudocode is included as Figure 12-3, which begins on the next page. Use it with the Data Division in Figure 12-2 as you write parts of the Procedure Division. The main-logic coding is given below. First code the CASE-UPDATE paragraph, using the form on page 262.

```
    PROCEDURE DIVISION.
    MAIN-LOGIC.
        OPEN INPUT UPDATE-INFO
            OUTPUT ERROR-FILE
            I-O INDEXED-FILE.
        PERFORM GET-UPDATE-INFO.
        PERFORM PROCESS-UPDATES
            UNTIL INFO-EOF = 'Y'.
        DISPLAY 'NORMAL ENDING'.
        CLOSE UPDATE-INFO
            ERROR-FILE
            INDEXED-FILE.
        STOP RUN.
    PROCESS-UPDATES.
        PERFORM CASE-UPDATE THRU CASE-EXIT.
        PERFORM GET-UPDATE-INFO.
    PUT-PROBLEM-RECORD.
        MOVE UPDATE-RECORD TO PROBLEM.
        WRITE ERROR-LIST FROM LISTING.
```

Main-logic.
Open files
Get update info
PERFORM UNTIL no more updates
　　Process updates
ENDPERFORM
Print 'NORMAL ENDING'
Close files
End program

Process-updates
PERFORM case-update
Get update info

CASE:　 Update
Case1:　Add record
Case2:　Add charge
Case3:　Subtract credit

ENDCASE

Add record
Set up ISAM record
IF　 Key valid
　　Put record in ISAM file
ELSE
　　Move 'DUPLICATE KEY' to output record
　　Put output record
ENDIF

Add Charge
Get ISAM record
IF　 not in file
　　put 'NOT IN FILE' in output record
　　put output record
　　branch to endcase
ELSE
ENDIF
Put UPDATE-ACTION in AMOUNT
Add AMOUNT to balance due
IF　 balance due > max bill
　　move balance due to max bill
ELSE
ENDIF
IF　 max bill NOT < MAXIM
　　put 'VERIFY CREDIT STANDING' in output record
　　put output record
ELSE
ENDIF

(continued on the next page)

(continued from page 261)

        Put ISAM record back in file.
        IF   key not valid
            put 'CHARGE-INVALID KEY' in output record
            put output record
        ELSE
        ENDIF

    Subtract Credit
        Get ISAM record
        IF   not in file
            put 'NOT IN FILE' in output record
            put output record
            branch to endcase
        ELSE
        ENDIF
        Subtract action from balance due
        Put ISAM record back in file
        IF   key not valid
            put 'CREDIT-INVALID KEY' in output record
            put output record
        ELSE
        ENDIF

Figure 12-3

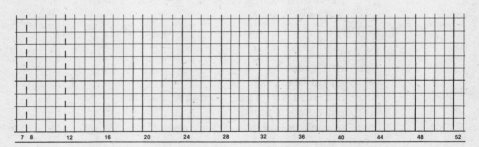

```
CASE-UPDATE.
    GO TO ADD-RECORD
         ADD-CHARGE
         SUBTRACT-CREDIT
      DEPENDING ON TRANSACTION-CODE.
    MOVE 'INCORRECT CODE' TO E-MESSAGE.
    PERFORM PUT-PROBLEM-RECORD.
    GO TO CASE-EXIT.
```

25. Consider the paragraphs referenced in the CASE-UPDATE paragraph. Code any ISAM file I/O statements you would need in the ADD-RECORD paragraph.

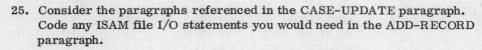

- - - - - - - - - - - - - - - - - -

```
WRITE ISAM-RECORD
     INVALID KEY MOVE 'DUPLICATE KEY' TO E-MESSAGE
        PERFORM PUT-PROBLEM-RECORD.
```

26. The paragraphs ADD-CHARGE and SUBTRACT-CREDIT will contain (or reference) similar I/O statements for the ISAM file. Code the statements for the ADD-CHARGE paragraph.

- - - - - - - - - - - - - - - - - -

```
READ INDEXED-FILE
     INVALID KEY MOVE 'NOT IN FILE' TO E-MESSAGE
                   PERFORM PUT-PROBLEM-RECORD
                   GO TO CASE-EXIT.
     :
     :
REWRITE ISAM-RECORD
     INVALID KEY MOVE 'CHARGE-INVALID KEY' TO E-MESSAGE
                PERFORM PUT-PROBLEM-RECORD.
```

27. Now code the GET-UPDATE-INFO paragraph. Be sure to set the NOMINAL key.

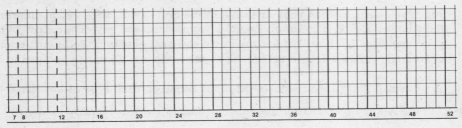

- - - - - - - - - - - - - - - - - -

```
GET-UPDATE-INFO.
    READ UPDATE-INFO
        AT END MOVE 'Y' TO INFO-EOF.
    MOVE CARD-NUMBER TO NOM-KEY.
```

Various compilers implement ISAM, VSAM and other direct files somewhat differently. If you have an opportunity to use what you have learned here,
be sure to review the COBOL reference manual for the computer installation.

In this chapter, we've looked at the three general types of random access
file: relative, direct, and indexed files. We've discussed key requirements
for all three file types. The indexed sequential access method (ISAM) type of
indexed random access file was covered in detail, including techniques and
statements needed for coding complete COBOL programs to create and use
such files.

SELF-TEST

After you have written your answers to the Self-Test, check your answers in
the Answer Key that follows. Be sure you understand any differences between
your answers and ours before you begin the next chapter. Following each suggested answer is a frame reference in parentheses, in case you need to review.

1. Identify the random access file that requires each type of key given below.

    (a) A key embedded in the record, that is used to identify it.

    _____

    (b) A value that corresponds to the position of the record relative to the
    first record in the file. _____

    (c) A two-part key, including both location and record identification.

    _____

2. Which type of random access file permits quickest direct access?

    _____

3. How can you tell if an ISAM record has been deleted?

    _____

4. Code Environment Division clauses to set up the following for an ISAM
    file:

    (a) Direct access of records

(b) A value ISAM-KEY in the data record that will be unique in each.

```
 7 8    12      16      20      24      28      32      36      40      44      48
 |       |
 |       |
```

(c) A value WS-IDENT in the Working-Storage Section that will be set to the value of the record you want.

```
 |    |       |
 |    |       |
 |            |
```

5. When an ISAM file is being created, what conditions activate the INVALID KEY clause? _____

6. Under what conditions do you use REWRITE in reference to ISAM files?

   _____

7. What condition activates the INVALID KEY clause on READ?

   _____

8. (a) What I/O statement(s) and clause(s) are needed to delete a record randomly from an ISAM file?

      _____

      _____

   (b) How would you delete the record?

      _____

   (c) How could you access that record later if you needed it?

      _____

9. Name two Environment Division entries that are different for a VSAM file than for an ISAM file? _____

   _____

10. How do you delete a record from a VSAM file? _____

   _____

Answer Key

1. (a) indexed file (ISAM and VSAM)   (4)
    (b) relative file   (2)
    (c) direct file   (3)

2. relative file   (4)

3. the first position contains HIGH-VALUES   (6)

4. (a) `ACCESS IS RANDOM`   (7)
   (b) `RECORD KEY IS ISAM-KEY`   (7)
   (c) `NOMINAL KEY IS WS-IDENT` or
       `SYMBOLIC KEY IS WS-IDENT`   (13)

5. a duplicate or out-of-sequence key   (9)

6. updating randomly   (15)

7. the record desired isn't in the file   (14)

8. (a) READ with INVALID KEY   (14)
       REWRITE with INVALID KEY   (15)
   (b) move HIGH-VALUES to the delete flag   (16)
   (c) randomly   (16)

9. any two: ORGANIZATION INDEXED
       ACCESS IS DYNAMIC
       PASSWORD (optional)
       STATUS (optional)   (19)

10. use a DELETE statement; set RECORD KEY to value   (21)

CHAPTER THIRTEEN
Running COBOL Programs

In this book, you have learned to write fairly complex structured COBOL programs. This chapter will give you some techniques and guidelines that will help you run your programs. We can't help you with the control language for any particular computer system, but we can give you an overview of some techniques for running and testing programs. COBOL provides some statements to help you, and every COBOL compiler will give you some feedback on your statements.

When you complete this chapter you will be able to:

- interpret common COBOL compiler diagnostics;

- create test data for a COBOL program;

- suggest ways of ensuring that program logic is correct;

- code COBOL TRACE and EXHIBIT statements to aid in program testing; and

- incorporate debugging mode into a COBOL program.

CORRECTING PROGRAMS

Between a program written on coding sheets and a successfully running program are many steps—and much frustration for the programmer. First the program is keyed onto cards, disk, or terminal. Then it must be compiled, or translated into machine language. This can only be done if the program adheres to the rules of the COBOL language. It is linkage-edited, then run with sample data until consistently good results are obtained. You get to fix your program at three major points—but you need to backtrack every time you correct an error.

Figure 13-1, on the next page, shows the process. At point 1 we check for typos or careless errors. At point 2, the computer gives us compiler diagnostics to help locate and correct errors. Point 3 is the hardest—the test plan and the program structure affect the difficulty encountered here. We'll be dealing with all three, in sequence, in this chapter.

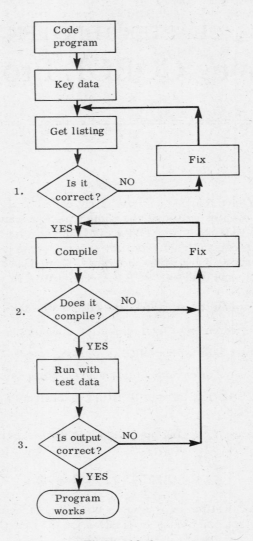

Figure 13-1

Before Compilation

1. After a program is coded, it is generally punched onto cards or entered on a terminal. It's a good idea to "desk-check" a listing of the cards or terminal entries before you submit it to the computer for compilation. Check for periods, correct spellings, and correct data-name usage. Be sure every paragraph you PERFORM is actually coded in the program. Trace the IF logic to verify it. And, of course, pick up data entry errors such as typographical errors or omitted lines of code. If you have adhered to structure conventions, desk-checking should be relatively easy.

For practice, assume the coding below is part of a card listing. Desk-check it and mark any errors.

```
FD   IDENTIFICATION
     LABLE RECORDS ARE STANDARD.
     BLOCK CONTAINS 12 RECORDS.
01   ID-RECORD
02   ID-NUMBR                    PIC 9(8)
02   ID-CODE                     PIC X(7)
02   FILLER.
WORKING STORAGE SECTION.
01   EOF/SWITCH                  PIC N.
```

- - - - - - - - - - - - - - - - - - -

These errors are included:

       IDENTIFICATION is a reserved word.
       LABEL is spelled wrong; this clause must not have a period
       01 level must have a period
       02 levels must begin in area B
       02 levels must end with periods
       FILLER needs a PIC clause
       WORKING-STORAGE needs a hyphen
       / is not a valid character in a name
       N is not a valid picture character

2. The more errors you correct before you first submit a program, the easier the whole process will be. Another technique for early detection and correction of errors is the structured walkthrough. The walkthrough involves sitting down with one or more other people and verbally walking through the problem and the program you have created to solve it. Actually, a walkthrough is often held at the design stage—when a structure chart or pseudocode has been developed. The people concerned determine that the design reflects a valid solution. After the program is written, another walkthrough helps to ensure that the program carries out the intent of the design. The walkthrough is more concerned with the logic of the program than with the syntax of COBOL.

(a) How could you do a walkthrough of a program by yourself?

    _____

    _____

(b) What precompilation technique identifies COBOL syntax errors?

    _____

(c) What precompilation technique identifies program logic entries?

    _____

- - - - - - - - - - - - - - - - - - - -

(a) There are a number of possibilities; you might explain the program to yourself or you might trace sample data all the way through the program.

(b) Desk-checking

(c) Walkthrough

Compilation

After precompilation corrections are made, the program is ready to be submitted to a COBOL compiler. Every manufacturer's compiler is slightly different. You will need to find out the specific control cards or entries for the compiler and system you will be using.

A compiler run produces output—a compiler listing of your COBOL program with errors identified. Other information may be included as well, but we'll focus here on the types of errors identified by the compiler.

3. A compiler listing identifies statements that include errors—or what it thinks are errors—by line numbers. Every compiler has a reference manual that details the possible diagnostic messages and gives likely causes. Most of these diagnostic messages are self-explanatory, however.

Line numbering is one reason structured COBOL uses only one COBOL verb per line. If an IF were coded entirely on one line, a diagnostic message on that line could refer to any of its parts. When the condition and action(s) are on separate lines, they can be indicated separately by the compiler.

Each COBOL statement below raised the diagnostic message shown. See if you can identify the error in each.

(a)
```
        WORKING STORAGE SECTION.
```
diagnostic: `'WORKING' SHOULD NOT BEGIN IN A MARGIN.`

cause: _____

(b)
```
        MOVE FINAL-RESULT TO OUT-RESULT.
```
diagnostic: `FINAL-RESULT NOT UNIQUE.`

cause: _____

(c)
```
        00021  FD  RESULT-FILE.
        00022      LABEL RECORDS ARE STANDARD.
```
diagnostic: `22 INVALID WORD LABEL.`

cause: _____

- - - - - - - - - - - - - - - - - - -

(a) no hyphen in WORKING-STORAGE

(b) apparently FINAL-RESULT wasn't defined in the Data Division

(c) statement 21 shouldn't have a period

4. The statement flagged by the COBOL compiler is frequently not the one with the error. Question (b) in frame 2 is an example of where the fault

clearly lies elsewhere in the program. Nevertheless, the diagnostic helps us find it. Question (c) also shows an error that is not in the flagged statement. Notice that 22 was flagged, but the error was in 21. The compiler flags the statement where it notices an error. If the Data Division includes a data-name called FINAL-RESULTS, that is a valid name. If you then refer to FINAL-RESULT in the Procedure Division, it won't be recognized. Spelling conflicts are identified where the conflict occurs.

The omission of the hyphen in WORKING-STORAGE actually would generate many more messages than the one shown here. The system doesn't recognize the entry, so it thinks you are still in the File Section. Hence, some REDEFINES and VALUE clauses may be invalid. Every 01 level is interpreted as being an implicit redefinition of the record for the last FD entry.

For each diagnostic below, identify whether it is a problem in the statement, or generated by the missing hyphen in WORKING-STORAGE.

```
00027  WORKING STORAGE SECTION.
00028  01  SWITCHES.
00029      02  EOF-MASTER          PIC   X
00030                              VALUE 'N'.
00031      02  EOF-TRANS           PIC   X
00032                              VALUE 'N'.
00033  01  HEADING
00034      02  CONTROL             PIC   X.
00035      02  FILLER              PIC   X(10).
              .
              .
              .
```

diagnostics:

(a) 30 VALUE CLAUSE TREATED AS COMMENTS. _____

(b) 32 VALUE CLAUSE TREATED AS COMMENTS. _____

(c) 33 PERIOD MISSING. ASSUMED.   _____

(d) 34 CONTROL INVALID WORD.   _____

- - - - - - - - - - - - - - - - - - - -

(a) and (b) were generated by the incorrect WORKING-STORAGE heading.
(c) and (d) are separate errors in the statement.

You have seen the types of messages provided by a COBOL compiler, and you have seen how to go from a diagnostic to the statement, and farther if needed, to correct the error. The standard reference manual or programmer's guide for the compiler you will use has additional diagnostic information. When you get a compiler run from your system, this documentation will be a great help in correcting all the errors to get a clean compile with no errors. As indicated above, most of the messages are self-explanatory and a check of the statement will reveal the source.

Testing COBOL Programs

5. After a program compiles correctly, you know its syntax is correct. But compilation doesn't touch the program logic. A program may not run at all the first time, but may abend (computer jargon for abnormal end). Or it may run but work incorrectly. Before a program is finished, it must be tested to be sure it will work under all circumstances.

    A test plan involves testing all the possible conditions in a program, both usual and extreme conditions for all arithmetic fields, end-of-file processing, and error-handling. The more complex a program, the more testing it will need. A program to list card images will need only limited test data, for example, while a program to count, sequence-check, and print card images will need considerably more. Consider such a program.

    List three conditions your test data might check.

    _____

    _____

    _____

- - - - - - - - - - - - - - - - - - -

    Any three:

        duplicate card number
        out of sequence card number
        normal sequence
        no cards
        too many cards

6. The first run of a program often produces an abend. There are various types of abends, but the most common has to do with numeric data items that aren't numeric. If you try to do arithmetic on a value that isn't numeric, the computer stops your program. Most computers call this a "data exception" (code 0C7). Others may give you "NON-NUMERIC DATA" as a message. Most systems will also tell which statement was executing when the error occurred. When a data exception is raised, you first check the input data. Then you desk-check your program logic to trace the numeric data items through the program.

    (a) Consider the program that sequence-checks, counts, and prints card images. Suppose the identifying card number is described as PIC X(6). When the program is run the first time, a data exception is raised. Can you determine a possible source of error?

    _____

    _____

    _____

(b) What technique might you use for ensuring that input data is numeric before attempting to do arithmetic?

_____

- -

(a) The counter may not have been initialized; any data should be okay on input; perhaps the counter was also described with X's.

(b) Check with a NUMERIC condition.

COBOL Debugging Aids

COBOL compilers offer special statements you can use as debugging aids. These are not part of the standard (ANS) COBOL, but are implemented in many computers that range in size from microcomputers to the IBM 370. Chances are excellent that you will be able to use these techniques with your system.

7. The COBOL trace mode causes the name of each paragraph of the Procedure Division to be printed each time the paragraph is entered. The printed list of names helps you to detect logic errors. And, in case of abend, the last paragraph named contains the fatal statement. The trace is initiated by the statement READY TRACE, and turned off with the statement RESET TRACE. It is normally off.

(a) What statement(s) would you use to cause a complete listing of paragraphs for a run? _____

(b) Where would you insert the statement(s)?

_____

(c) Suppose your program is a typical disk file update (as in Figure 9-4) and you want to trace the update logic, but not the end-of-file processing. What statement(s) would you insert?

_____

(d) Where? _____

_____

- - - - - - - - - - - - - - - - - - - -

(a) READY TRACE

(b) As the first statement in the Procedure Division

(c) READY TRACE and RESET TRACE

(d) READY before the main processing routine
RESET before the end-of-file routine

8. Another useful statement is EXHIBIT. This statement can be used to print the name of a data item with its value each time it is executed. It can also selectively print values only when they change.

```
EXHIBIT NAMED PART-NUMBER, ITEM-CODE.
```

Each time this statement is executed, the data-names and their values will be printed. During debugging, this can help you track values as your program is executed. The statement below will print only those values that have changed since the last EXHIBIT.

```
EXHIBIT NAMED CHANGED PART-NUMBER, ITEM-CODE.
```

You can specify literals in EXHIBIT, and as many data-names as you need.

(a) Write a statement to print the names and values of STUDENT-NAME, STUDENT-CLASS, and MAJOR-CODE.

(b) Write a statement to print just the values.

(c) Write a statement to print the names with their respective values, only if the value has changed since the last time the statement was executed.

- -

```
(a)  EXHIBIT NAMED STUDENT-NAME, STUDENT-CLASS, MAJOR-CODE.
(b)  DISPLAY STUDENT-NAME, STUDENT-CLASS, MAJOR-CODE.
(c)  EXHIBIT CHANGED NAMED STUDENT-NAME, STUDENT-CLASS,
                                              MAJOR-CODE.
```

DEBUGGING MODE

You may want statements such as TRACE and EXHIBIT executed during debugging, but such entries can slow down run times. Many compilers provide a debugging mode that lets you tell the computer when to recognize certain statements. We'll look at COBOL's debugging mode in this next section.

9. The COBOL debugging mode requires you to use the SOURCE-COMPUTER paragraph in the Configuration Section of the Environment Division. This

section is usually optional, as you know. The Environment Division framework is shown below.

```
ENVIRONMENT DIVISION.
CONFIGURATION SECTION.
SOURCE-COMPUTER.   comp-name   WITH DEBUGGING MODE.
[OBJECT-COMPUTER. comp-name.]
[SPECIAL-NAMES.
     special-name IS mnemonic-name.]
INPUT-OUTPUT SECTION.
    .
    .
    .
```

The source and object computer paragraphs were used in early days of COBOL to document the systems on which a program was compiled (SOURCE) and run (OBJECT). They are optional today, but may still be used for documentation. The comp-name depends on the computer system. IBM-370, 6800, and PDP11 are valid comp-names, as they're treated as comments.

The clause WITH DEBUGGING MODE lets you use COBOL's debugging mode. You include any extra statements you want to use in testing, such as DISPLAY, EXHIBIT, READY or RESET TRACE. And you include a "D" in column 7 of those statements. During testing, they are all executed.

When the WITH DEBUGGING MODE line is removed after testing, the compiler ignores statements that contain a "D" in column 7. So when your program works perfectly, you can simply remove the SOURCE-COMPUTER paragraph and your debugging statements will be ignored. You don't have to remove the extraneous statements.

(a) What is the effect of the WITH DEBUGGING MODE clause?

_____

(b) Suppose you accidentally punch "D" into column 7 of the READ statement for a master file. What will be the effect during testing in

debugging mode? _____

(c) What is the effect after the debugging clause is removed?

_____

- - - - - - - - - - - - - - - - - - -

(a) causes the system to recognize and execute statements with "D" in position 7;   (b) no effect;   (c) the READ will be ignored

10. Write statements to accomplish the following:

(a) Print the names of paragraphs entered.

(b) Modify the statement you just wrote to take effect only under debugging mode.

(c) Write the complete entry that allows the system to recognize debugging mode.

- - - - - - - - - - - - - - - - -

(a) READY TRACE

(b) D   READY TRACE (D in column 7, READY in column 12 or later)

(c) SOURCE-COMPUTER. ALTOS WITH DEBUGGING MODE.

(Your computer name may be different.)

In the next sequence of frames, we'll walk through a series of trials of a program. The program is similar to one you worked with at the end of Chapter 5. We'll compile it first and make any necessary corrections. Then we'll create a set of test data, and make a few test runs using COBOL debugging aids.

11. Figure 13-1, which begins on the next page, shows the program listing as it comes from a first compiler run. Notice that the lines are numbered, and those numbers are used to identify the messages. These messages were reproduced by a microcomputer COBOL compiler, but they are fairly clear. What would you do to the program to correct each error?

52	_____
0029	_____
0041	_____
0048	_____
0054	_____
0055	_____

- - - - - - - - - - - - - - - - -

52	put in space between filename
0029	put hyphen in GROSS-VALUES
0041	correct spelling of SPACES
0048	put hyphen in CALCULATE-OUTPUT (line 54)
0054	fixed by 0048
0055	fixed by 0029

```
 1   IDENTIFICATION DIVISION.
 2   PROGRAM-ID.
 3       SALARY.
 4   ENVIRONMENT DIVISION.
 5   INPUT-OUTPUT SECTION.
 6   FILE-CONTROL.
 7       SELECT CARD-FILE
 8           ASSIGN TO DISK.
 9       SELECT PRINT-FILE
10           ASSIGN TO PRINTER.
11   DATA DIVISION.
12   FILE SECTION.
13   FD  CARD-FILE
14       DATA RECORD IS CARD-RECORD
15       LABEL RECORDS ARE STANDARD.
16   01  CARD-RECORD.
17       02  C-NUMBER          PIC 9(9).
18       02  C-NAME            PIC X(28).
19       02  FILLER            PIC XXX.
20       02  C-HOURS           PIC 99V9.
21       02  FILLER            PIC XX.
22       02  C-WAGE            PIC 99V99.
23       02  FILLER            PIC X(31).
24   FD  PRINT-FILE
25       LABEL RECORDS ARE OMITTED.
26   01  PRINT-LINE            PIC X(121).
27   WORKING-STORAGE SECTION.
28   01  EOF-CARD              PIC X          VALUE 'N'.
29   01  GROSS VALUES.
30       02  GROSS             PIC S999V99    VALUE ZERO.
31       02  TOTAL-GROSS       PIC S9(6)V99   VALUE ZERO.
32   01  EMPLOYEE-LINE.
33       02  FILLER            PIC X(10)      VALUE SPACES.
34       02  E-NAME            PIC X(28).
35       02  FILLER            PIC X(12)      VALUE SPACES.
36       02  E-GROSS           PIC 999.99.
37       02  FILLER            PIC X(65)      VALUE SPACES.
38   01  SUMM-LINE.
39       02  FILLER            PIC X(20)      VALUE SPACES.
40       02  OUT-GROSS         PIC 9(6).99.
41       02  FILLER            PIC X(92)      VALUE SPCES.
42   PROCEDURE DIVISION.
43   MAIN-LOGIC.
44       OPEN INPUT CARD-FILE
45           OUTPUT PRINT-FILE.
46       READ CARD-FILE
47           AT END MOVE 'Y' TO EOF-CARD.
48       PERFORM CALCULATE-OUTPUT
49           UNTIL EOF-CARD = 'Y'.
50       MOVE TOTAL-GROSS TO OUT-GROSS.
51       WRITE PRINT-LINE FROM SUMM-LINE.
52       CLOSE CARD-FILE, PRINT-FILE.
```

(continued on the next page)

```
**** PUNCT?
  53              STOP RUN.
  54          CALCULATE OUTPUT.
  55              COMPUTE GROSS ROUNDED = C-HOURS * C-WAGE
  56                  ON SIZE ERROR DISPLAY C-NAME.
  57              MOVE GROSS TO E-GROSS.
  58              MOVE C-NAME TO E-NAME.
  59              WRITE PRINT-LINE FROM EMPLOYEE-LINE.
  60              ADD GROSS TO TOTAL-GROSS.
  61              READ CARD-FILE
  62                  AT END MOVE 'Y' TO EOF-CARD.
0029:  UNRECOGNIZABLE ELEMENT IS IGNORED.   VALUES
0041:  INVALID VALUE IGNORED.   SPCES
0048:  PROCEDURE-NAME IS UNRESOLVABLE.   CALCULATE-OUTPUT
0054:  /W/ PERIOD ASSUMED AFTER PROCEDURE-NAME DEFINITION.
0054:  UNRECOGNIZABLE ELEMENT IS IGNORED.   OUTPUT
0055:  ERRONEOUS QUALIFICATION; LAST DECLARATION USED.   GROSS
0055:  ILLEGAL MOVE OR COMPARISON IS DELETED.
```

Figure 13-1

12. Suppose we made all those corrections and the program compiles perfectly. Now we need some test data. Two sample records are shown below. Add three or four input records that will test other aspects of the program.

```
376401494RUTH ASHLEY              400   1234
111111111JUDI N. FERNANDEZ        255   3456
```

_____

_____

_____

_____

- - - - - - - - - - - - - - - - - -

```
376401496RUTH ASHLEY                     400   1234
111111111JUDI N. FERNANDEZ               255   3456
222222222BARBARA TABLER                  777   7777
333333333SOMEBODY ELSE                   000   0000
444444444AND ANOTHER NAME                010   0010
123456789ABCDEFGHIJKLMNOPQRSTUVWXYZAB     345   1525
```

(Your test data will be somewhat different. Be sure you included very large and very small values.)

13. We ran our slightly modified program (Figure 13-2) with the test data above. The printed output follows on page 280.

```
IDENTIFICATION DIVISION.
PROGRAM-ID.     SALARY.
ENVIRONMENT DIVISION.
INPUT-OUTPUT SECTION.
FILE-CONTROL.
    SELECT CARD-FILE       ASSIGN TO DISK.
    SELECT PRINT-FILE      ASSIGN TO PRINTER.
DATA DIVISION.
FILE SECTION.
FD  CARD-FILE
    DATA RECORD IS CARD-RECORD
    LABEL RECORDS ARE STANDARD.
01  CARD-RECORD
    02  C-NUMBER           PIC 9(9).
    02  C-NAME             PIC X(28).
    02  FILLER             PIC XXX.
    02  C-HOURS            PIC 99V9.
    02  FILLER             PIC XX.
    02  C-WAGE             PIC 99V99.
    02  FILLER             PIC X(31).
FD  PRINT-FILE
    LABEL RECORDS ARE OMITTED.
01  PRINT-LINE             PIC X(121).
WORKING-STORAGE SECTION.
01  EOF-CARD               PIC X            VALUE 'N'.
01  GROSS-VALUES.
    02  GROSS              PIC S999V99      VALUE ZERO.
    02  TOTAL-GROSS        PIC S9(6)V99     VALUE ZERO.
    02  OUT-GROSS          PIC 9(6).99.
01  EMPLOYEE-LINE.
    02  FILLER             PIC X(10)        VALUE SPACES.
    02  E-NAME             PIC X(28).
    02  FILLER             PIC X(12)        VALUE SPACES.
    02  E-GROSS            PIC 999.99.
    02  FILLER             PIC X(65)        VALUE SPACES.
PROCEDURE DIVISION.
MAIN-LOGIC.
    OPEN INPUT CARD-FILE
        OUTPUT PRINT-FILE.
    READ CARD-FILE
        AT END MOVE 'Y' TO EOF-CARD.
    PERFORM CALCULATE-OUTPUT
        UNTIL EOF-CARD = 'Y'.
    MOVE TOTAL-GROSS TO OUT-GROSS.
    DISPLAY 'TOTAL PAID IS ', OUT-GROSS.
    CLOSE CARD-FILE, PRINT-FILE.
    STOP RUN.
CALCULATE-OUTPUT.
    COMPUTE GROSS ROUNDED = C-HOURS * C-WAGE
        ON SIZE ERROR DISPLAY C-NAME.
    MOVE GROSS TO E-GROSS.
    MOVE C-NAME TO E-NAME.
    WRITE PRINT-LINE FROM EMPLOYEE-LINE.
    ADD GROSS TO TOTAL-GROSS.
    READ CARD-FILE
        AT END MOVE 'Y' TO EOF-CARD.
```

Figure 13-2

Here is the printed output.

```
RUTH ASHLEY                             493.60
JUDI N. FERNANDEZ                       881.28
BARBARA TABLER                          881.28
SOMEBODY ELSE                           000.00
AND ANOTHER NAME                        000.10
ABCDEFGHIJKLMNOPQRSTUVWXYZAB            526.13
```

During execution, two messages were displayed:

```
BARBARA TABLER
    TOTAL PAID IS      002782.39
```

(a) Did the program run correctly? _____

(b) Examine the program and the output. Can you locate any errors?

_____

_____

- - - - - - - - - - - - - - - - - - -

(a) no; (b) The SIZE ERROR option was activated, but the previous value of GROSS is used again.

14. Suppose you want to print values of C-NAME, C-WAGE, and C-HOURS before the GROSS is calculated, in the form "name = value".

(a) Code the statement.

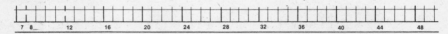

(b) How could you make sure the statement is executed only during debugging without removing it? _____

_____

- - - - - - - - - - - - - - - - - - -

(a) EXHIBIT NAMED C-NAME, C-WAGE, C-HOURS.
(b) Put a D in column 7, then use a SOURCE-COMPUTER paragraph WITH DEBUGGING MODE during testing.

15. Suppose we modify paragraph CALCULATE-OUTPUT in Figure 13-2 to look like this:

```
CALCULATE-OUTPUT.
    COMPUTE GROSS ROUNDED = C-HOURS * WAGE
        ON SIZE ERROR MOVE 1 TO SIZE-OVER.
    IF SIZE-OVER = 1
        DISPLAY C-NAME
```

(continued on the next page)

```
        ELSE
            MOVE GROSS TO E-GROSS
            MOVE C-NAME TO E-NAME
            WRITE PRINT-LINE FROM EMPLOYEE-LINE
            ADD GROSS TO TOTAL-GROSS.
        READ CARD-FILE
            AT END MOVE 'Y' TO EOF-CARD.
```

We also define SIZE-OVER in the Working-Storage Section.

Do you think the program will run correctly now? _____

- - - - - - - - - - - - - - - - - - - -

The program doesn't run correctly. The next frame shows the result.

16. These values are printed:

```
    RUTH ASHLEY          493.60
    JUDI N. FERNANDEZ    881.28
```

All other names are displayed, as is a TOTAL of 1374.88. Can you identify the remaining error in the coding in the last frame?

_____

- - - - - - - - - - - - - - - - - - - -

We need to reset SIZE-OVER to zero. (Figure 13-3, which begins below, shows the final program.)

```
IDENTIFICATION DIVISION.
PROGRAM-ID.     SALARY.
ENVIRONMENT DIVISION.
INPUT-OUTPUT SECTION.
FILE-CONTROL.
    SELECT CARD-FILE      ASSIGN TO DISK.
    SELECT PRINT-FILE     ASSIGN TO PRINTER.
DATA DIVISION.
FILE SECTION.
FD  CARD-FILE
    LABEL RECORDS ARE OMITTED.
01  CARD-RECORD.
    02  C-NUMBER          PIC 9(9).
    02  C-NAME            PIC X(28).
    02  FILLER            PIC XXX.
    02  C-HOURS           PIC 99V9.
    02  FILLER            PIC XX.
    02  C-WAGE            PIC 99V99.
    02  FILLER            PIC X(31).
FD  PRINT-FILE
    LABEL RECORDS ARE OMITTED.
01  PRINT-LINE            PIC X(121).
```

(continued on the next page)

```
WORKING-STORAGE SECTION.
01  EOF-CARD              PIC X           VALUE 'N'.
01  SIZE-OVER            PIC 9           VALUE ZERO.
01  GROSS-VALUES.
    02  GROSS            PIC S999V99     VALUE ZERO.
    02  TOTAL-GROSS      PIC S9(6)V99    VALUE ZERO.
    02  OUT-GROSS        PIC 9(6).99.
01  EMPLOYEE-LINE.
    02  FILLER           PIC X(10)       VALUE SPACES.
    02  E-NAME           PIC X(28).
    02  FILLER           PIC X(12)       VALUE SPACES.
    02  E-GROSS          PIC 999.99.
    02  FILLER           PIC X(65)       VALUE SPACES.
PROCEDURE DIVISION.
MAIN-LOGIC.
    OPEN INPUT CARD-FILE
        OUTPUT PRINT-FILE.
    READ CARD-FILE
        AT END MOVE 'Y' TO EOF-CARD.
    PERFORM CALCULATE-OUTPUT
        UNTIL EOF-CARD = 'Y'.
    MOVE TOTAL-GROSS TO OUT-GROSS.
    DISPLAY 'TOTAL PAID IS ', OUT-GROSS.
    CLOSE CARD-FILE, PRINT-FILE.
    STOP RUN.
CALCULATE-OUTPUT.
    COMPUTE GROSS ROUNDED = C-HOURS * C-WAGE
        ON SIZE ERROR MOVE 1 TO SIZE-OVER.
    IF SIZE-OVER = 1
        DISPLAY C-NAME
        MOVE ZERO TO SIZE-OVER
    ELSE
        MOVE GROSS TO E-GROSS
        MOVE C-NAME TO E-NAME
        WRITE PRINT-LINE FROM EMPLOYEE-LINE
        ADD GROSS TO TOTAL-GROSS.
    READ CARD-FILE
        AT END MOVE 'Y' TO EOF-CARD.
```

Figure 13-3

The steps in compiling and debugging larger programs are much the same as you've seen in this short sequence.

If you have access to a computer system, you may want to test out one or more of the programs you wrote as you worked through this book. The program you wrote at the end of Chapter 6 (frames 38 through 42) would be a good one to try. Running it will give you excellent feedback about whether you have met the objectives of this chapter, as well as the objectives of the first six chapters.

If you have a chance, you may want to test some of the later programs, especially those dealing with disk files, as well. There will be no Self-Test for this chapter.

SUMMARY

You have now completed this Self-Teaching Guide. You are able to code structured COBOL programs to solve many types of common computing problems. You know enough COBOL now to function in the real world of computer programming. Appendix C includes a summary of formats for the COBOL statements covered. You'll be able to learn the rest easily from COBOL reference manuals.

There is more to programming than knowing the language, however. Practice and experience, actual running of programs you have written, are needed. The structured COBOL approach you have learned will make debugging easier for you and speed you on your way to becoming a programmer.

ANS COBOL Reserved Words

The words listed in this appendix are reserved words in ANS COBOL. Most of these words are reserved in all such compilers, but some may be permitted in some installations. Most installations will also have special words they have reserved. None of these reserved words may be used in a name that a programmer creates, as a program-name, a paragraph-name, or a data-name.

ABOUT
ACCEPT
ACCESS
ACTUAL
ADD
ADDRESS
ADVANCING
AFTER
ALL
ALPHABETIC
ALPHANUMERIC
ALSO
ALTER
ALTERNATE
AND
APPLY
ARE
AREA
AREAS
ASCENDING
ASSIGN
AT
AUTHOR

BEFORE
BEGINNING
BITS
BLANK

BLOCK
BOTTOM
BY

CALL
CANCEL
CD
CF
CH
CHARACTER
CHARACTERS
CLOCK-UNITS
CLOSE
COBOL
CODE
COLLATING
COLUMN
COMMA
COMMUNICATION
COMP
COMPUTATIONAL
COMPUTE
CONFIGURATION
CONSOLE
CONSTANT
CONTAINS
CONTROL
CONTROLS

COPY
CORR
CORRESPONDING
COUNT
CURRENCY

DATA
DATE
DATE-COMPILED
DATE-WRITTEN
DAY
DE
DEBUGGING
DECIMAL-POINT
DECLARATIVES
DEFINE
DELETE
DELIMITED
DELIMITER
DEPENDING
DESCENDING
DETAIL
DISPLAY
DIVIDE
DIVISION
DOWN
DUPLICATES
DYNAMIC

EGI
ELSE
EMI
ENABLE
END
END-OF-PAGE
ENTER
ENVIRONMENT
EOP
EQUAL
EQUALS
ERROR
ESI
EVERY
EXAMINE
EXCEPTION
EXIT
EXTEND

FD
FILE

FILE-CONTROL
FILE-LIMIT
FILE-LIMITS
FILLER
FINAL
FIRST
FOOTING
FOR
FROM

GENERATE
GIVING
GO
GREATER
GROUP

HEADING
HIGH-VALUE
HIGH-VALUES

I-O
I-O-CONTROL
IDENTIFICATION
IF
IN
INDEX
INDEXED
INDICATE
INITIAL
INITIATE
INPUT
INPUT-OUTPUT
INSPECT
INSTALLATION
INTO
INVALID
IS

JUST
JUSTIFIED

KEY

LABEL
LAST
LEADING
LEFT
LENGTH
LESS
LIBRARY
LIMIT

LIMITS
LINAGE
LINAGE-COUNTER
LINE
LINE-COUNTER
LINES
LINKAGE
LOCK
LOW-VALUE
LOW-VALUES

MEMORY
MERGE
MESSAGE
MINUS
MODE
MODULES
MOVE
MULTIPLE
MULTIPLY

NATIVE
NEGATIVE
NEXT
NO
NOMINAL
NOT
NOTE
NUMBER
NUMERIC

OBJECT-COMPUTER
OCCURS
OF
OFF
OH
OMITTED
ON
OPEN
OPTIONAL
OR
ORGANIZATION
OTHERWISE
OUTPUT
OVERFLOW

PAGE
PAGE-COUNTER
PERFORM
PF

PH
PIC
PICTURE
PLUS
POINT
POINTER
POSITION
POSITIVE
PRINTING
PRIORITY
PROCEDURE
PROCEED
PROCESSING
PROGRAM
PROGRAM-ID
PROTECT

QUEUE
QUOTE
QUOTES

RANDOM
RANGE
RD
READ
RECEIVE
RECORD
RECORDING
RECORDS
REDEFINES
REEL
REFERENCES
RELEASE
REMAINDER
REMARKS
REMOVAL
RENAMES
REPLACING
REPORT
REPORTING
REPORTS
RERUN
RESERVE
RESET
RETURN
REVERSED
REWIND
REWRITE
RF

RH
RIGHT
ROUNDED
RUN

SAME
SD
SEARCH
SECTION
SECURITY
SEEK
SEGMENT
SEGMENT-LIMIT
SELECT
SEND
SENTENCE
SEPARATE
SEQUENCE
SEQUENTIAL
SET
SIGN
SIZE
SORT
SORT-MERGE
SOURCE
SOURCE-COMPUTER
SPACE
SPACES
SPECIAL-NAMES
STANDARD
START
STATUS
STOP
STRING
SUBTRACT
SUM
SUPERVISOR
SUPPRESS
SYMBOLIC
SYNC
SYNCHRONIZED

TABLE
TALLY
TALLYING
TAPE
TERMINAL
TERMINATE
TEXT
THAN
THEN
THROUGH
THRU
TIME
TIMES
TO
TOP
TRAILING
TYPE

UNEQUAL
UNIT
UNSTRING
UNTIL
UP
UPON
USAGE
USE
USING

VALUE
VALUES
VARYING

WHEN
WITH
WORDS
WORKING-STORAGE
WRITE

ZERO
ZEROES
ZEROS

APPENDIX B
Collating Sequence
of COBOL Characters

The collating sequence, and even the characters considered, may vary among installations. One typical sequence (EBCDIC) is presented here. The specific sequence must be checked when you run programs in an actual installation. In this sequence, 9 has the highest value, and the blank (ƀ) the lowest.

$$
\left.\begin{matrix} 9 \\ \vdots \\ 0 \end{matrix}\right\} \quad \text{(numeric characters)}
$$

$$
\left.\begin{matrix} Z \\ \vdots \\ A \end{matrix}\right\} \quad \text{(alphabetic characters)}
$$

"	(quotation mark)
=	(equal sign)
'	(single quote)
>	(greater than)
,	(comma)
/	(slash)
–	(minus or hyphen)
;	(semicolon)
)	(close parenthesis)
*	(asterisk)
$	(dollar sign)
+	(plus)
(	(open parenthesis)
<	(less than)
.	(decimal point or period)
	(blank, indicated often by ƀ)

APPENDIX C
Summary of Formats

This appendix includes the formats of all Procedure Division statements discussed in this guide. In addition, a complete format for the Identification Division and for the FILE-CONTROL paragraph of the Environment Division are included. All of these formats use the following conventions.

— Words in all capitals are reserved words. Those that are underlined must be included in that format.
— Words in all small letters are to be supplied by the programmer.
— Components enclosed in brackets [ ] are optional; if used, they must be complete.
— Components enclosed in braces { } indicate that one and only one of the items in the braces must be included.
— Punctuation, where shown, is required.

Identification Division Formats

IDENTIFICATION DIVISION.

PROGRAM-ID. program-name.

[AUTHOR. comment-entry.]

[INSTALLATION. comment-entry.]

[DATE-WRITTEN. comment-entry.]

[DATE-COMPILED. comment-entry.]

[SECURITY. comment-entry.]

[REMARKS. comment-entry.]

Environment Division, FILE-CONTROL paragraph entries

SELECT file-name   (all files)

ASSIGN TO system-name   (all files)

ACCESS IS $\begin{Bmatrix} \text{SEQUENTIAL} \\ \text{RANDOM} \end{Bmatrix}$ (required for random access)

ACTUAL KEY IS data-name   (direct files only)

NOMINAL KEY IS data-name   (indexed files only—IBM)

RECORD KEY IS data-name   (indexed files only)

SYMBOLIC KEY IS data-name   (indexed files only)

Procedure Division Statement Formats

ACCEPT data-name [FROM $\left\{ \begin{array}{l} \text{CONSOLE} \\ \text{mnemonic-name} \end{array} \right\}$].

(a) ADD $\left\{ \begin{array}{l} \text{data-name-1} \\ \text{literal-1} \end{array} \right\}$ TO data-name-2

  [ROUNDED]

  [ON SIZE ERROR statement].

(b) ADD $\left\{ \begin{array}{l} \text{data-name-1} \\ \text{literal-1} \end{array} \right\}$ $\left\{ \begin{array}{l} \text{data-name-2} \\ \text{literal-2} \end{array} \right\}$ GIVING data-name-3

  [ROUNDED]   [ON SIZE ERROR statement].

CLOSE file-name-1 file-name-x.

COMPUTE data-name-1 [ROUNDED] = $\left\{ \begin{array}{l} \text{data-name-2} \\ \text{literal} \\ \text{arithmetic-expression} \end{array} \right\}$.

  [ON SIZE ERROR statement]

DISPLAY $\left\{ \begin{array}{l} \text{data-name-1} \\ \text{literal-1} \end{array} \right\}$ $\left\{ \begin{array}{l} \text{data-name-x} \\ \text{literal-x} \end{array} \right\}$ [UPON $\left\{ \begin{array}{l} \text{mnemonic-name} \\ \text{CONSOLE} \end{array} \right\}$].

(a) DIVIDE $\left\{ \begin{array}{l} \text{data-name-1} \\ \text{literal-1} \end{array} \right\}$ INTO data-name-2

  [ROUNDED]   [ON SIZE ERROR statement].

(b) DIVIDE $\left\{ \begin{array}{l} \text{data-name-1} \\ \text{literal-1} \end{array} \right\}$ $\left\{ \begin{array}{l} \text{INTO} \\ \text{BY} \end{array} \right\}$ $\left\{ \begin{array}{l} \text{data-name-2} \\ \text{literal-2} \end{array} \right\}$

  GIVING data-name-3

  [ROUNDED]   [ON SIZE ERROR statement].

EXIT.

(a) GO TO paragraph-name.

(b) GO TO paragraph-name-1 paragraph-name-2 paragraph-name-x

  DEPENDING ON data-name.

IF condition statement.

(a) MOVE $\left\{ \begin{array}{l} \text{data-name-1} \\ \text{literal} \end{array} \right\}$ TO data-name-2.

(b) MOVE $\left\{\begin{array}{l}\underline{\text{CORR}}\\ \underline{\text{CORRESPONDING}}\end{array}\right\}$ data-name-1 $\underline{\text{TO}}$ data-name-2.

(a) MULTIPLY $\left\{\begin{array}{l}\text{data-name-1}\\ \text{literal-1}\end{array}\right\}$ $\underline{\text{BY}}$ data-name-2

  [$\underline{\text{ROUNDED}}$] [ON $\underline{\text{SIZE}}$ $\underline{\text{ERROR}}$ statement].

(b) MULTIPLY $\left\{\begin{array}{l}\text{data-name-1}\\ \text{literal-1}\end{array}\right\}$ $\underline{\text{BY}}$ $\left\{\begin{array}{l}\text{data-name-2}\\ \text{literal-2}\end{array}\right\}$ $\underline{\text{GIVING}}$ data-name-3

  [$\underline{\text{ROUNDED}}$] [ON $\underline{\text{SIZE}}$ $\underline{\text{ERROR}}$ statement].

OPEN $\left\{\begin{array}{l}\underline{\text{INPUT}}\\ \underline{\text{OUTPUT}}\\ \underline{\text{I-O}}\end{array}\right\}$ file-name.

(a) $\underline{\text{PERFORM}}$ paragraph-name-1 [$\underline{\text{THRU}}$ paragraph-name-2].

(b) $\underline{\text{PERFORM}}$ paragraph-name-1 [$\underline{\text{THRU}}$ paragraph-name-2]

  $\left\{\begin{array}{l}\text{data-name}\\ \text{integer}\end{array}\right\}$ $\underline{\text{TIMES}}$.

(c) $\underline{\text{PERFORM}}$ paragraph-name-1 [$\underline{\text{THRU}}$ paragraph-name-2]

  $\underline{\text{UNTIL}}$ condition.

(d) $\underline{\text{PERFORM}}$ paragraph-name-1 [$\underline{\text{THRU}}$ paragraph-name-2]

  $\underline{\text{VARYING}}$ data-name-1 $\underline{\text{FROM}}$ data-name-2 $\underline{\text{BY}}$ data-name-3

  $\underline{\text{UNTIL}}$ condition.

READ file-name [$\underline{\text{INTO}}$ data-name]

  $\left\{\begin{array}{l}\text{AT } \underline{\text{END}}\\ \underline{\text{INVALID}} \text{ KEY}\end{array}\right\}$ statement.

$\underline{\text{STOP}}$ $\underline{\text{RUN}}$.

(a) $\underline{\text{SUBTRACT}}$ $\left\{\begin{array}{l}\text{data-name-1}\\ \text{literal-1}\end{array}\right\}$ $\underline{\text{FROM}}$ data-name-2

  [$\underline{\text{ROUNDED}}$] [ON $\underline{\text{SIZE}}$ $\underline{\text{ERROR}}$ statement].

(b) $\underline{\text{SUBTRACT}}$ $\left\{\begin{array}{l}\text{data-name-1}\\ \text{literal-1}\end{array}\right\}$ $\underline{\text{FROM}}$ $\left\{\begin{array}{l}\text{data-name-2}\\ \text{literal-2}\end{array}\right\}$

  $\underline{\text{GIVING}}$ data-name-3

  [$\underline{\text{ROUNDED}}$] [ON $\underline{\text{SIZE}}$ $\underline{\text{ERROR}}$ statement].

(a) <u>WRITE</u> record-name [<u>FROM</u> data-name]

$$\left[\left\{ \begin{array}{l} \underline{\text{BEFORE}} \\ \underline{\text{AFTER}} \end{array} \right\} \quad \text{ADVANCING} \quad \left\{ \begin{array}{l} \text{data-name LINES} \\ \text{integer LINES} \\ \text{special-name} \end{array} \right\} \right].$$

(b) <u>WRITE</u> record-name [<u>FROM</u> data-name]

    <u>INVALID</u> KEY statement.

Index

A, 39
Abends, 272
ACCEPT statement, 42
ACCESS clause, 247
Actual decimal point, 79
ADD statement, 80
ADVANCING options, 117
AFTER ADVANCING options, 117
ALPHABETIC, 132
Alphanumeric editing, 107
Arithmetic operators, 85
Arithmetic statements, 78
ASCENDING KEY clause, 237
ASSIGN clause, 63
    unit record files, 96
    sequential files, 143
    indexed files, 247
Asterisk (*) edit character, 104
AT END option, 68
AUTHOR paragraph, 95

B, 107
BLOCK CONTAINS clause, 119
Blocking of records, 142

Card-to-tape program, 149
Carriage control character, 102
Case Structure, 207
Class condition, 132
CLOSE statement, 66
Coding sheet, 23
Collating sequence, 129
Comma, 104
Comment entries, 95
Comparisons, 129
Compilation, 270
COMPUTE statement, 85
Condition-name condition, 131

Conditions
    Class, 132
    Compound, 132
    Condition-name, 131
    Relation, 128
Configuration Section, 96, 274
Control structures, 9
CORRESPONDING option, 195
Counting, 53
CR, 108

Divisions, 21
Data Division header, 21
DATA-RECORD clause, 145
DATE-COMPILED paragraph, 95
DATE-WRITTEN paragraph, 95
DB, 108
Debugging Mode, 247
Decimal point
    actual, 79
    implied, 78
Delete flag, 245
DEPENDING ON option, 208
Desk-checking, 268
Direct files, 243
DISPLAY statement, 42
DIVIDE statement, 80
Dollar sign ($), 105

Editing problems, 4
Elementary data items, 100
End-of-file processing, 169, 176,
      179, 182
Environment Division header, 21
EXHIBIT statement, 274
EXIT statement, 206

FD, 64
Figurative constants, 40

FILE-CONTROL paragraph, 63
File description entry, 64
File Section, 64, 97
FILLER, 39, 101
Floating insertion, 105
Format Notation, 32

GIVING option, 82
GO TO statement, 207
    DEPENDING ON option, 208
Group data items, 100

Heading records, 114
Hierarchy, 7
HIGH-VALUES, 246

Identification Division header, 21,
        94
IF statement, 26, 50
    Nested, 136
Implied decimal point, 78
Independent data items, 113
Index of table, 233
Indexed files, 244
INDEXED BY clause, 233
Input, 3
INPUT option, 65
Input-Output Section, 63
INSTALLATION paragraph, 95
INVALID KEY
    Read, 253
    Rewrite, 254
    Write, 248
I-O option, 147
ISAM files, 244

Key clauses
    RECORD, 247
    NOMINAL, 252
    SYMBOLIC, 252

LABEL RECORDS clause, 98
Level numbers, 99, 113
Literals
    non-numeric, 45
    numeric, 45
LOW-VALUES, 246k

Microcomputers, 150
Mnemonic names, 96
MOVE statement, 44

MULTIPLY statement, 80

Names, 24
NOMINAL KEY clause, 252
NUMERIC, 132

OBJECT-COMPUTER paragraph, 257
OCCURS clause
    single-level, 219
    double-level, 229
OMITTED option, 98
ON SIZE ERROR option, 80
OPEN statement, 65
Output, 3
OUTPUT option, 65

PASSWORD, 256
PERFORM statement
    THRU option, 206
    TIMES option, 202
    UNTIL option, 28, 48
    VARYING option, 202
PICTURE clause, 39, 98
Problem types, 4
Procedure Division header, 21
Processing, 3
PROGRAM-ID paragraph, 95
Program-names, 24
Pseudocode, 11

Qualified names, 194

RANDOM option, 256
READ statement, 68
RECORD KEY clause, 247
RECORD CONTAINS clause, 145
Record matching structures
    access only, 165
    adding records, 173
    deleting records, 178
    updating records, 181
REDEFINES option, 197
Relation condition, 52, 128
Relational operators, 52
Relative files, 243
REMARKS paragraph, 95
Repetition structure, 9, 28
Report problems, 4
Reserved words, 24
REWRITE statement, 254
ROUNDED option, 83

S, 79
SEARCH ALL statement, 238
SEARCH statement, 235
SECURITY paragraph, 95
SELECT clause, 63, 96
Selection structure, 9, 26
Sequence checking, 152
Sequence structure, 9, 26
SEQUENTIAL option, 247
SET statement, 234
Signed values, editing of, 108
SOURCE-COMPUTER paragraph, 275
SPACES option, 40
Spacing 31
SPECIAL-NAMES paragraph, 96
STANDARD option, 145
STATUS, 256
STOP RUN statement, 48
Subscripts, 219
SUBTRACT statement, 80

Summary problems, 4
SYMBOLIC KEY, 252

Table description entries, 219
TRACE statements, 273

Update problems, 4

V, 78
VALUE clause, 41
Vertical spacing options, 117
VSAM coding, 256
VSAM file, 244

Walkthrough, 269
Working-Storage Section header, 113
WRITE statement, 66

X, 39

Z, 103
ZERO, 40
Zero suppression characters, 103